GEORGE FORREST
Plant Hunter

GEORGE FORREST
Plant Hunter

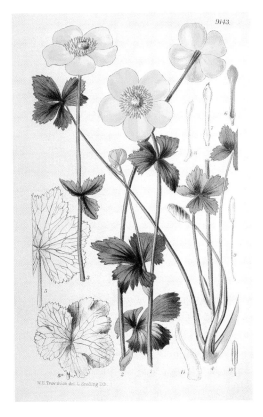

Brenda McLean

Antique Collectors' Club
in association with the Royal Botanic Garden Edinburgh

To Robert

ISBN 1 85149 461 8

British Library Cataloguing-in-Publication Data
A catalogue record for this book is available from the British Library

Frontispiece. George Forrest on his third expedition in Yunnan.
Title page. *Trollius yunnanensis,* a common plant of alpine meadows of Yunnan. The plant illustrated (*Curtis's Botanical Magazine* t.9143) was raised from Forrest's seed by Bees Ltd.

Printed in Spain
by the Antique Collectors' Club Ltd, Sandy Lane, Old Martlesham, Woodbridge, Suffolk

I confess that after reading your letter one of my first thoughts was – Why has Forrest not written a book upon his explorations? I hope now that you are able to look at all your surroundings with a mature mind and with more knowledge than any other explorer in these regions has had that you will put it all down as a story written in the natural manner of your graphic letters and issue it to the world. It is bound to have a great circulation and to be a great success.

Professor I.B. Balfour, Regius Keeper, Royal Botanic Garden Edinburgh
to George Forrest, 1 October 1917

To have lived down these years of high endeavour when Forrest stood pre-eminent among plant hunters, handling his beautiful material either in the herbarium or in the garden, must have been a rare privilege, a privilege the like of which is unlikely to be given to man again.

Dr. H.R. Fletcher, Regius Keeper, Royal Botanic Garden Edinburgh,
in Cowan, Dr. J. Macqueen,
The Journeys and Plant Introductions of George Forrest VMH
(Oxford University Press, 1952)

Contents

Preface

A garden stroll and the twinkle in an old lady's eye started me on the detective trail of George Forrest. The stroll was in the Botanic Gardens at Ness, near Chester, where their balm and beauty soaked in and a new curiosity welled up within me. The plant labels showed how plants had come from all over the world, and one particular post, next to a very handsome bush of *Pieris formosa forrestii*, proudly announced, 'This plant grew from the first packet of seed sent by George Forrest'. Who was he?

An exhibition explained that these gardens were founded by an enterprising Liverpool cotton broker, Mr A.K. Bulley, and here he started the new nursery of Bees Ltd, for which he paid George Forrest to go to the remote mountains of Yunnan, in south-west China, to collect seeds. Forrest set out in 1904 and found an unbelievably rich flora to which he returned on six more expeditions. Altogether he sent home mule-loads of seeds for our gardens, and 31,000 dried plant specimens for study. This was a mighty achievement and I set out to read more about him.

Unfortunately, Forrest never wrote a book about his travels and, although he is always mentioned in books about plant hunters in Asia in that period, there are only two books that concentrate on him. These are:

1. *George Forrest, VMH*, The Scottish Rock Garden Club (1935)
2. *Journeys and Plant Introductions of George Forrest VHM*, ed. J. Macqueen Cowan (OUP, 1952)

These books leave important questions unanswered. What motivated this man to keep on going back? What was he like? What was his life like? Who else paid for him to go on these expeditions, and was it only for plants? I became more curious, especially as the main hope of ever extending our information on him seemed to rest on his letters. Where could they be found?

When a friend's mother came for tea, she suddenly said with a twinkle, 'I have a niece in Inverness who has some letters from George Forrest'. I visited the niece and the neatly folded letters were safely housed in a biscuit tin. As I excitedly opened them on the kitchen table, George Forrest's accounts of his latest adventures, and near murder, came tumbling forth in his easily recognised writing. It was a magic moment. This famous plant hunter, who first set off to roam the wild, remote and misty mountains of south-west China one hundred years ago, was brought to life. Such nuggets nourished the urge to find more evidence.

A further thrill came with the opening of an attic trunk in Essex. It revealed documents that even Forrest's granddaughter had never seen before: Forrest's Chinese passports, his contracts for several expeditions, written in Forrest's hand and signed by his sponsors, together with Chinese currency of silver ingots. It was the stuff of a biographer's dream, and lit up the detective trail that has led to this book.

Prologue

In 1880 a thirty-four year old wealthy, English gentleman of extraordinary energy and vitality was already a widely travelled naturalist. This man of giant frame and booming voice, Henry John Elwes, had amassed a vast collection of birds, butterflies and plants. Inspired by the *Himalayan Journals* of Sir Joseph Hooker,[1] Elwes had recently collected in the Sikkim Himalaya. He loved gardening, lilies were one of his favourite plants, and it seemed an appropriate time to write a monograph about them. He produced a sumptuous folio work of great beauty, the first to bring together illustrations of every known species of the genus *Lilium*.[2]

On the basis of the evidence before him, Elwes wrote in the introduction to his monograph: 'I do not think many new species remain to be discovered; for … not more than three or four species have been added to the genus in the last four years'. As he surveyed the world in his mind, he made one important proviso:

> The only regions from which much novelty can be expected are the Eastern Himalayas and the immense tract of unexplored and difficult mountain country which surrounds our Indian Empire on the north and east, and which lies around the headwaters of the Irrawaddy, the Brahmaputra and the Yang-tse-kiang.

Thirty-five years later so many new lilies had been discovered in the Sino-Himalayan mountains that Elwes had to consider the preparation of a Supplement to the original volume.

George Forrest was one of the intrepid botanical explorers who rose to the challenge of these remote regions. His plant and seed collections contributed to this explosion in knowledge of the plants of the Sino-Himalaya. Not only new lilies, but new species of Primula and Rhododendron were also discovered on a scale never envisaged. It was a tremendously exciting time for gardeners and scientists as the new discoveries poured into Europe, and Elwes himself subscribed to one of Forrest's expeditions.

This book enters into the excitement, as we examine Forrest's life, the development of his career, and the motivation that led him to make seven long expeditions to the mountains of Yunnan in south-west China.

1. Hooker, J.D. *Himalayan Journals*, 2 vols., John Murray, 1854
2. Elwes, H.J. *A monograph of the Genus Lilium*, London, 1880

7216.

M.S.del, J.N.Fitch lith.

Vincent Brooks,Day & Son Imp

L.Reeve C°London.

10

Yunnan – a Botanist's Paradise

Yunnan is a home of beauties.
I. Bayley Balfour to A.K. Bulley, 31 March 1897

Airports and hotels now serve such a thriving tourist industry in the magnificent mountains of south-west China that it is difficult to appreciate how very inaccessible this area used to be. Colourful books, with beautiful pictures of the camellias, gentians, primulas and rhododendrons of Yunnan, make one forget that a hundred years ago many of these flowers were unseen by the outside world. This beautiful corner of China is so isolated by mountains and vast distances that foreigners reached here very late in the country's long history. Some Yunnan plants were known from herbarium specimens of dried plants; hardly any had been introduced to Europe as garden plants. The area still held great potential for George Forrest when he arrived in 1904.

A century before this, the wild plants and animals of the whole of inland China were almost unknown outside the country. Merchants and collectors were limited to the coastal ports of Canton and Macao, where one enterprising collector, Thomas Reeves, employed Chinese artists to paint plants, butterflies and animals (Plate 2). But only a trickle of horticultural plants reached Europe. The Celestial Empire was closed to foreigners; exploration inland was forbidden.

Step by step, against Chinese opposition, a series of treaties improved access to the interior. The first step was taken in 1842 with the signing of the Treaty of Nanking which opened five coastal ports for trade with foreigners. The next year the Horticultural Society (now the RHS) sent Robert Fortune to look for ornamental and useful plants in the vicinity of the newly opened ports. He collected abundantly from private, nursery and temple gardens, returning with plants such as *Anemone japonica* and *Trachycarpus fortunei*. But Fortune was mainly restricted to searching out horticultural plants near the coast. Foreigners could still only nibble at the edge of this vast country; the wild flowers inland were out of their reach.

The pressure on China to open up its borders continued through the 1850s and was helped by the decline of the oppressive Ch'ing dynasty. In 1858 Lord Elgin signed the Sino-British Treaty of Tientsin, which granted Britain the right to have an ambassador, secured the entry of missionaries and their protection by the Chinese authorities, and allowed unhindered and protected travel for British subjects on consular passports. British ships were given the right to trade on the Yangtze and more ports were opened. This breakthrough in the freedom of travel for the British was rapidly followed by the same concessions for the Americans, French, Germans, Dutch and Spanish.[1] As merchants, missionaries and explorers penetrated far inland, they discovered an unsuspected wealth of China's plants and animals.

Intrepid Russian explorers approached China from the north, Carl Johann Maximowicz probed the borderlands through Manchuria in 1854, and later Russian travellers such as Nicolai Przewalski explored widely in northern China. They collected for the Imperial Botanic Garden of St Petersburg, and some of their duplicates were exchanged with Kew, preparing the way for future collectors such as Farrer. But the Russians did not reach Yunnan.

Meanwhile, from the coast, Roman Catholic and Protestant missionaries penetrated to remote and inhospitable areas of China, enduring great hardship and ill health, harassment and humiliation, and facing hostility as foreigners and

Opposite:
Plate 1. *Primula poissonii.* A historic picture (1892) of one of the few species that came into cultivation in Britain, via Kew, from Père Delavay's seeds. The illustration is from *Curtis's Botanical Magazine.*

Plate 2. An early 19th century painting of Camellia and butterflies from John Reeves' collection, Canton. The first animals that Forrest collected in large numbers were butterflies.

Christians. The French Jesuits, in particular, made collections that revealed the huge diversity of plant and animal life in inland China.

Jean Pierre Armand David, who arrived in 1862, was one of the first and most outstanding French missionary collectors to go to China. His specimens were deemed so interesting that he was released from his apostolic work to concentrate on collecting plants, birds and mammals. He found the dove or handkerchief tree, *Davidia involucrata*, and the giant panda. He travelled more than 3,000 miles (5,000km) through north, central and western China, as far south as the Yangtze River. Despite introducing few plants to cultivation, he laid the foundation to our knowledge of the flora of China.[2] Classic publications of all his collections emanated from the *Muséum d'Histoire Naturelle* in Paris over twenty years, from 1868 to 1888, including the two-volume *Plantae Davidianae* produced by the hard-working director, Adrien-René Franchet.

Yunnan, however, was still largely unexplored and in 1875 Maximowicz reviewed what remained to be done in China and proposed the Tibet/China border as the next most important area for exploration. He told Joseph Dalton Hooker, Director of Kew, '*That* ought to be the exploring field for hardy and experienced travellers: Szetchuan [*sic*] and part of Yunnan'.[3]

Maximowicz was perceptive in pointing to the significance of these remote mountainous provinces. Again it was a Jesuit missionary, Jean-Marie Delavay, who pioneered plant collection in Yunnan. From 1882 he was stationed for nearly ten years near Tali (Dali) in north-west Yunnan, the 'Switzerland of China', where high snow-capped ranges with alpine flowers contrast with deep valley gorges containing subtropical plants (Plate 3). Delavay's enormous collections, compiled in his spare time, were a model for all those who followed. He repeatedly visited the same localities, collecting flowers and fruits of the plants, and even some seed. The well-known garden plants, *Deutzia discolor* and *Osmanthus delavayi*, were introduced

Plate 3. A satellite photograph of part of N.W. Yunnan. The crests of the north-south oriented mountains are highlighted by snow. The historic city of Dali lies about two-thirds of the way down the plain west of the large lake called Erhai. Both Père Delavay and George Forrest collected plants in this area.

by him, although unfortunately only a small proportion of his discoveries were raised successfully. Franchet estimated that Delavay sent back to Paris some 200,000 botanical specimens, representing more than 4,000 species, of which about 1,500 were new to science.[4] The size of his collection was overwhelming. Franchet never completed writing up all Delavay's plants, but he published results in several journals, most notably in *Plantae Delavayanae*, where the stunning Himalayan blue poppy (*Meconopsis betonicifolia*) was first described.[5]

News of such massive missionary contributions gradually spread in the 1880s and 1890s through scientific journals, correspondence and gossip. Their collections became one of the 'hot topics' among botanists and gardeners at the forefront of knowledge. A few of Delavay's plants were grown at Kew in the 1890s (Plate 1). Joseph Hooker referred to *Rhododendron rubiginosum* as 'another of the swarm of Western Chinese Rhododendrons discovered by the indefatigable Abbé Delavay'.[6] The possibility of a rich mountain flora in western China, mooted earlier by visionaries like Elwes, was becoming a reality. British focus on Szechuan and Yunnan was now sure to follow, especially as the expanding British Empire made possible a new, shorter, route into Yunnan.

In 1886 – the heyday of British imperialism – the Viceroy proclaimed that 'Upper Burma was annexed to the British Indian Empire'.[7] Burma provided the route into south-west China via the Irrawaddy river. The Irrawaddy Flotilla Company's steamers were immortalised in 1890 by Rudyard Kipling: 'Can't you 'ear their paddles chunkin' from Rangoon to Mandalay?'[8] The company received a Government subsidy for a regular and increased packet service for the 700 miles (1,120km) between Rangoon and Bhamo. From there the frontier of China and Yunnan was only thirty-five miles (56km) away, albeit by a mountainous mule track. Traders dreamed of a gateway to new markets; others dreamed of new plants and seeds. As we shall see, the route through Burma was to provide George Forrest's great opportunity to explore a 'botanist's paradise'.[9]

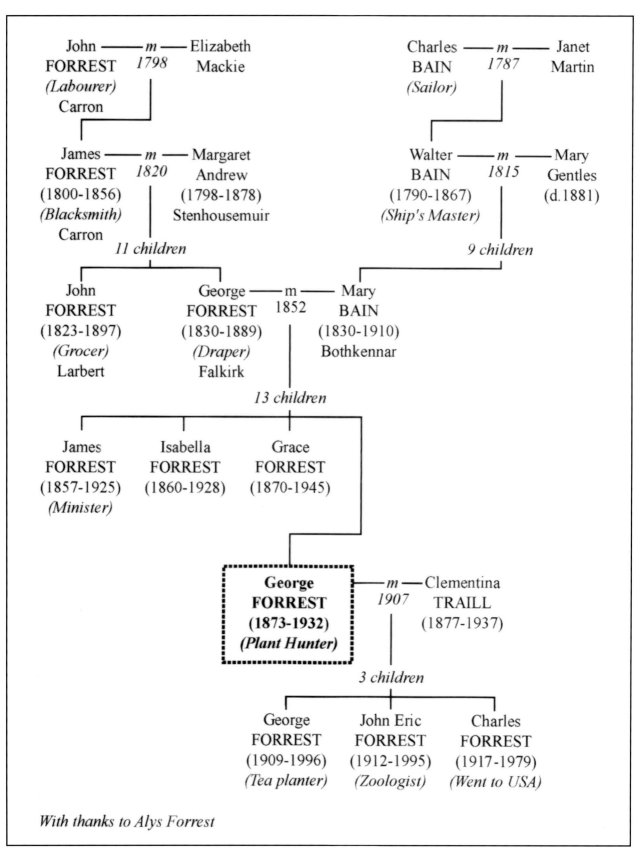

Plate 4. Simplified family tree of George Forrest.

CHAPTER ONE

Scottish Background

Time future contained in time past

T.S.Eliot[1]

The first thirty years of George Forrest's life are largely hidden from view, but there are welcome shafts of light that give us an insight into his background, upbringing and early manhood. Forrest's forebears were rooted in and around Larbert, near the Firth of Forth (Plate 5). As the general population became increasingly mobile in the nineteenth century, the family spread out but largely remained in Central Scotland, while Forrest himself was to adventure much further afield. We shall see glimpses of his forebears around Larbert, Forrest's early family life in Falkirk, his training in Kilmarnock, his adventures in Australia and his budding ambition to be a plant collector.

Family background

George Forrest was a vigorous and determined plant collector who trekked over rugged mountain ranges in south-west China on foot, horseback and mule, even through deep snow and dense mist, to find new flowers in cliff crevices or on boggy mountain passes. He did not spare himself and was renowned for his strong physique.

He was not the first in the family to lead a tough and physically demanding life. Three generations of men before him, either in the Carron Iron Works or as sailors, had years of work demanding great fitness and strength, and courage in the face of danger.

All his grandparents came from the Larbert area, north of Falkirk, and both his parents were baptised at Larbert Parish Church. When his father, who was also called George Forrest, and his mother, Mary Bain, married they united two families of contrasting characteristics and talents (see Plate 4). On his father's side were tough, skilled craftsmen and businessmen, high-class shopkeepers, property owners, all well

Plate 5. The Forrest family in Scotland.

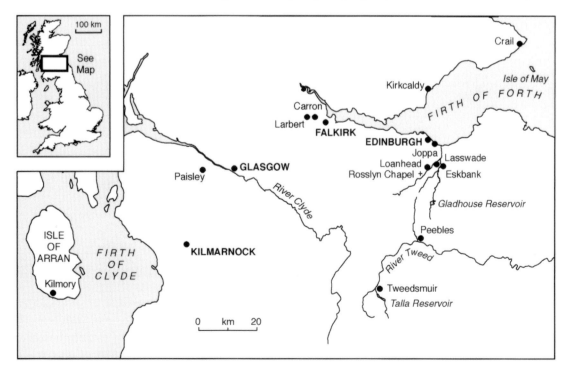

established in their communities. On his mother's side the Bains were a sea-faring family, including masters of sailing ships, who led adventurous and hazardous lives.

The Carron Iron Works, by the River Carron, was an important feature of life in the Larbert area. Established in 1759 to work and smelt iron on a large scale, it became Scotland's largest manufacturing plant and a significant employer. Many of the Forrest family worked with the smelted iron under the very tough conditions of its mighty blast furnaces, while the Bains sailed in Carron ships.

George Forrest's great grandfather was a labourer at Carron, his grandfather James Forrest was a blacksmith, three great uncles were in ironwork and two uncles were blacksmiths. Carron's most famous product was the Carronade, a short naval cannon of large bore, designed for close combat at sea and used effectively in battles of the Napoleonic Wars.

The Napoleonic Wars also changed the life of George's grandfather, Walter Bain, who became a legendary figure in the family. 'My grandfather fought against the French for many years in the Napoleonic Wars!' wrote Forrest when friendly with French missionaries in China.[2] The son of a sailor, Walter was only twelve years old when he first went to sea, sailing in ships of the Carron Company that were trading between Grangemouth and Liverpool. Then in 1810, aged twenty, he was press-ganged into the Navy[3] – one of the many that were forced into service to make up the crews of naval ships. Two years later, having been 'Prest' as an Able Seaman, he was on the Muster Roll for HMS *Duncan*.[4] The *Duncan* was a two-decker medium-sized ship carrying 74 guns, with 590 men on board.[5] Conditions on board were cramped and hard; desertion was not unknown, but Walter endured it until the end of the Napoleonic Wars.

Walter Bain's first two years on the *Duncan* were spent patrolling the waters off the east and south coasts of England. From there the ship went to the Mediterranean and in November 1814 she set sail for Brazil as flagship of Rear-Admiral Sir John P. Beresford (1766-1844), to escort the exiled Prince Regent of Portugal, Dom Joao, back to Lisbon. They were at sea for two months before waiting four months in Rio de Janeiro, but returned without the Prince Regent and sailed back to Portsmouth in the summer of 1815. Walter was then free to marry Mary Gentles, but the following year he was at sea again, on the Carron ship *Proserpine,* one of the fast-sailing schooners trading to London. He served twenty-three years on this ship as mate, followed by a further thirteen years as master. His wife bore him nine children and one of his sons, James Gentles Bain, also joined the ships of the Carron company, becoming master of the screw steamer *Derwent*. So three generations of Bains sailed from ports on the River Carron.

Meanwhile, Walter Bain's family had moved from Carronshore to the next-door parish of Bothkennar, and in Bothkennar Church, on 9 November 1852, the two local families, the Bains and the Forrests, were joined when Mary Bain married George Forrest. They were both twenty-two years old and were to be the parents of the plant hunter, George Forrest.

Falkirk bairn

George's father was a grocer in Paisley when he married Mary Bain and they had their first six children there. But tragedy struck the family. Their firstborn died when nearly a year old, two boys died in infancy and another child was stillborn. After this loss of four infants, Mr and Mrs Forrest moved with their surviving two children to make a fresh start in Grahamston, Falkirk. They were part of the young migrant population that was moving from one swiftly growing town to another in search of employment, and Mr Forrest became apprenticed to a draper in

THE FAMILY REGISTER

George Forrest, & Mary Bain
(born 9th June 1830) (born 9th June 1830)
*were married by,
The Revd. R. G. Rutherford, of
Dundee, on the
9th November. 1852.*

Births.

*Mary, Georgina, Forrest. born 25 October 1853.
Margaret, Malvina, Andrew, Forrest,
= born 4th January 1855.
James Forrest, born 28th January 1856.*

EXCEPT THE LORD BUILD THE HOUSE
THEY LABOR IN VAIN THAT BUILD IT

BIRTHS

SUFFER LITTLE CHILDREN TO COME UNTO ME

*James Forrest, born 19th March 1857.
Walter, Bain, Forrest, born 20th March 1858.
Isabella, Campbell, Forrest, born 24 March 1860.
Mary, Georgina, Forrest, born 7th April 1862.
Elizabeth, MacKie, Forrest, born 16 March 1864.
Janet, Bow, Mitchell, Forrest, born 16th January 1866.
Annie Bain Forrest, born 30th October 1867.
Grace Robertson Forrest, born 4th January 1870.
George Forrest, born 13th March 1873.*

BLESSED IS THE MAN THAT HATH HIS QUIVER FULL OF THEM

Falkirk. Together they had a further seven children and, when our plant hunter, George Forrest, was born at Falkirk on 13 March 1873, he was the last of thirteen children (Plate 6). His mother had borne children for nearly twenty years but, when young George arrived, his parents had only one other surviving son, James. George's birth must therefore have been a particularly happy addition to the family. James was then sixteen years old and he was later to take on special responsibility for his young brother.

When George was born his parents and their eight surviving children were living at 32 Grahams Road, Falkirk, and they no longer had a domestic servant. Their neighbours were a tobacco spinner, a shoemaker, and another draper: other traders of the lower middle class in the very stratified society of those Victorian times. In 1876, when another draper's shop became vacant, Mr Forrest rented these premises and set up a 'New Drapery Establishment'[6] at no. 124, on the north side of the High Street, advertising 'Drapery Goods of every description'. Six years later Mr Forrest also became an agent for the flourishing Pullars' dyeworks at Perth. He was bettering himself and, when no. 34 Grahams Road became vacant, the Forrest household moved into this improved accommodation.

Mr Forrest promised 'prompt and careful attention' in his shop and honest hard work was expected of everyone in the household. A sense of duty, caring and seriousness of purpose permeated the family and was linked to their religious beliefs. George Forrest's parents embraced the dynamism and vitality of Victorian religion and were staunch supporters of the Evangelical Union, a branch of the Free Church which had a special appeal among the skilled artisans and upwardly mobile middle class in Scotland. Their daily toil was uplifted by joyous religious fervour, and thrift went hand in hand with voluntary 'givings' to church missionary funds.[7] There was a huge release of missionary energy in Britain and missionaries in Africa and China had a leading role in overseas explorations.

Plate 6. Register of births in Forrest family Bible. (One stillborn child was not recorded.)

In Falkirk George's father played a prominent part in the local church and an elder sister accompanied the singing on the harmonium, an instrument popularised by the American evangelists, Moody and Sankey, in their revival campaign of 1873–74. George's elder brother, James, went to Edinburgh to train for the E.U. Church Ministry. Young George was therefore accustomed to an atmosphere of evangelical zeal, long before he stayed with missionaries in China. No wonder he felt at home among missionaries, as well as grateful for their hospitality and assistance.

As George was a 'lad o' pairts', his parents set great store on giving him a good education. Schooling in Scotland, at that time, was compulsory only up to the age of thirteen, but George was to continue until the age of eighteen. He began at the Southern School in Falkirk, but had to move as in 1885 his father gave up the shop because of failing health. Young George (aged twelve) and his elder four unmarried sisters moved with their parents to Kilmarnock to join the eldest son, James, who, having completed his training, was now a minister there. In the long term the move turned out well for the younger son and he always stayed particularly close to his unmarried sisters, Isabella and Grace, and to his brother, James, with whom he shared his time in Kilmarnock.

Kilmarnock influences

Moving to Kilmarnock was a major change for the young George Forrest. He left behind a large network of family and friends and set up home with his brother James. His brother was now the Revd James Forrest, MA, pastor of Clerk's Lane Church, and he took his family responsibilities seriously. He was truly and literally 'my brother's keeper', which was most fortunate for young George Forrest.

Kilmarnock provided an important training ground for this budding teenager up to his early years of manhood. Forrest benefited from a supportive home, an excellent school and a climate in which enquiry was encouraged. There was opportunity for natural history exploits and learned societies, and he gained his first job there.

Forrest attended the Kilmarnock Academy and received a broad education, subsidised by government grants. This was a privilege as, at that time, only about four to five per cent of the age group was able to benefit from secondary education, far less a good school.[8] The Rector of Kilmarnock Academy, Dr Hugh Dickie, was an exceptional and much respected person, a learned and outstanding teacher. By the time George Forrest arrived, Dr Dickie had established the Academy's good reputation. He cultivated a high standard of teaching and was keen on promoting science. In 1887 a new science laboratory was opened. This was the first science laboratory in Ayrshire and it made the Academy a pioneer in the teaching of science in the west of Scotland.[9] Furthermore, Dr Dickie had a 'marvellous power of communicating a knowledge of science and leading young people to take an interest in it and attain a proficiency in it'.[10] This obviously worked for George Forrest.

Everyone at the Academy studied a wide range of subjects that included geology, physical geography, botany, practical inorganic chemistry, mathematics, French, German and Latin.[11] This background later enabled Forrest to gain mastery of botanical Latin – the *lingua franca* of all botanists worldwide – and to converse, albeit somewhat hesitatingly, with the French missionaries in China.

The Revd James Forrest also provided plenty of stimulus for his brother. He was sixteen years older than George and a man of deep thinking and strong views. He wrote articles in the local newspapers on Home Rule, Socialism and John Ruskin.[12] While pastor of Clerk's Lane Evangelical Union Church in Kilmarnock he was tried for heresy, resulting in him and his church members leaving the Evangelical Union and joining the Unitarians.[13] Unitarianism was associated with progressive causes and welcomed intellectual debate and, in 1890, as an enthusiastic recent convert, James was sponsored by the Trust of William McQuaker to give lectures on Unitarianism. It was said that 'his high scholarship and argumentative powers' made him a valuable lecturer.[14] Argumentative powers were also a feature of his younger brother, George, and later would almost wreck his career.

Meanwhile, the health of their father deteriorated further. Before Christmas 1888 he became paralysed on one side of his body and in early September the following year he slipped into a coma. On the morning of 14 September 1889 the sixteen year old George Forrest woke to learn that his father had died. From then on the close relationship between the two brothers seemed to lead George to regard his older brother more like a substitute father.

The year their father died, the Revd James Forrest became a member of the Glenfield Ramblers' Society. Could this have been partly to take his energetic younger brother out of the house, to share in an activity which the lad enjoyed? James was an enthusiastic naturalist who is reported to have fostered his brother's interest.[15] The Glenfield Ramblers' Society was active and popular in the town[16] and both Hugh Dickie and David Murray, George's mathematics master, were members. There were plenty of enthusiasts in Kilmarnock from whom George could learn more about the wildlife of the countryside.

One outstanding naturalist in Kilmarnock, who was also the Hon President of the Glenfield Ramblers, was the Revd David Landsborough II (1826-1912) (Plate 7). He had contributed to a revised edition of his father's book, *Arran: its Topography, Natural History, and Antiquities*. He discovered new species of algae, shells and fossils in Ayrshire and some discoveries were named after him. When the University of Glasgow conferred an honorary degree of LL.D. on David Landsborough II in 1901, it was said in the presentation that 'his untiring energy and enthusiasm…had endeared him to many students and made his name a household word throughout Ayrshire'.[17]

It is likely that the teenage George Forrest was one of those students in Kilmarnock who benefited from the zeal and passion of the Revd David Landsborough II. Landsborough had three brothers in Australia[18] and tales of them may even have inspired Forrest to go there. One of Landsborough's particular enthusiasms was the introduction of Australian and other exotic plants to the Isle of Arran.[19] He received seeds of gum trees direct from Ferdinand von Mueller (1825-1896),[20] the leading Australian botanist of the nineteenth century. It would be utterly surprising if Landsborough's passions had not rubbed off on Forrest, who was later to discover new species, introduce many of them to Britain, and even to take his own family for holidays on the Isle of Arran.

However, when George Forrest left school, aged eighteen, his future as a natural history collector was not mapped out. He did not go to university, although the Academy prepared students for university entrance, and we can only speculate on the reasons why. (Maybe further academic study did not appeal, or financially he had to find a job.) He took work in the well-established and prospering family business of Messrs Rankin and Borland, pharmaceutical chemists.[21] This enterprise was not simply a local apothecary's concern. It had a most extensive stock of chemicals, drugs, proprietary and patent medicines, and a factory manufacturing 'aerated waters' on an extensive scale. It was in the heart of Kilmarnock by the Town Cross and it had local and country trade, wholesale and retail.

The proprietor, Mr John Borland (Plate 8), an influential member of the Glenfield Ramblers, was a keen scientist, a professional analyst and a member of the Pharmaceutical Society of Great Britain. Plant-derived drugs and products were important in pharmacy at that time and it has been said that George Forrest

collected plants, drying, labelling and mounting them while working at the
pharmacy.[22] There are no records to confirm this, although we know that he was
very familiar with *A Manual of Botany* by Professor Robert Bentley, an Honorary
Member of the Pharmaceutical Society and one of the three editors of the *British
Pharmacopoeia*, 1885. The *Manual* was a textbook of especial value to medical and
pharmaceutical students, being a work of reference for those who required
'accurate and condensed information on the Properties and Uses of plants'. George
Forrest did not become a qualified pharmacist,[23] although his eldest son said that
he 'made pills' while at the pharmacy. Certainly, when first in China, George
Forrest asked his brother to send a copy of the *Manual* out to him. He found it a
boon when first sorting out the Chinese flora, as the plant classification in the
Manual was based on the *Genera Plantarum* used in the Flora of Bentham and
Hooker, which he knew.

Australia – a formative experience

The year of 1898 fortuitously gave Forrest his first big chance of adventure, as he
received a small inheritance from a prosperous uncle. He used the money to travel
to Australia and his experiences there were to have a profound influence on the
young man. He gained a taste for life in the wild and he would later refer to it
when on his plant hunting expeditions in China.

The wealthy uncle was John Forrest, a grocer and wine merchant in Larbert who,
having inherited monies and property through his mother's family, himself bought
land and property. He owned many properties at Larbert Crossroads, including the
Red Lion Hotel and the large tenement block known as Forrest's Buildings. He
died on 25 November 1897 without having any children. In his will a share was
given to George Forrest's late father, to be divided equally among his children. At
the end of February 1898 it was confirmed that a small legacy (probably about
£50, equivalent to approximately £2,800 today, taken as Nov. 2003 throughout)
was available for George.[24] This was sufficient to buy a ticket to Australia and the
twenty-five year old George set off on his first great adventure in foreign lands.

George visited relatives in Australia and tried sheep farming and gold digging. After
the Californian Gold Rush of 1849 the Australian discoveries of gold had become

headline news. Many books had been published giving advice on where to go and how to survive when camping in the outback. Perhaps inspired by these, George Forrest joined in the last flurry of gold digging in New South Wales. It was a rough, tough life and, although he discovered at least one sizeable nugget,[25] a fortune in gold eluded him, though he was fortunate that, out of the blue, he inherited a second small legacy at the end of 1898, from another of his uncles, James Forrest of Larbert.

George's love of exploration also surfaced in other ways and these new adventures had their challenges. After some time in the interior, George attempted to reach the coast by crossing a desert area but, as the watering-places on which he relied had dried up, he got into desperate straits and almost died of thirst before he got through.[26]

George Forrest was a risk taker and a survivor, a man who coped in the rough and precarious conditions of the outback, travelled miles on horseback and found a happy challenge in firing his Winchester rifle at distant kangaroo. Overall, his time in Australia was a crucial, formative experience in a wild and hazardous environment, and he emerged a man of the 'right grit' for a natural history collector.

Forrest returned to Scotland via South Africa, richer in experiences if not in gold, toughened up and eager for more travel and the outdoor life. The appeal of exploration combined with adventure in the wild had been strongly aroused, though the way ahead was not clear. This was a pattern that was to repeat itself many times in his life, one expedition after another.

Back in Scotland

We next find Forrest, aged thirty, living with his seventy-three year old mother and three unmarried sisters in Linden Cottage, 16 High Street (Linden Place), Loanhead,[27] a small coal-mining village in the parish of Lasswade, six miles (9.5km) south of Edinburgh (Plate 10). The beautiful wooded banks of the North Esk valley were nearby, with fishing and walking on the Pentlands and beyond. The primary landmarks of Loanhead were the Reformed Presbyterian Church, with its new clock, and the community was proud of its even newer cast-iron fountain with its horse drinking trough, and a street lamp to light the main cross-roads. The Forrests' neighbours included several miners, a chemist and two greengrocers, a millworker, papermaker, mason and engineer.[28] There were two 'smiddies' (blacksmiths' workshops) in the High Street, shoeing horses and 'ringing' wooden cart wheels, and a large engineering workshop's noise clashed with the clatter of horses' hooves as they passed along the High Street. After Forrest's travels it must have seemed a staid, provincial, conservative community, kirk and school being the centres of most peoples' lives.

Later, when Forrest looked back at 'dear old dirty Linden Cottage',[29] it was with affection; his family had always provided a vital security. As in so many Scottish burghs, despite the strong feeling of community it was not unusual for a person to go overseas. Loanhead men took up management positions in India and went to far-flung corners of the world to mine coal, gold, diamonds and tin. Others went as missionaries to Arabia and China and one worked as a river pilot on the Irrawaddy in Burma – which was to become Forrest's main route into China.[30] We don't know what influences this had on Forrest, but in this expansive era people were confident and enterprising in working abroad within and beyond the Empire.

Back in Scotland, Forrest's elder brother, James, was again helpful and influential. He introduced George to a Glasgow natural history society for which George was to collect local Scottish plants. This was to be of significant importance for future developments, yet it was only a flickering glow compared with the outcome of the following unexpected series of coincidences.

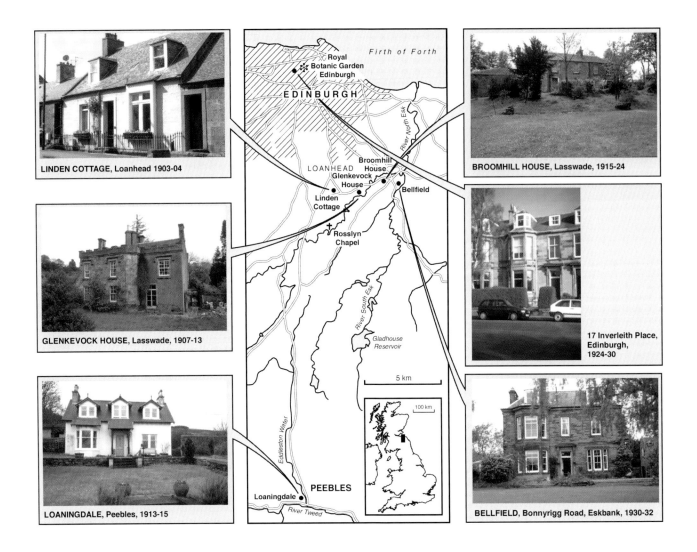

LINDEN COTTAGE, Loanhead 1903-04

GLENKEVOCK HOUSE, Lasswade, 1907-13

LOANINGDALE, Peebles, 1913-15

BROOMHILL HOUSE, Lasswade, 1915-24

17 Inverleith Place, Edinburgh, 1924-30

BELLFIELD, Bonnyrigg Road, Eskbank, 1930-32

Firth of Forth

Royal Botanic Garden Edinburgh

EDINBURGH

River North Esk

LOANHEAD

Broomhill House

Glenkevock House

Bellfield

Linden Cottage

Rosslyn Chapel

River South Esk

Gladhouse Reservoir

5 km

100 km

Eddleston Water

PEEBLES

Loaningdale

River Tweed

Plate 10. Homes of George Forrest, 1903-32.

An important letter

There is an element of luck in every life, but the quality of an individual is shown in the way chance is used. George Forrest made the most of the luck that came his way.

The turning point in his life came in Scotland in June 1903 with his chance discovery of some human bones. This led to an amazing chain of events and a vital introduction to the Regius Keeper of the Royal Botanic Garden Edinburgh. The story illustrates Forrest's two essential characteristics: an explorer with an enquiring mind and a collector contributing to knowledge.

Forrest was on a fishing trip at Gladhouse Reservoir, south of Edinburgh, when he noticed the corner of a stone coffin or cist projecting from an eroded bank. He investigated and found that the end-slab had fallen off and there was a skeleton inside. Thrilled, he took a few bones to the Keeper of the Museum of National Antiquities in Edinburgh (now part of the National Museums of Scotland). He was soon returning to the site of discovery with the Hon John Abercromby, secretary of the Society of Antiquaries of Scotland. Abercromby was a retired and friendly gentleman of leisure, a scholar with wide-ranging interests, including archaeology. He liked to see what was going on.[31] There was also something appealing about Forrest, an open, friendly and persuasive young man, utterly lacking in pretence and pretentiousness, and exuding an eager curiosity. The two men started digging and uncovered three long stone cists, each containing a skeleton laid on its back, but in varying states of decay.[32] The cists were probably from the early Christian period – the second part of the first millennium AD.[33]

Being a sociable man in the 'small world' of Edinburgh, as it was then, Abercromby was also acquainted with Professor Isaac Bayley Balfour, the Regius Keeper of the Royal Botanic Garden Edinburgh (RBGE). Impressed by Forrest, and learning of his background and ambitions, Abercromby decided to help him by writing to this Professor.[34] It was a crucially important letter:

June 21 1903

Dear Prof. Balfour

Do you know of any person or society that wants a collector to collect for them abroad any kind of botanical specimens. [?]

I have recently come to get slightly acquainted with a young fellow of the name of Forrest who lives out at Loanhead. At present he is collecting specimens of the plants in the three Lothians for some society in Glasgow with which his brother, who is a minister in Glasgow has to do. He would rather travel than stay at home and has had some experience of roughing it as a gold digger in N. South Wales…

If you would care to see him I will tell him. He looks the right sort of man.

Yours sincerely,

John Abercromby

This letter 'rang bells' for the fifty year old Balfour. Years before, he had even invested £100 in gold mining in Queensland, inspired by tales of 'Flakes of gold as big as a man's hand…slicing it off with cold chisels. By jingo it's more like Arabian nights than modern gold mining'.[35] Balfour also understood the urge to collect plants overseas, having collected on the island of Socotra, in the Indian Ocean, in his youth. However, although new exotic plants were being reported from abroad, Balfour could find no immediate opening for a collector.

Months passed and Forrest waited anxiously before asking Balfour politely for news. Balfour was abroad and did not receive the letter immediately. Then, on 1 September 1903, Balfour helpfully made Forrest a tentative offer:

It has …occurred to me …it might be possible to give you, should you care for it, some work temporarily in the garden here – in connection say with the Herbarium of dried plants, where at any rate you could acquire further knowledge of plants and could learn the methods of preservation and arrangement of collections. It so happens that I have a vacancy on our Staff just now. The lad who has left has been receiving pay at the rate of 10/- per week and for a start I should be glad to give that to you as a beginner… Should a post of this kind suit you I shall be glad to hear from you. You might begin work at once if you care to come.[36]

Forrest leapt at the chance. The job offered valuable training and experience that would increase his skills as a collector. He replied by return of post, 'I shall be most pleased to accept the position you offer, and trust to fill it with satisfaction to you. After this week I shall be free and at your service'.

'Dear Sir,' replied Balfour, 'If you will come to the Garden on Monday next the 7th Sept. you will find the Assistant in the Herbarium prepared to give you instructions as to your work – Come between 9 and 10 a.m.'

This was only a humble, temporary job. The wage was no better than a sixteen year old could earn in a nursery. Forrest was probably earning more as an apprentice pharmacist in Kilmarnock. At Kew the minimum wage for an adult gardener and labourer was 21/- in 1895. But it was as if the genial and kind Abercromby, with all his experience of life, had turned a key to open the door to fresh opportunities for Forrest, unlocking his potential. Forrest's life was to open up in an exciting way that no-one could have envisaged.

Left:
Plate 11. Professor Isaac Bayley Balfour, Regius Keeper of the Royal Botanic Garden Edinburgh, 1888 to 1922, and mentor to George Forrest for nineteen years.

Below:
Plate 12. The Herbarium where George Forrest met Clementina Traill. Shown is Helen Miller who knew Forrest and worked on his specimens.

CHAPTER TWO

George Forrest and the Lure of China

*He is a strongly built fellow and seems to me
to be of the right grit for a collector*
Professor Isaac Bayley Balfour, 28 April 1904

When Forrest walked into the Royal Botanic Garden Edinburgh (RBGE) on 7 September 1903 he was entering a new world that would change his life in two fundamental ways. The RBGE was the ideal training ground for a plant collector and it was also the place where Forrest would meet his future wife. The RBGE was a vibrant place to be and it provided a rich learning environment under the Regius Keeper, Professor Bayley Balfour (Plate 11). Balfour had many contacts in the worlds of botany and horticulture and he was to be the link between Forrest and his two loves, his wife and China.

In the Herbarium

Balfour was a dynamic leader, he was superbly qualified and dedicated to the advancement of the RBGE. He had studied in Germany and had been Professor of Botany in Glasgow and Oxford. Now aged fifty, he had been making progressive improvements in the Edinburgh Garden for fifteen years. He was resolute, hardworking and had good relations with his staff.

When Forrest arrived at the RBGE Balfour had recently appointed three young men who were contemporaries of Forrest: Harry Tagg in the Museum, William Wright Smith on the teaching staff and Robert Adam as an assistant head gardener. All three were to be Forrest's loyal colleagues and life-long friends. He would return to them time and again after his expeditions. Thus, unknown to any of them, the foundations for the future were forming as soon as Forrest stepped into the Herbarium.

At that time the Herbarium was in the Caledonian Hall, a small Victorian building at the southern end of the Garden, which was the hub of the Garden's taxonomic work. Dried, pressed plants that represented a huge diversity of floras were sent there from all over the world. Specimens were treated with chemicals to prepare them for permanent storage, and they had to be carefully mounted, labelled, examined and sorted (Plate 12). Forrest was taught the great value of a complete specimen, with its flowers and fruit, its stems and leaves and even roots. He was honing his skills and gaining new expertise that was to be invaluable to him in the future. He would later become renowned for the quality of his dried specimens and the care with which they were pressed, dried, and arranged for mounting.

Forrest learned of tropical and temperate plant families and worked on genera that he had never heard of before. He handled Himalayan specimens and saw North American plants that do not grow naturally elsewhere. It was enriching to come across this huge spectrum of plant life. His interest and curiosity were aroused.

Stimulus abounded in this confined space. Rows of three-tiered cupboards stored dried pressed specimens. The walls were lined with journals and books that helped the people there to classify, describe and name the incoming plants, some of which were newly discovered. Forrest had expert tuition from specialists who were at the frontier of knowledge and he saw that being a collector was part of something bigger: using the system of Linnaeus to bring order to the profusion of the world's plants. His time at the RBGE made him all the more determined to go off across the world to discover plants that were so far hidden from the European gaze.

Plate 13. Clementina Traill (far right) outside the Caledonian Hall which housed the Herbarium. John F. Jeffrey, in charge of the Herbarium, is second from the left.

Clementina

A young lady of twenty-six was already working at the Herbarium when the thirty year old George Forrest arrived at the RBGE in 1903. Her name was Miss Traill, Harriet Clementina Mary Wallace Traill. She was tall and slim, smartly but demurely dressed, with a quiet smile (Plate 13). She was a charming and gracious person of retiring disposition, but, as they worked together in this small building by the rock garden, Forrest won her trust and confidence and the two colleagues gradually learned more about one another.

Clementina was familiar with the passions of plant collecting; it was in her blood. A love of natural history was a skein that threaded through three generations of Traills in the nineteenth century. The family owned land and lived in the Isles of Orkney in the days when the sea-shores of Britain were a happy hunting ground for ardent collectors. Clementina's grandfather was William Traill of Westness and Woodwick, and his wife Harriet collected seaweeds with their children. One of these children, Dr William of Woodwick, became a surgeon who collected beautiful Eastern shells from Madras to Malacca, and in China and Singapore.[1]

Another child was Clementina's father, George W. Traill. He filled his spare time with the collection and study of marine and freshwater algae.[2] He spent forty-two years in the head office of the Standard Life Assurance Co. at grand premises in George Street, Edinburgh,[3] and has been variously described as a clerk, bookkeeper and accountant. Clementina, the third of George Traill's four children, was born in 1877. Soon afterwards the family moved from Edinburgh to Joppa on the Firth of Forth, where the rocky shores were clothed in rich carpets of green, brown and red seaweed. There the children acquired from their father the skills of detailed,

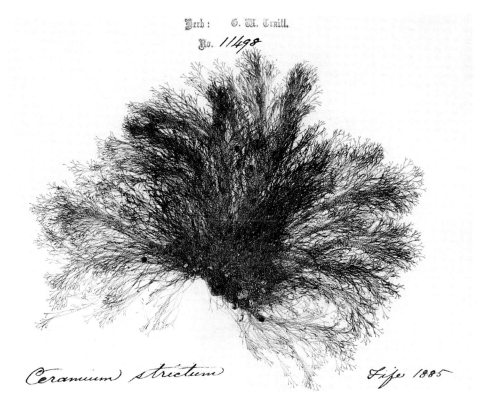

Herb: G. W. Traill.
No. 11498

Ceramium strictum

Fife 1885

Plate 14. George Forrest's father-in-law, George W. Traill, was an authority on algae. This seaweed, *Ceramium strictum,* is one of the rarer species he collected in Fife in 1885 as number 11,498 in his Herbarium.

accurate observation and they were used to the long hours he spent studying and arranging his international collection of specimens. He was an intrepid collector, even with declining health and failing eyesight,[4] and he wrote ten papers on the marine algae of Joppa, the Firth of Forth and the Orkney Islands.[5] Seaweeds were named after him, including the genus *Trailliella*[6] and species such as *Phyllophora traillii*.

Balfour knew Traill through the Botanical Society of Edinburgh. They visited each other to see their respective algal collections in the Traill home and the RBGE,[7] and before Traill died in 1897 he donated part of his algal collection to the RBGE (Plate 14).[8] Balfour knew Clementina from when she was twelve years old and later offered her a job in the Herbarium where her father's collection of algae was lodged.[9]

Friendship between Clementina and George Forrest soon developed and blossomed. They found that they both lived with widowed mothers and shared a sense of humour. She was intrigued by tales of his adventures in Australia and her quiet steadfastness complemented his zestful spirit. As the bond between them grew, Clementina's mother sometimes invited Forrest to their home for meals. It was springtime. Clementina was a keen walker and naturalist and they shared a love of the countryside.

Yunnan beckons

It is possible that Forrest had no special interest in China before he arrived at the RBGE. If so, that was soon to change. The Regius Keeper, Bayley Balfour, was alert to the continuing revelations of the rich Chinese mountain flora and keen to grow new introductions. More than ten years before Forrest arrived at the RBGE, the Garden was competing for seeds that Abbé Delavay had sent from Yunnan to the Jardin des Plantes in Paris. The Garden obtained seed from Delavay's newly discovered *Rhododendron racemosum* and in 1893 Balfour proudly sent this flower for illustration in *Curtis's Botanical Magazine*. It was an early hint of the many rhododendrons in Yunnan awaiting seed collection for our gardens.

Balfour had an impressive web of contacts at home and abroad to keep him up to date with developments in the fields of botany and horticulture, and as an eminent botanist he was elected to membership of scientific societies on the Continent and in Britain.[10] He was Fellow of the Linnean Society which published, in 1892, the known plants of China. The long list included over thirty species of *Primula* that Delavay had found, providing mounting evidence of the huge diversity of plants that existed in Yunnan.[11] No wonder that botanists and gardeners were anxious to obtain more seeds from there. But how?

One of Balfour's more unusual correspondents who wanted seed from Yunnan was a Liverpool cotton broker, Arthur K. Bulley (Plate 15). Bulley was a catalyst who made things happen and he was to be a most unexpected and fortuitous influence on Forrest's career.[12] He was an exceptionally keen and knowledgeable gardener and a lively, colourful character. He was a cultured man of great individuality, with an unkempt look and a trilby hat among the smartly dressed, bowler hat brigade at the Cotton Exchange. Bulley was the only Liverpool cotton broker with strong socialist leanings, in those pioneering days of the Labour party, and he later canvassed (unsuccessfully) as a Labour candidate in municipal elections and as a Women's Suffrage candidate for parliament.

Bulley and Balfour had a matching enthusiasm and fascination for introducing new flowers to Britain. Bulley, as an amateur gardener, had a very special collection of alpine and hardy plants in his garden and he used every means possible to add to its rarity value. In the 1890s he circulated a lithographed letter to anyone who might be useful, from a Customs man or Consul to a representative in the cotton trade:

> I am an enthusiastic and devoted lover of wild flowers which are hardy enough to stand the cold of an English winter out of doors … All hardy plants are interesting to me – the smallest gentian or Saxifrage of the mountains, as much as the tallest Lily or Rose of the woods and plains.
>
> Now for the main question. Have you any natural love of flowers? Or, if not, do you know of any people in your part of the world who have. Because, if so, and you would let me have their addresses, I would gladly write to them and say, that if they have nothing more important to do, to gather and send me a few seeds or bulbs of anything they may consider beautiful growing in their neighbourhood, I would with pleasure pay the carriage, and send them in return seeds of the best things which grow in English gardens. Gardening is my hobby and delight. And truly it would be a pleasing thought that one had been instrumental in adding to the store of beauty in hardy flowers available for poor men's gardens.[13]

This was a huge gamble, but in Bulley's global quest for seed he wrote more personal, pleading letters to other enthusiasts, botanic gardens and nurserymen and he surprised Balfour by the wide variety of plants that he offered to the Botanic Garden in Edinburgh.

One of Bulley's sources of seed was Augustine Henry, recruited as a young man to the Imperial Maritime Customs Service in China (see Plate 94). He was posted in lonely and virtually unexplored territory in central China and then Yunnan and, as an antidote to boredom, Henry offered to collect herbarium specimens for Kew in his spare time, employing native collectors to help him. He sent Bulley some seeds, confiding to a friend, 'I don't know [Bulley], but he wrote to me for seeds … He is an enthusiast. I have a weakness for enthusiasts, cranks and the like.'[14]

Extracts from Henry's Yunnan letters to the Director of Kew were published in the *Kew Bulletin* in 1897, for all to see:

Plate 15. Cartoon of Arthur K. Bulley, Liverpool cotton broker, with a socialist document in his pocket.

As regards botany, this region is, I imagine, the most interesting in the world. It is evidently the headquarters of most of the genera which are now spread all over Europe and Asia in great part … I intend to go on collecting vigorously, and hope to rival Delavay in Yunnan. His 3,000 species will be hard to beat.[15]

Henry's enthusiasm was infectious and he reported that his shoes were nearly worn out from all the trekking, but mules were cheap and he had just had a tent made for trips.

Bulley was gradually being persuaded of the desirability of focusing on Yunnan. He wrote to Henry, 'I've just been reading Hosie's book, 'Three years in Western China'… I found the general description of Szechuan and Yunnan very clear and helpful. What he said about the Flora of Tali [Dali] has made my mouth water.'[16]

The same year Henri Correvon, a leading light on alpine plants, confirmed this by writing Bulley a firm postcard in his idiosyncratic English:

> If you know somebody which is in Yunnan you must write … All the plants of Delavay come from there. Read the publication of Franchet on the new Primula; … Gentians, Paeonies, Anemones, Iriss [irises], etc. of the Yunnan. I always wish to hear that somebody would go there … if you have a friend there ask him for seeds of Primula and Paeonies etc. etc., faithfully yours H.Correvon.'[17] (Plate 16.)

Ever eager, Bulley wrote to missionaries who were stationed at Tali [Dali], in the area where Delavay had been based in Yunnan: 'I've written to the C.I.M. [China Inland Mission] people there offering all sorts of bribes. Shortly I shall tackle the papists.'[18]

But Augustine Henry became adamant that so much time and patience were needed to collect seeds as well as herbarium specimens that full-time collectors were required. He tried to persuade the Director of Kew, William Thiselton-Dyer, 'so great is the variety and beauty of the Chinese flora and so fit are the plants for [the] European climate, that an effort ought to be made to send out a small expedition.'

In the 1899 issue of the *Kew Bulletin* Henry echoed the thoughts of the experienced collector, Henry John Elwes, saying, 'until the great region north-east, as it were, of the Himalayas is explored, people will have no idea of the richness of the world in beautiful plants.'[19] He wished that he could be sent to Tengyueh, near the border between Burma and Yunnan, where he had heard that a Customs House was to be established: 'A little more north there are higher mountains, and I think there would be quite a new flora there'. In his next published letter in the *Kew Bulletin* he was even more precise, 'there would be a chance of rivalling Delavay's collections from the mountains near Tali'.

Such news was tantalising to people like Balfour and Bulley. They ached to get their hands on more seed from Yunnan. Balfour, as director of the RBGE, was bound by the terms of the Treasury not to raise money for such a venture, whilst Bulley, who had only just bought the land for Ness Gardens, was resistant to starting his own commercial nursery. Meanwhile, in 1899, the nursery firm of Messrs James Veitch & Sons, Chelsea, sent E.H. Wilson to central China to collect seed of the handkerchief tree, *Davidia involucrata*, gaining advice from Augustine Henry on the way.

In 1901 Augustine Henry visited Bulley at Ness and reiterated his thoughts on the need for a full-time collector in Yunnan. Both men realised that the recent opening of a Customs post at Tengyueh provided a shorter route through Burma into Yunnan. As they walked and talked, Augustine Henry gave his constant advice: 'Don't waste money on postage – send a man'.[20] Bulley eventually decided late in 1903 that he would start his own nursery, named from his initials: A. Bee & Co. A special feature of his nursery would be a professional, full-time collector to gather seeds of hardy and alpine plants from the mountains made famous by Delavay.

The decision now made, Bulley wasted no time. He wrote an advertisement for a collector in the *Gardeners' Chronicle* and wrote to Balfour at the Royal Botanic Garden Edinburgh.

Wanted: a plant collector

On 30 April 1904 a highly compressed message in fairly small print appeared low down in a 'Trade' column under 'Situations Vacant' in the *Gardeners' Chronicle*. It was seven months since Forrest started at the RBGE and it was to be a life-changing message:

WANTED, a YOUNG MAN well up in Hardy Plants, to go out to the East and Collect. – Box 15, G.P.O., Liverpool

Bulley wrote this advertisement as a nurseryman intent on finding the best possible person to harvest the hardy and alpine flora of the Yunnan mountains.

Even better for Forrest, three days earlier, Bulley had also written to Balfour to ask him whether he had a suitable man on his staff for such an expedition. The answer from Balfour was very positive.

> Royal Botanic Garden
> Edinburgh
> 28 April 1904
>
> Dear Mr Bulley,
>
> There is a man, Forrest, here who is on the lookout for a billet such as you describe. I have given your letter to him and he will write to you.
>
> He was recommended to my notice by John Abercromby, the Naturalist, as a man who was collecting plants for some Society in Scotland and who wished to go abroad as a collector. I could find nothing for him in that line but took him on my staff in the Herbarium so that, whilst of use to us, he might gain a wider knowledge of plants. He has been working here for about 6 months and I have found him an excellent industrious and steady man. He has had opportunity here of getting to know a good deal about the plants of the world and he seems to have profited by it. The Head of the Herbarium speaks very highly of him.
>
> He is a strongly built fellow and seems to me to be of the right grit for a collector.
>> Yours very truly,
>> Isaac Bayley Balfour[21]

Delighted at such good news, Bulley immediately asked Balfour for more details, which he sent on the very day that the advertisement came out in the *Gardeners' Chronicle*. Forrest had a head start.

> 30 April 1904
>
> Dear Mr Bulley,
>
> Forrest should be all right in the way of health, honesty, steadiness, devotion to work, general knowledge of plants. Of his gardening powers I know nothing; he has not been on our gardening staff. I should say that if he knew what you want he would do well for you…
>> Yours
>> Isaac Bayley Balfour[22]

With such an endorsement Bulley didn't hesitate to hire Forrest. Forrest would set off for China as soon as possible, on behalf of the nursery firm, A. Bee & Co. This was the kind of job he had hankered after, but which only a few months earlier had

Plate 16. The tree peony, *Paeonia delavayi,* discovered in N.W. Yunnan by Père Delavay in 1884, and important in breeding garden hybrids.

seemed impossible to find. At last he had the chance to prove what he could do. And there were extraordinary parallels to the way in which, five years earlier, E.H. Wilson had been hired to collect seed in China. Then the Director of Kew recommended Wilson to the nursery firm of Veitch, just as Forrest was now being recommended to Bulley and his nursery.

The only thing that could have stopped Forrest leaving for China was his love for Clementina. However, she saw Forrest's dilemma, knowing his present job was only temporary, not well paid or ideal for him. Having experienced her father's enthusiasm for collecting, Clementina understood Forrest's desperate wish to set out exploring for plants. Not only had her uncle, William Traill, collected in China, but on her mother's side of the family travel was part of life. Her grandfather, Henry Trew, had held government appointments in the West Indies and was married in Dominica. Her mother had been born in Antigua.

Mrs Traill did not approve of Forrest as a suitor for her daughter. It seems that in those socially hierarchical times her proud mother thought that Clementina would be marrying beneath her. Clementina came from a long lineage of Traills, traced back to their seat in Orkney, and the Trews had moved in colonial society. Forrest's father was only a draper and in his job he only went to the back door of any 'Big House'. Moreover, what security of income could Forrest possibly provide as a plant collector?

However, a strong bond had grown up between the two young people in the Herbarium and there was nothing that Mrs Traill could do about it. George Forrest and Clementina Traill became engaged before he left for China in the spring of 1904. In those Edwardian days, the combined ethos of Christianity and benevolent imperialism imbued exploration overseas with high ideals of manliness, courage and service. Clementina was quietly proud of Forrest and they accepted separation as a necessary sacrifice in a good cause. They were two people of complete integrity who trusted each other and were prepared to face three years apart, knowing they would be married on his return. Forrest's life in Australia had been carefree; now a new sense of responsibility was on his shoulders. The young couple's closeness, loyalty and love were to be tested more than either of them could possibly have foreseen.

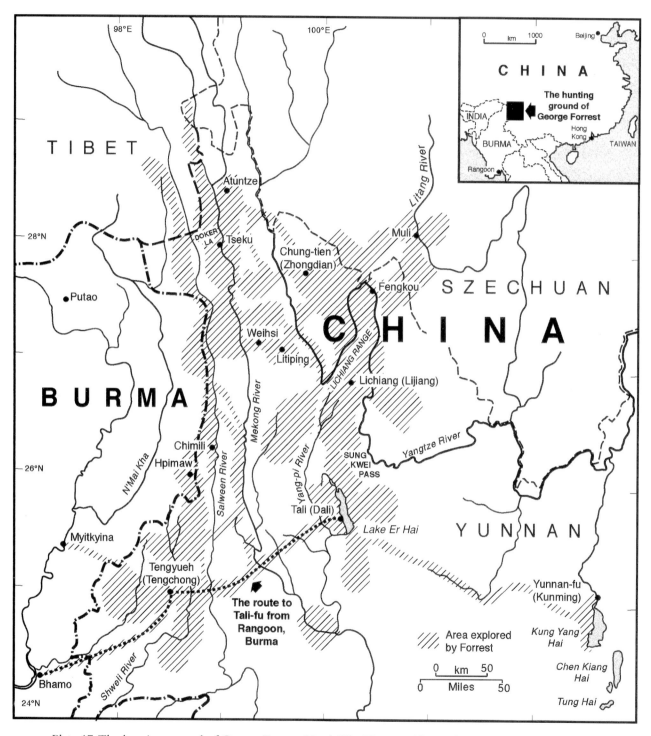

Plate 17. The hunting ground of George Forrest, North West Yunnan, China. The names are those used by him and contemporary plant hunters.

CHAPTER THREE

To China for Bees Ltd, 1904

Let us, then, be up and doing,
With a heart for any fate.

H. W. Longfellow

Forrest left the Royal Botanic Garden Edinburgh on Saturday 14 May 1904. He felt exhilarated and eager to be off. He was beckoned by the unknown, and ready for the challenge. 'Beware the rainy season in Burma', warned Bulley, but Forrest could not wait. He booked the quickest passage to Rangoon, via the Suez Canal and India, and boarded the P&O passenger liner SS *Australia* bound for Bombay (Plate 18). He left his mother in the care of his sisters, his brother in charge of his money and Clementina (Clem) with his much thumbed Bentham and Hooker until they met again.

Keen to reach China

Forrest had a long journey ahead of him, by ship, rail, paddle steamer and mule caravan. The first stage, in the luxury of a modern liner, gave no idea of what was to come. He was to face new experiences in other cultures and climates before reaching his destination. But he was prepared for anything – a friend had given him two revolvers – and he was determined to reach Delavay's former hunting ground, around Tali [Dali] in Yunnan, as soon as possible. The Board of the RBGE contacted the Foreign Office to request the co-operation of the Consuls in China.

Before the ship reached Aden, Forrest discovered that one of the head stewards knew a plant collector in Australia. Forrest immediately asked the steward for a package to be sent to Balfour in Edinburgh, on the off chance that it might be useful. In an explanatory note to Balfour he wrote, 'Thanking you for all your kindness in the past,'[1] little realising that their lives would be entwined for years to come.

Forrest arrived at Bombay, the flourishing terminus of the India route, on

Plate 18. A letterhead used by George Forrest, outward bound on S.S. *Australia* in 1904.

Plate 19. George Forrest relaxing on his travels.

Saturday 4 June 1904 and sent Clem a card from the stylish Watson's Esplanade Hotel. In those Edwardian days of the Raj it was mainly patronised by British army officers. He was in for a culture shock. The extremes between European luxury and the natives' poor status struck him forcibly. He wrote home:

No European thinks of walking, at least during the heat of the day. Gharries as they are called, are to be had for 8 annas ½ rupee = 8d per hour, so it is hardly worth one's while walking. These gharries are really rubber-tyred victorias [4 wheeled carriages]. The drivers being natives called gharry-wallahs…All the native servants are called boys irrespective of age or positions, and in my opinion most servile. They are continually salaaming the sahib and it makes one feel most uncomfortable at first, at least it did me…In my opinion they work very cheaply in fact almost for nothing…I think it is a shame but apparently they are quite pleased with such payment, and to give them more, as I felt inclined to do, only makes them lose respect for you…In fact one has hardly to do anything for oneself. I believe they would have washed and dressed me if I had allowed it…

Forrest admired the exceptionally fine buildings of Bombay, notably the Victoria

Terminus of the Great Indian Peninsular Railway that had been elaborately ornamented and completed only sixteen years before, and the carefully planned streets lined with mangrove and other flowering trees, and the palm decorated gardens. However, the contrasts within the populace perturbed him:

> The streets of the city are swept by natives, men, women carting away the refuse in baskets on their heads to carts drawn by buffaloes…All the lower caste natives go practically naked, the children entirely so. The men have nothing on but a loin cloth, and a turban…[while] The police of Bombay are dressed in khaki trousers, blue putties and jacket and brilliant canary yellow turban…The pest of the place is…the beggars. These, in most cases, are afflicted with some disabling and generally loathsome disease, which they make the most of. They are most persistent and will only leave off on threat of being kicked. They seemed to think nothing of being pummelled by a white man. On the launch coming ashore from the steamer, I saw the captain kick and hammer one of the porters until I thought he intended killing him, for a most trivial offence…but I don't think although I can swear at them and order them about now that I shall ever reach the kicking stage.

Forrest's sensitivities were being tested and stretched by the attitudes and callousness he witnessed. Nurtured in a strong Protestant tradition, he had a powerful sense of justice and morality, and his own personal discipline and loyalty were shown by his reactions to what he saw next, when a fellow Indian traveller took him for a drive to another area of Bombay late on the Saturday night.

> I thought I knew a lot regarding the viciousness of the world in general, but that drive only showed me my own ignorance. In the native quarter the streets are very narrow, no pavements, the houses generally of two stories, and very small…The stench is indescribable in places…a mixture of sweaty bodies and all sorts of reeking abominations;…the streets, altho' it was nearing midnight, were densely crowded and all places were in full swing, so much so in fact, that it was impossible for our gharry to go at more than a walking pace. I never knew what it was Hasan intended showing me and therefore it came all the more as a shock…the part that we drove through is simply one vast brothel. Each of these rooms on the ground flat… had a bedstead in the background with a curtain which could be drawn when in use, I suppose. In front of each room seated on chairs or walking about in front importuning women of all ages and nationalities. On the upper story at each window was seated a woman and also in the background could be seen a bed on the floor. I never thought it possible for vice to be paraded so openly anywhere. We were continually being tackled by the women, some of whom even went the length of trying to get into the carriage beside us. As far as I could see the different nationalities kept pretty well by themselves there being a native, Japanese, and English or European quarter or districts…Altho' an experience, it was most disgusting and sad, and I was pleased when once we got back out of it…I should say roughly that there are three miles [5km] of streets devoted to nothing else…All the women are of course very gaily dressed, and a number of them very good looking, but what a life to lead…I pity the poor wretches, how they live the life I don't know, it must be awful.

A long train journey to Madras followed, and daily, for two weeks after leaving Bombay, he had to be inspected for plague and carry a plague passport. Over one million people died from plague in India in 1904 and, as it was present in Bombay, strict precautions were being taken. In Madras he met men from the Upper Burma survey department who were a 'wreck with fever' and full of awful yarns about the Burmese country Forrest had to pass through. He consoled himself that these might be gross exaggerations, but there had been a long history of disputes along the northern border between 'the peaceful Shan, less peaceful Kachin, and head-hunting Wa'.[2] Augustus Raymond Margary (1846-1875), the first Englishman to traverse the route between Burma and Yunnan, was murdered near the border.

There had also been endless difficulties in defining the boundary between Burma and China. Surveys of the Burma-China boundary commission in 1897-8 linked on to the great Survey of India pursued with such determination by William Lambton and George Everest throughout the first half of the nineteenth century.[3]

Forrest crossed to Rangoon in bad weather, in an overcrowded, dirty boat in a stench in which 'one child died and was thrown overboard like a bundle of brown paper'. The engines kept breaking down and as darkness fell over the delta of the Irrawaddy river the powerless steamboat waited for a rescue launch – and Forrest felt heartily sick of the voyaging 'that takes me away from all I love and I have nothing to do but think'.

The heavy rain and heat in Rangoon were 'atrocious':

> a rain that makes the opposite side of the street appear as through a mist, every day accompanied by heavy thunderstorms…I never heard such thunder, not even in Australia…It was like whole batteries of artillery firing together.

Though everything was 'simply steaming', he visited the magnificent, gilded 'Shive Dagone' pagoda and nearby lakes, as well as running round the city getting things together for the journey and the work to come. He bought a rifle and revolver and 200 rounds of ammunition for each, besides blankets, waterproof sheet, camp bedstead and medicines, before setting off by train to Mandalay, which is 450 miles (700km) from the sea. There he chose to continue the next 350 miles (550km) to Bhamo by the cheaper and pleasanter paddle steamer of the Irrawaddy Flotilla Company, enjoying the magnificent river scenery.

The small town of Bhamo, in Upper Burma, was the limit of steamer service up the Irrawaddy. Beyond the hills lay China, only about thirty miles (50km) away. Since 1867 the British had the right to station a commercial agent at Bhamo, to profit from overland trade across the frontier, but in 1904 there was still no road taking wheeled transport into China. After the first ten miles (16km) there was only a mountain track along which caravans of laden mules and ponies carried the goods of two empires. A steep path from the river led straight to the huge caravan camp, which in the dry season would be full of tethered animals, heaps of Chinese saddles, and an exciting atmosphere with a mixture of races and the flow of traffic. However, Forrest arrived in early July, at the height of the monsoon, and the (British) Deputy Commissioner at Bhamo strongly advised him to go back to Rangoon and wait until October when conditions would be better.[4] This was the last thing that Forrest would do; he urgently wanted to press on to Tengyueh (Tengchong), the first walled town beyond the frontier. He was given a letter of introduction to Mr Litton, who was Consul at Tengyueh and a particular friend of Bulley. Forrest gained permission to put up at the daks (government bungalows) provided along the route in Burma and he bought tinned food and other stores. He had his photograph taken in his new garb and sent copies to his brother, mother, Clem and a friend. The anticipation was immense. He wrote home:

> If I can manage, of course, once I get right into China I shall put on the regulation Chinese dress, big baggy trousers reaching to the calf and a loose blouse with a big hat and Chinese shoes. Minus the pigtail of course, altho' I could buy one.

(This hairstyle of a long plait was imposed by the conquering Manchus in 1644.) Some Protestant missionaries in China at the time used to wear this apparel to seem less foreign and sixty years earlier a Scottish plant collector, Robert Fortune, had worn Chinese dress to escape recognition when he ventured beyond the recognised limit for Europeans. In 1904 Europeans could have permits to travel inland. Indeed only one photograph of Forrest shows him wearing Chinese costume when, like Fortune, he needed a disguise. As he set off from Bhamo he was simply relishing the thought of this totally new adventure and loved telling his family about it.

> I have been advised by nearly everyone here to buy a young Burmese girl and take her with me as a bedmate and help. You never knew of that kind of thing before, did you? It is the regulation thing in this country and especially here and on such a journey as I am going. They run from 100 to 1,000 rupees according to their attractiveness and purity. All the [unmarried] officers in the regiments stationed here, and there are three regiments, besides all the civil authorities… keep them. The girls are simply delighted with having a European for a husband, if you like to call it that, and I could get a dozen tomorrow if I wanted them, ranging from 10 or 12 to 20. I have been laughed at several times for protesting against it …but I wouldn't touch any of them with a tarry stick. There is only one woman in the world for me and that is Clem, and she is white all through…I have kept straight all my life and I have every reason in the world to keep straighter than ever.[5]

With that reassurance he sent fondest love and kisses to all the family and set off for the frontier.

For this first experience of the main Burmese trade route into China Forrest kept a daily diary in an exercise book.[6] In this he vividly recounted for his family the terrible conditions of his journey, the countryside through which he passed and the people he met. As it was the only diary he ever kept and holds such intrinsic and historic interest, some details will now be given to show the experience through his eyes, as he encountered a new culture and landscape. It is a record not only of the problems he had to overcome, but of the way he solved them. One early lesson was that the essential co-operation of both man and beast was not easily won, especially in the monsoon. He wrote home that 'The stubbornness of the Chinese muleteer is proverbial here and only equalled …by his animals'. However, frustrating delays were turned into opportunities to meet people, drink with them and learn his first words of Chinese. Ordeals could be forgotten in the joy of watching wildlife or examining an orchid. Then his spirits would lift, making all seem worthwhile, as if the discovery re-energised him to go on.

This adventurous naturalist never knew the phrase 'I give up!' He had a mission he took seriously and an utter determination to fulfil his task. His instinct was to be alert, adapt and to consider risks and challenges as the spice of life. The diary reveals his keen observant eye, his quick sizing up of situations and his astuteness of reaction to dangers and difficulties. Very few Europeans entered China by this route, so he also aroused much curiosity among the local people. He was offered hospitality and exchanged gifts, even though to some, as a European, he was a 'foreign devil'.

None the less, when he arrived in Tengyueh he wrote to his mother admitting the journey had been most trying and had taken not the nine days that he had anticipated, but twenty-three days to cover 150 miles (240km). 'I think if I had known what I know now of the road, I would have taken Mr Bulley's advice and stayed in Bhamo for the winter.'[7]

The inexperienced Forrest knew no Chinese or Burmese and could not find an interpreter to go with him, so he took two servants, one Chinese who could speak Burmese and one Hindu who could speak Burmese and very little English. The muleteers objected strongly to travelling in the rain, and caused a day's delay, but eventually Forrest set off with nineteen bullocks and mules loaded for the Consular and Customs service in Tengyueh, as well as his own twelve bullocks, three mules,

Plate 20. Caravans being loaded in a compound. Note the loaded wooden box saddles on the ground.

a pony and nine muleteers. Each animal was laden with a wooden box saddle and frame carrying loads of up to 2 cwt (100kg) divided into two packages placed like panniers on either side. At night this frame with the load could be lifted out of the wooden saddle and placed on the ground (Plate 20).

The road was bounded either side by an almost impenetrable wall of wet and marshy tropical jungle: tall teak and wild mango, bamboo, shrubs, tall grasses and innumerable creepers. There were not many flowers in bloom, but when he stopped to examine one he was captivated by an approaching green and brown whip snake. He watched curiously. 'Nothing that I have ever seen', he wrote, 'equals the agility and beauty of motion of these snakes. They seem to glide over the leaves and small stems of a plant, travelling along a stem and not around it as is popularly supposed'. He killed one that was about 4ft.6in. (1.4m) long and as thick as his little finger.

The muleteers were dressed in their cool, loose Shan trousers and big grass or cane hats and Forrest gradually stripped off some clothes as the daytime temperature rose. He alternated riding and walking the ten miles (16km) to the foot of the hills, where there was a village of about a hundred cane huts, each raised above the ground on teak poles, the main frame of teak supporting walls of interwoven patterns of split bamboo. The filthy main street had wide gutters piled with mud, bullock dung and village refuse and Forrest was not surprised to hear that cholera was rampant, as it was in Bhamo. He lodged comfortably in a dak bungalow, the muleteers sleeping on the ground beneath, their animals safe in the compound. As darkness fell he examined the flickering fireflies, 'one of the prettiest sights of this country'. He timed their flashes of light and wrote a detailed description of one he captured in a matchbox.

Their journey through the hills was more of a nightmare. He summarised it in a letter to his mother:

> The roads were frightful, miles [of] nothing but streams and ditches sometimes belly deep and whilst on the hills we had to negotiate numerous landslips and heavy mountain torrents. Most of these had no bridge and had to be forded.[8]

As they left the village overnight heavy rain caused the head muleteer to avoid the valley road and steer for the heart of the hills. Even so the track was very boggy, in many places under water. Forrest rode a mule, admiring the strength, endurance and agility of these animals.

> The mule I rode, to avoid a sloughy piece of ground, clambered up an almost perpendicular bank over 5ft. [1.5m] high before I could stop it or in fact knew what it was going to do…walking along a few paces [it] jumped down on to the road again. It was an awful drop for such an animal, and I fully expected to come a cropper but it landed quite easily.

The hills were wreathed in mist and the rain poured down, and Forrest was pleased when they arrived at a dak with a view across the Irrawaddy to the mountains.

As they climbed higher, the delightfully cool air on the ridges contrasted with the 'disgustingly muggy' valleys, but the track cut on the side of the hill demanded their concentration, as the mules seemed to insist on walking on the very edge, with a drop of 600-700ft. (180-210m) down to the river below.

> I know I can stand a lot of that sort of thing without light headedness, but at last the one I was riding fairly frightened me. Its hind near foot slipped at a crumbly place, and I thought my time had come at last. It was only with a great struggle that it recovered itself and you may be sure I got off for a bit then.

The next day Forrest had his first experience of a flimsy bamboo bridge across a small mountain stream, the bamboos having no fastenings, one set simply being laid across the other. They covered twenty miles (32km) that day and Forrest felt 'rather done-up' on reaching their destination. 'It is no joke sitting for such a long time in the saddle in a blazing sun and moist heat'. He was dosing one of his boys with quinine and antefebrine and hoped he would not succumb himself as he watched the jungle swarming with monkeys on the far side of the river. The next day the boy was almost unconscious and they were not able to ford a flooded river that had no bridge. 'One of the muleteers stripped at my request and tried to ford it taking a rope across, but was nearly swept away'. Forrest summarised his position: 'Heavy rain, flooded rivers, beastly roads, and fever, with the chance of taking it badly myself. However, with the exception of a slight depression at not being able to proceed, I never felt better in my life'. This was after a 'lively night' with bugs the size of lentils swarming in his bed.

His bravado was tested when Forrest decided that a three feet (a metre) overnight drop in the water level, was sufficient for them to ford the stream:

> It took us about two hours to get everything safely across. The muleteers were all naked and it took two to pilot each bullock safely across. Most of the things got wet, more or less, and a number of my films got completely spoilt and also a part of a side of bacon. I had to swim my pony over part of the way bare-backed to keep the saddle dry, and was wet up to the waist before I was finished with the job.

As heavy rain then continued for the rest of the day, even Forrest admitted, 'I haven't even the spirit left in me to keep my eyes open for flowers. It took me all I knew to keep my pony on its feet the path was so rough and slippery'. As they arrived for the night at a 'dismal hole', everything and everyone soaking, he began to wish he had heeded advice to wait another month. 'I will just have to make the best of it and push thro'...If all goes well we will reach the frontier tomorrow.'

More troubles were in store. About two miles (3km) from camp a large landslip had carried away three-quarters of a mile of track. They had to strike across a ridge by a jungle path and every rider had a fall, including Forrest. Luckily even the boy weak with fever escaped serious injury and they clambered round other landslips, although walking through the tall grass disturbed the clegs, horseflies that drove them nearly crazy. Forrest 'killed a very pretty snake today of a beautiful bottle green, as it was crossing the path in front of us. It was about three feet [a metre] long.'

About midday they met two Chinese soldiers of the frontier guard. Each was armed with a fearsome dha, a Burmese weapon with a double handed, slightly curved single-edged blade about two feet (60cm) long, carried in a wooden scabbard slung by a heavy cord, high up on the shoulder, so that the weapon rested below the armpit. Forrest and his men were told they could go no further. 'Like the man in the song', wrote Forrest, 'we had come to a river that we couldn't get across'.

Forrest cursed inside while much talking went on and then the gentlemanly senior soldier, with a pigtail down to his knees, brought Forrest a bottle of rice spirit, called arrack, for his refreshment, and offered him one of the bamboo and grass huts. The whole encounter made a great impression on Forrest, who later described the man's dress: the usual baggy blue trousers, with a loose, plum coloured silk jacket, figured over with Chinese designs and figures in black, and long loose black sleeves and gold buttons. He wore an agate bracelet on each wrist, had enormously long fingernails and saluted Forrest 'by shaking hands with himself, and bowing'. A three-cornered conversation followed, helped by one of Forrest's boys. Forrest later wrote, 'You would have died if you had seen us each trying to outdo the other in politeness, and a circle of 40 or 50 muleteers and soldiers admiring us'. Forrest explained his work and the senior soldier said he would at once call out all the coolies of the neighbouring villages and get a bridge built, but it would take at least four days. At that moment there was only a narrow bamboo footbridge slung across the raging torrent about 30ft. (10m) above the water.

A visit of three local headmen was preceded by a gift of a duck, a fowl, five dozen eggs and three visiting cards each comprising a strip of red coloured paper on which their names were printed in black in large Chinese characters. Two men wore Chinese dress, black silk with canary coloured sashes and blue trousers, and had come to superintend the building of the bridge. The other, a senior soldier, was particularly kindly and polite, offered Forrest hospitality in his village and tried to teach Forrest his first few phrases of Chinese. The first was 't'sing t'so', or 'pray be seated'. In return Forrest opened a bottle of cherry brandy and proffered some biscuits and cigarettes and an immensely happy hour ensued until the men took their leave and about fifty coolies began to use their dhas to cut the timber and bamboo for the bridge.

The next day Forrest received more gifts of chickens, ducks and eggs before the same gentlemen reappeared with an extra headman and two servants as bodyguards armed with very long, handsomely mounted dhas. The new man offered hospitality in his home and a pony. Forrest refused, though tactfully offering a tin of fruit and a bottle of whisky. 'I do wish I could speak the language', wrote Forrest, 'They seem so pleased when I appear to understand anything they say'. He knew it would help him, too, for he later privately admitted in Tengyueh, 'I have felt horribly depressed at times…For one thing I had no one to speak to in all that time and I took to *mooning* which isn't good for anyone'.

Two days later Forrest opened another bottle of whisky and a tin of plums to welcome his three friends and they wrote down his name in Chinese. They ordered two soldiers to attend to Forrest and his servants, but this turned out to be a mixed blessing as they smoked opium and gambled most of the day and one night they had a row, one of them receiving two stab wounds that Forrest had to attend to.

Despite almost incessant rain, the bridge was completed in five days and Forrest persuaded his reluctant bullock men to continue their journey to the nearby village of Man-Hsien, where they had to report to the customs house of the frontier. Forrest described the filth and stench of this village as making any ordinary manure heap at home seem sweet and beautiful, but luckily the head-man's house was perched on a nearby hill and he kindly offered Forrest his own bed for the night while he slept on the floor. (Unlike in Burma, no bungalows were provided for travellers by the Chinese government.) Because the continuous heavy rain made the roads almost impassable, with deep, dangerous water-filled holes and enormous corrugations, this kind man tried to persuade Forrest to stay a few days, but Forrest still pressed on, after exchanging a tin of fish for their eggs and fowl. A letter of introduction was sent on to the next village and Forrest had an escort of two soldiers to take him to Tengyueh.

Once in China they had days of heavy marching through paddy fields along the 'bunds' between terraces. Even on horseback Forrest was soaked up to the knees and splashed to the hat with mud. The small villages they passed through were a sea of mud on either side of the causeway and the black pigs wallowed and fed on the excrement and refuse. 'I used to be rather partial to pork', wrote Forrest, 'but never again after what I have seen here'. However, they were hospitably welcomed at the next stopping point and Forrest found a bed already made up for him at the back of a temple behind the main shrine, after receiving more eggs, a fowl and two pineapples.

He did not foresee what would happen next morning. He was woken at about 4 a.m. by the head priest beating on a large tom-tom hung at the side of his bed and an immense bell ringing in the nearly temple. Four joss sticks were lighted above his head and a large pile of paper was lit between his bed and the shrine, to make an offering to the gods on behalf of the dead. Nearly choking, Forrest lay there bemused as the gong and bells began again, more paper was burned and prayer mats were placed on the floor, only five feet from his bed, and people began to troop in to prayers.

> I thought then that it was time to get up and was sorry I had not done so earlier as I had to dress in front of innumerable men and women who were praying all over the place…this went on all the time I was having breakfast, a continual stream of men and women passing to and fro. I was very uncomfortable but couldn't help smiling when I thought of what you people would have said could you have seen me.

Before Forrest left a large crowd had gathered in the courtyard and he dispensed calomel and quinine to about twelve people. Having tipped the head priest, he then departed as the tom-toms and bells were played in his honour. Twenty miles (32km) later they were housed in a more secluded temple and were able to keep out the curious and rested the bullocks for a day. Bands of armed robbers called dacoits were reported to be roaming the nearby hills, so he was offered an extra escort of ten soldiers, but to save money on tips he took only two, to add to the two he had already, having one in front and one behind and two with the bullocks. They acted as guides and made everyone stand to one side and dismount to clear the way. As the next thirty miles (48km) were rough going, mostly along the side of a gorge, there was no time to pay attention to anything but their own foothold on the track. That day Forrest was ten hours in the saddle, with only a drink of water after 6 am. He was welcomed at the next stop with a meal and he used chopsticks for the first time, with an audience to watch him. He was then entertained with the villagers to the headman's five-hour shadow play, 'a sort of marionette show with the shadows of the figures being cast on a screen'. He likened it to a Punch and Judy show with lots of fighting accompanied by cymbals and gongs.

The bullocks were footsore and the rain continuous, so Forrest had to endure an enforced three-day wait that was frustrating after pushing on so valiantly through the gorge. He also learned that Litton had passed through in the opposite direction, so would not be at Tengyueh to greet him. None the less, Forrest was anxious to get on and when they found the next proposed stopping place was 'filthy and vermin ridden' he resolved to reach Tengyueh that night, however long it took to cover the next ten miles (16km). His men objected strongly, so he closed discussion by getting on his pony and setting off alone to cross the fertile plain. This was a gamble, but it worked. His men had a meal and then decided to join him. They arrived at 10.30 p.m., worn and weary, travel stained but safe. Forrest put up at an 'inn' for the night and tucked in to a 'make-do' meal of rice and hard-boiled eggs. He had had no food for fifteen hours. Now he could relax, and he 'turned in dead tired'. He had come by a long and treacherous route, a three-week foolhardy struggle at the worst time of year, but his strong constitution had favoured him and he had no fever. He had reached his first destination, the walled town of Tengyueh (Tengchong), in the Yunnan province of China (Plate 21).

Launched by Litton

Forrest was now in the 'Flowery Land' of China known for its cultural appreciation of flowers, in gardens, designs, and symbolic associations such as summer with the lotus flower and August with pear blossom. However, he entered Imperial China towards the end of the Manchu-led Qing dynasties (1644-1911), when Imperial control was weak. He also entered the province of Yunnan, in the remote south-west of China, where there were many ethnic minority groups with their own traditions and cultures. Nevertheless, each district of Yunnan had its own Chinese civil official who wore a traditional, Chinese Imperial costume. This included a symbolically embroidered rank badge or mandarin square in which the image of the sun symbolised the emperor and the official's rank was represented by a particular animal, turning towards the sun, just as the official turned towards the emperor. All travellers had to pay respects and dues to the Chinese official, although ease of travel was also at the mercy of social unrest over which officialdom had little control.

The province of Yunnan had long remained virtually unknown to the British. Tengyueh was one of the most recent and remote of the treaty ports created in China to serve British and other Western interests in trade, diplomacy and evangelism. It had only been staffed since 1899. The Union flag flew from the flagstaff of British consulates and His Majesty's consul at Tengyueh was a 'listening ear' near the Burma border, keeping an eye on trade and social and political unrest, ready to deal practically and legally with emergencies involving British subjects. When Forrest arrived, the acting British consul of Tengyueh, Mr G.J.L. Litton, had

Opposite:
Plate 21. Tengyueh street with a city gate in the distance. A Forrest photograph, December 1905.

been based in Tengyueh for three years (Plate 22). An enterprising and energetic man, he had a special aptitude for the post. He travelled widely in Yunnan, venturing through mountainous, unmapped areas almost unknown to Westerners. Litton reported to the Foreign Office in London on such varied affairs as the salt trade, the army and the possibility of opening up further communications with Burma. He attended annual Sino-Burmese meetings to settle issues arising from tribal raids across the border. Indeed, he had been nearly killed on the Burmese frontier when attacked and knocked unconscious by Wa tribesmen with stones and crossbows. When he came to, the two British men with him were apparently dead and Wa were hacking at their heads 25 yards (23m) away. He shot one man who came towards him brandishing a sword.[9]

In 1904 Tengyueh had a population of only 1,400 people including four British residents: Mr G.J.L. Litton in the Consular Service and three men employed by the Imperial Maritime Customs Service. A fourth man had recently died of malignant smallpox. The Commissioner of Customs, the Hon Cecil Napier, was the eighth son of Robert Cornelius Napier (1819-1890)[10] who was created 1st Baron Napier of Magdala and given the rank of Field Marshal after commanding the Abyssinian Expedition and capturing the fortress of Magdala.[11] The pomp of his state military funeral in St. Paul's Cathedral was said to have been the most imposing spectacle since that of the Duke of Wellington's funeral in 1852.

Compared with the older, larger, coastal treaty ports, Tengyueh was a lonely and difficult European posting. For communications the staff relied on the telegraph lines and postal services dependent on mules and runners. In this tiny foreign community, isolated from family and friends, people were thrown upon each other's company. There were no pleasant social diversions, like the races held in the larger treaty ports, so travellers were especially welcome, bringing fresh companionship and news. Forrest had plenty of stories to tell and was overjoyed to converse in English again.

At Litton's invitation, Forrest settled comfortably at the consulate and explored the town with a soldier escort. He wrote home that the city was surrounded by a 'real, fired brick, wall', 30ft. (9m) high and about 40ft. (12m) thick, with four gates. Food from the surrounding plain was brought to the market every five days, attracting crowds of people to the stalls displayed under two lines of bamboo and paper umbrellas along each side of the main street. He was aware of some insults being thrown at him and, like the other Europeans, he was always armed and got through the crowds by having the soldier 10ft. (3m) in front of him, shouting and pushing people out of the way. At night the Europeans had an escort of four soldiers and a procession of servants carrying Chinese paper lanterns. Forrest made light of this to his family, but he also reported Litton's explanation, 'If it wasn't for the punishment which they know would be meted out to them our lives would not be worth a moment's purchase'.

Forrest spent six busy days in Tengyueh. There were so many basic practical matters to be attended to, as he learned and adapted to the way of life in Imperial China, accumulating the necessary paperwork, currency and other articles necessary for his travels. Litton wrote and spoke Chinese fluently, having learned both Cantonese and Mandarin. He proved to be a most lively, helpful friend and Forrest acknowledged his good fortune in having Litton's assistance.

Litton and Napier, who were both about Forrest's age, had the fun of deciding Forrest's honorary Chinese name, Fu Lishi (Plate 23). They translated it as 'Fu the learned scholar'. ('Rather ridiculous, isn't it?' wrote Forrest.) His new name was

carved on a wooden block, to be used as a seal or 'chop'. Forrest then obtained two enormous passports, made of good quality paper, written in vertical columns of Chinese script. The first was nearly two foot (60cm) square and stated that Article 9 of the Tianjin Treaty allowed British people to hold a passport for travel and business. Forrest's Chinese name was inserted, together with his simple title, 'Employee from Britain'. In the top right-hand corner Litton wrote in his own hand, 'Mr G. Forrest, granted Aug. 12, 1904 for 1 year. Good for Yunnan, Kweichow and Szechuan'. Litton personally signed it and gave it the official stamp of the British Consulate, Tengyueh. Two days later Forrest visited the chief military official to receive a supporting passport/visa, giving advice to travel only on the main roads for his safety – a tall order for a plant hunter as determined as Forrest. The first passport was then verified with a special red stamp in ancient Chinese calligraphy. Now at last Forrest was equipped with the necessary papers to show to Chinese officials of every district he passed through in the coming year.[12]

Litton advised him to open an account with a merchant who acted as a banker

Plate 22. Consul Litton ready for his travels with two Lissoo sepoys, 1905.

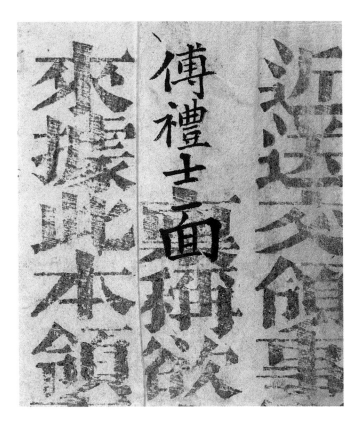

Plate 23. George Forrest's Chinese name, Fu Lishi, inserted in black Chinese script reading downwards, on Forrest's 1905 provincial passport.

of the 'Happy Spring' bank and Forrest made a deposit of 800 rupees, to draw on when he got to Talifu, as well as keeping his account with Cook & Son in Rangoon. His bank dealings were to be recorded in a Chinese bank 'book' that opened like a concertina and Litton introduced him to the Chinese currency. Forrest often withdrew his money in taels of silver. (In 1904 he paid his cook 8 taels and 3 taels for food or 'rice money' per month, his 'number two boy' and his groom each getting 3 taels and 3 taels for food.) For larger transactions at that time he required silver currency ingots or sychee cast in Yunnan from refined silver

Plate 24. Silver ingots: currency used by George Forrest in Yunnan under Imperial rule on his first two expeditions.
Above: 'Yuansi' ingots cast in rounded iron moulds. All have concentric ripple marks on their surface and bubble marks on the underside.
Right: 5-ounce (140g) 'fangbian', or saddlepack ingots stamped with silver marks and made in Yunnan. The scale is in centimetres.

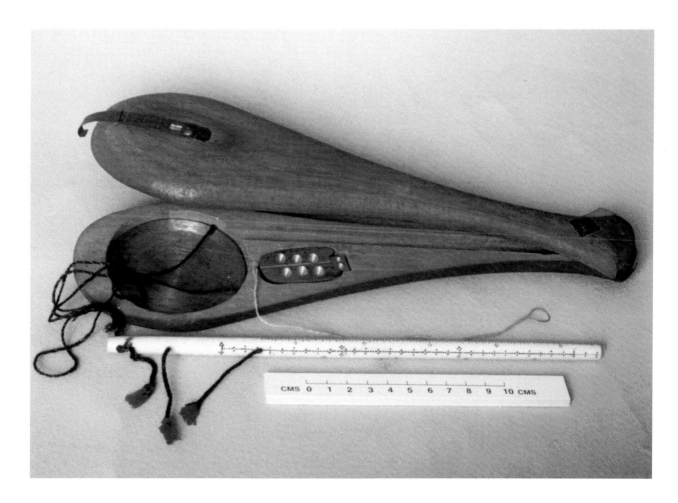

bullion (Plate 24). The main ingots used to pay taxes were the *fangbian*, known in English as 'Yunnan saddlepack ingots'. They were reliably tested for the purity of their silver and stamped with the names of the responsible bank and official assayer. Other *yuansi*, or 'fine silk oval ingots', were unstamped.[13] Even the saddlepack ingots were not all exactly the same weight, so Forrest, like every traveller, banker, merchant or shopkeeper, acquired small portable money scales, called 'dotchin' by foreigners. Forrest could not even visit the market without one. The 'dotchin' was a hand-held balance with a single pan and a counterweight that would be suspended and slid along an ivory beam with markings like a scale. An ingot that was too big for a certain transaction would have some silver clipped off it. Once used, the dotchin would be neatly packed into its hinged wooden case, shaped like two spoons held together by their handles (Plate 25).[14]

Plate 25. George Forrest's portable scales or 'dotchin' used to weigh silver and enclosed in a wooden case.

Fortunately for Forrest, Litton was unhampered by routine and he offered to travel with Forrest to Talifu (Tali, now Dali), and helped him to hire mules and procure fresh servants, including a good Chinese cook. Litton even asked Forrest to pick some local flowers to demonstrate his job, in order to dispel rumours that Forrest was a magician who was going to Tali to get gold and pearls from Erhai, the nearby lake.

At the end of August 1904 they headed 200 miles (320km) eastwards to Tali, crossing the gorges of the mighty Salween and Mekong rivers that flow south from the snowy, windswept heights of the Tibetan plateau. These deeply entrenched rivers flow parallel for hundreds of miles, sometimes only fifty miles (80km) apart, and Forrest described the rough road to Tali as crossing a 'regular see-saw of immense ranges of mountains and deep valleys'. On reaching the walled town of Tali Forrest thought that, but for the filth of the place, it would be a paradise on earth. It lay between a range of mountains towering to over 13,000ft. (4,000m) and

Plate 26. The historic town of Tali (Dali) where Forrest often stayed at the China Inland Mission and hunted for plants on the nearby mountains, the Tali Range (Cang Shan).

the shore of the lake called Erhai with its harbour and fishing boats (Plate 26). This was within the area of Père Delavay's former plant hunting and Tali was to be a base for many of Forrest's expeditions. As Forrest approached this mountain range for the first time, Litton told him that probably no plant collector had yet been to the top of these mountains. Indeed, many were unsurveyed (Plate 27). This encouraged Forrest's hope that, despite the previous good work of Delavay, he would still find hardy and alpine plants totally new to British science and horticulture.

A preliminary canter
Forrest had originally intended to settle at Tali for the winter and learn Chinese. However, Litton was travelling to the annual horse and mule fair held at Sung Kwei (Songgui/Songkui), north of Tali, on the seventh moon, in September. Forrest went with him and fresh plans emerged.

Earlier in the year an American traveller, Mr E. Nichols, had arrived at Tengyueh,

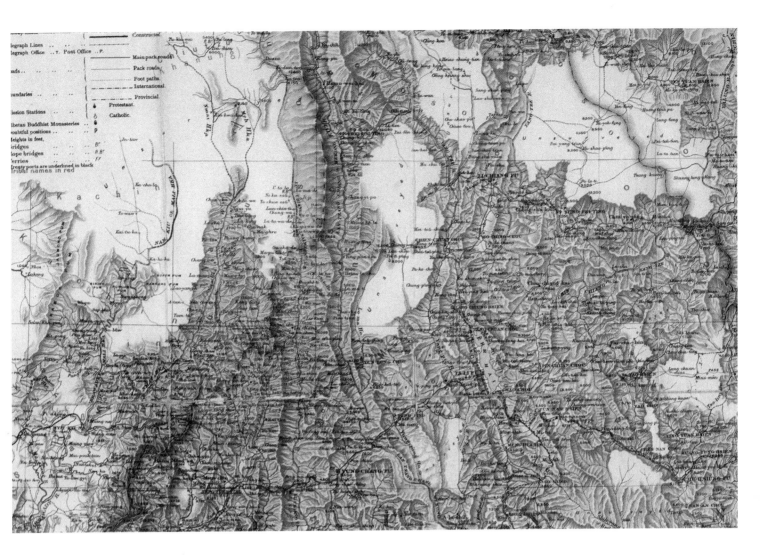

dressed in Tibetan costume, having spent several months further north in Chinese Tibetan country between Tachienlu (Kangding) and Batang. He had made friends with the lamas in the area and spoke Tibetan. He reported to Litton that Chinese influence was declining in those borderlands and emissaries of the Grand Lama were openly urging the Tibetans to cast off their allegiance to the Chinese. Also, the current British Expedition to Lhasa, led by Younghusband,[15] was exciting the Tibetans and anti-English and anti-Chinese feeling was very strong.[16]

When Litton met Mr Nichols again at Sung Kwei horse fair he decided he had better see for himself what was happening in the Tibetan borderlands. He offered to take Forrest, warning him that they would be pressed for time, but they would go by horseback. Forrest leapt at the opportunity to see more of Yunnan with him. He relished the chance to traverse the northern ranges to gain a bird's eye view of the land, its people and its wildlife, especially as Bulley had recently acknowledged his 'British pluck' and given him a free hand to go where he liked. (On the other hand, the Consul General, W.H. Wilkinson, told them not to go and later wired to say he 'washed his hands' of them.[17]) Litton and Forrest were mobbed at the fair and had to draw their revolvers in self-defence; some of their horses and mules were stolen. Once these were replaced, the two friends were nearly ready. Litton was tall and thin compared with Forrest's stocky figure and they came from different backgrounds, Litton having private means and going from Eton to Oxford University. But they were glad of each other's company, enjoyed the same humour and shared a love of exploration and adventure.

The little party set off for the Chungtien (Zhongdian) plateau on their way to

Plate 28. Zhongdian (Chungtien) plateau in autumn with euphorbia and autumn gentians. The brilliant red of the euphorbia reminded Consul Litton of reading about vegetation from Mars in *The War of the Worlds*.

Opposite:
Plate 29. The west side of the Yulong Shan (Lichiang Range) looking over the Yangtze river from near Tiger Leaping Gorge. Forrest wrote that it was 'a most impressive scene. It makes one wonder where all the water comes from. Here at over two thousand miles [3,200km] from the sea it is fully 600 yards [550m] broad and very deep and swift.'

the borderlands with Tibet. They camped a mile from the Yangtze River (Jinsha Jiang) ferry and Forrest had his first view of this great River of Golden Sand, one of the longest in the world, where the mountains force its turbulent flow in huge bends squeezed between gigantic cliffs (Plate 29). They crossed by ferry, 'an immense flat bottomed structure more like a raft than a boat, capable of holding about 30 horses and propelled by 6 oars, each worked by 3 or 4 men'. In twenty minutes the current forced the boat about two miles (3km) downstream. They then made an eight hour ascent through dense forest over a chilly pass of yak pastures and descended to the plateau of Chungtien. As they approached the valley of Chungtien, Litton described the picturesque view of fields and marsh with dark pine woods on the lower slopes and bare mountain tops above the sparkling mountain streams, reporting to London that it 'reminded my companion, a Scotch botanist, of a cultivated highland valley in his native land'.[18] Litton got carried away, writing lyrically about 'a species of Euphorbia which in the autumn turns so brilliant a red that readers of *The War of the Worlds* might think that the vegetation of the valley came from Mars' (Plate 28).

Forrest was thrilled to be there, telling Balfour that the plateau 'is blank on the maps, and Litton and I were the first Europeans to pass up it.'[19] He excitedly told his mother, 'I have never seen any place to equal it for flowers in all my travels. It is one huge flower garden'. Despite the rain, he was collecting and numbering plant specimens and pressing them between drying papers, and harvesting seed whenever he could, while Litton, like Forrest, admired the pastures richly carpeted with masses of blue gentians. They estimated altitude by using a last boiling point thermometer. (The boiling of water falls about 1°C degree for every 1,000 feet

Plate 30. The autumn gentian, *Gentiana sino-ornata*. It is one of Forrest's best known discoveries and has been adopted by Ness Botanic Gardens (once the home of A.K. Bulley) as their logo.

(300m) of altitude.) At 14–15,000ft. (4,500m) above sea level, Forrest collected specimens of *Gentiana sino-ornata*, one of the most popular deep blue autumn flowering gentians in gardens in Britain today (Plate 30). Further on, at about 12–13,000ft. (3,800m), near the town of Chungtien (Zhongdian), he picked another new species of gentian, one that he was to name after his fiancée, *Gentiana trailliana*[20] (now *Comastoma traillianum*). They were running short of stores and, as the countryside was teeming with game, they kept 'the pot going' with their guns and had 'some lovely shooting on the Chungtien plateau', in one afternoon bagging close on fifty brace of pheasants.

Plate 31. *Gentiana sino-ornata* photographed by Forrest on his second expedition, 2 October 1910.

As they crossed the plateau they met more and more Tibetans. They mainly stayed in Tibetan headmen's houses, and one whose company Forrest particularly enjoyed was a

Plate 32. *Gentiana georgei* discovered by George Forrest on his first expedition. Professor Diels, in Marburg, named the flower in Forrest's honour.

> regular savage beauty, just like a pirate out of Gilbert & Sullivan. Clad in a coarse Tibetan scarlet cloak, open at the neck with immense sleeves…matted black hair hanging down to his shoulders, no pigtails here now, huge Tibetan top boots and a pair of scarlet puttees on his legs. On top of all this a cap just the same pattern as the cap of Liberty and dirt *ad libitum*.[21]

Forrest and Litton themselves were the centre of curiosity and had very little privacy. Indeed, Forrest confessed to his family that during his travels,

> I have got so callous that I can stand and have a bath with a crowd looking on. It was Litton who broke me into that. This is no exaggeration. We have both stood stark naked in the open taking a bath with a crowd around us and not only that but women in the crowd. What do you think of that [?] The first time I turned pink as a lobster all over…

It was certainly a contrast to his strict Victorian upbringing.

As they approached Chungtien they sent their calling cards ahead and were received in great state with a line of soldiers from the garrison and a salute of three guns for the Consul. Official visits came with gifts of food, and in return they gave presents of silver. The Chinese military and civil officials offered them each an escort of a dozen soldiers, but they only took two as they continued their journey. Sometimes they started at 4 or 5 a.m., by moonlight, to cover new ground on a long day's haul, as they headed for the ferry that crossed the Yangtze River.

After ferrying the Yangtze, they started on a six-day march through the mountains of the Mekong-Yangtze divide, climbing to the flowery alpine pastures of the Kari pass at over 15,000ft. (4,600m). 'First time crossed by Europeans', wrote Forrest to his brother. The scenery was magnificent and for two days they followed a river 'larger than the Clyde' with white water rapids rushing over beds of boulders and steep cliffs rising up to 2,000ft. (600m) on either side. Further on, when a tremendous climb took them to about 16,000ft. (5,000m), they were rewarded by

Plate 33. The turbulent Mekong river flowing under a precipice.

a view that entranced them. Forrest wrote home:

> The morning was wonderfully clear and we could see for hundreds of miles on all sides. Nothing but range after range of tremendous mountains, many of the peaks capped with snow, and all glistening in the early morning sunlight like gems. Add to this billows of vapour rolling about in ceaseless movement in all the valleys, and above all the intense stillness at this elevation, not even the rustle of a blade of grass ... One feels in a situation such as that, that one is nearer something, call it by any name you like. I could have sat drinking it in for hours ...

But that peaceful serenity was soon broken when a sudden gust of wind blew his hat off, his pony shied in fright and careered down a boulder strewn slope, jumping

over the boulders with Forrest fearfully hanging on and Litton helplessly convinced that horse and rider would be killed. However, this former polo pony kept his feet and all was well as they contemplated the descent into the Mekong valley.

Litton wrote dramatically:

> We were able to look down a mighty limestone precipice on the Mekong (Lancang Jiang), over 7,000 feet [2,000m] below us… In 3½ hours careful going, we came down 6,500 feet by a dark and narrow gorge like the descent to Avernus in the bowels of the earth.[22]

The descent was so steep that the mules and ponies had to be led part of the way down, and Forrest reckoned that they dropped 5,000ft. (1,500m) in less than three miles (5km).

In the Mekong valley, confined between two mountain ranges, they headed north where the 'road' in the cliff of the narrow gorge was sometimes hundreds of feet above the river (Plates 33 and 34). There were no barricades. In the worst places, brackets were inserted in the cliffs, the path was made of logs, and travellers made their way perilously across the logs through which they could see the deep and rapid river rushing along below. 'It was here', explained Forrest to his family, 'that Prince Henry of Orleans lost 2 of his mules'.[23]

Their destination was Tsekou (Chigu), a hamlet of a dozen houses and a French mission station, at about latitude 28°N. To cross the mighty Mekong River to reach

Plate 34. This 'road', cut from rock, is probably the one Forrest used in 1904 on his way north up the Mekong valley to Tsekou.

Plate 36. *Pieris formosa forrestii* growing at Ness Botanic Gardens. It was raised by Bees' nursery from the first packet of seed sent by George Forrest from Western China.

the mission they had to use a rope bridge, where the rope of twisted bamboo skin was stretched between two strong posts either side of the great river. Forrest went first; two green cowhide slings were looped around his body and passed through a wooden 'runner' that slid along the rope, the runner and rope being well greased. He described to Balfour:

> One sling is placed round the right shoulder and under the left armpit, the other below the hips. Hanging on to the runner, lift off the feet, [and] the slope of the rope with the weight of the body carries one across. The speed at first is tremendous…over in a very few seconds, about 50-70 feet [15 to 20m] above the river. The sensation is very peculiar at first but one soon gets used to it.

On reading this, Balfour may well have smiled, pleased that he was not trying this assault course. Forrest's family was told dramatically that when the passenger puts his hands on the runner, the wrists and face have to be kept well away from the rope because the speed was so great that 'the slightest graze would mean being cut to the bone'. He admitted that it felt as if your inside were falling out. It was a rollercoaster ride with no safety net and Litton would only cross with experienced assistance.

The mules were also slung on a runner by a 'belly band' and given a kick to start them. Litton wrote, 'before the unlucky beast knows what is happening, he has been whirled half across the river and is suspended like the Prophet between heaven and earth….'[24] Three Tibetans were sent down by the French Fathers to assist them, and the party of seven beasts, two Europeans, six Chinamen, four loads and one dog were safely passed over the river in about 1½ hours.

The mission was built round four sides of a 40 yard (36.5m) square, the chapel forming one side, and the living rooms on the upper floor were approached by a verandah. Here Forrest and Litton enjoyed two days of generous hospitality, being treated like princes by the three French Fathers residing there, and sleeping, according to Forrest, in the room Prince Henry of Orleans had once used. Forrest said that the eldest missionary, Père Dubernard, had been there for sixty years. Only one spoke a little English, the others speaking French and Tibetan. 'All are thorough gentlemen, in fact come of very good families', wrote Forrest, but they lived in dangerous times and only eighteen months previously the mission had been the object of a Tibetan raid by about two hundred men armed with rifles and cartridges. The Fathers 'got wind of it' and, aided by their converts, ambushed the would-be attackers.[25]

The French Fathers tantalised Forrest by showing him botanical specimens from the next mountain range to the west, forming the Mekong-Salween divide. Prince Henry of Orleans had reported on the rich flora[26] and now this was vividly confirmed. Forrest learned that these mountains were exceptionally rich in the species that he was searching for: rhododendrons, gentians, androsaces and primulas. 'They say', wrote Forrest, 'there are at least 7 or 9 species of Primula on the hills behind their station.'[27] He collected a few gentians while he was there and determined, there and then, that he would return to Tsekou the following February or March, to work the hills as the snow melted. He was particularly intent on this when he saw the poor quality of the herbarium specimens that the Fathers were sending to the Paris Herbarium. He was confident that he knew more botany and in a short time he could do better, both in quality and number of specimens. It seems to have been 'anything you can do I can do better'. Moreover, when he heard that Bulley was in correspondence with them, he was even keener to collect plants before they did! Yet Forrest was in a dilemma: 'I gave them a good deal of

information but not too much, as I don't want to spoil my own chances'. He could see that the Fathers were desperately poor financially and would be glad of money if Bulley paid them, yet he was also anxious to please his sponsor, feeling fearful and insecure lest Bulley should be dissatisfied with him and send him home before his contract was completed. He compromised. As they had never succeeded in sending lily bulbs home in good condition, he gave them advice on when and how to pick, dry and pack bulbs to send to Bulley and Balfour, hoping they would be paid. And he accepted a very pressing invitation by Père Dubernard to make the old man's house his home when he returned to collect the following year.

Forrest's next goal was set. Despite the area's turbulent past and lawless state, it seemed safe enough to plan a return visit.

Meanwhile, Litton and Forrest completed their round tour via the Weihsi (Weixi) pass at 14,000ft. (4,500m) where they could hardly believe the beauty of a moor that was 'as if painted the richest imaginable blue by one species of gentian'. The magnificent scenery and flora made an indelible, deep impression on Forrest. This 'preliminary canter', as he called it, enabled him to see so many contrasting habitats and places, from the ravines to the snowy heights. He would never have seen all this so soon without Consul Litton to lead him. He completed the journey by sending Bulley a box of seed of 78 species and Balfour a parcel of 380 dried specimens, dispatched to Bhamo, Burma, by special runner, and he was happily aware that this was only a small fraction of the potential. He had the promise of rich pickings ahead of him and he knew that Bulley would be pleased.

Self-doubt creeps in

Forrest had not had a proper rest since he entered Burma and endured the exhausting journey in the monsoon rains. He reckoned that on his latest trip with Litton they had covered 900 miles (1,440km) in fifty-three days. He received kind offers of help from Balfour in Edinburgh and Augustine Henry at Kew, but the constant travel and demands were beginning to wear him down. Bulley unwittingly made things worse by suggesting to Forrest that he should make botanical notes that Bulley could publish in the *Gardeners' Chronicle*. Forrest doubted that he would have time and he reacted badly. 'It is disgusting and I don't feel inclined to do it. I didn't come out here on a job of that kind.' After all, he had already given up writing his diary because of pressure of time. After long weary days on horseback, it was very difficult to maintain all his correspondence, with evenings spent sorting, drying, pressing and packing plants and seeds. And correspondence was a high priority and necessity, to keep precious contact with Bulley and Balfour and his family. Indeed, once November had come he was writing to his brother asking him to send, on his behalf, a cheque for £5 (about £275 today) to Clem for a Christmas and New Year present.

Anxiety added to his sense of weariness. Deep down, Forrest lacked confidence. He was still worrying that Bulley might not be satisfied with his efforts and might recall him. Unfortunately, he had already found that his photographs could not be developed in Tali, because all his films and glass plates had been destroyed by damp, so he had to write to Bulley to request that more ¼ plates be sent from England. Then he went to collect plants near Lichiang and was heavily thrown from his pony, landing on his head and right shoulder. When he wrote home in his exhausted and shaky state, his inner turmoil rose to the surface:

I am heartily sick of China and everything Chinese, but will have to stick to my guns. If I was only assured of success I wouldn't mind but I have always the fear of failure haunting me and when I think of all it means for me, I get very heartsick. The fact is I am only beginning to see what a muddle I have made of my life. I thought I realised it before, but it is being thrust more and more before me day by day. If this proves a failure I think I will end it all, only I will then have the awful regret of having spoiled two lives instead of only one.

There are plenty of wolves here. It is now 2 in the morning and they are busy howling for all their worth just on the hills behind my tent. I wish I could get a shot at one. It might relieve me a bit to kill something.

With love and lots of kisses to you all and thanks for being kind to Clem.

From your ever loving son and brother

George.[28]

What we have to remember is that earlier in this long letter he had written spiritedly about his plans, and joked about the state of his dirty, scabby red face. 'I doubt if you would recognise me if you saw me. I must be hideous. I believe if Clem saw me she would chuck me at once'. But he knew she wouldn't, and it would take more than a temporary bout of homesickness and despair to force Forrest from his plant-hunting mission. Greater tests were to come.

Plate 37. *Androsace bulleyana*. Forrest's patron, A.K. Bulley, considered this plant 'one of the very finest of Forrest's things'.

Plate 38. George Forrest sets out from Tali, spring 1905. He wrote: 'I bought a pony, a very nice one... It is piebald biscuit and white... It is a tricky little devil... but I like a pony with some fun in it.'

CHAPTER FOUR

Death and Determination

I simply cannot leave those flowers to be discovered by
and named after Frenchmen.

G. Forrest to his brother, 30 December 1905.

The best laid schemes…

At the dawn of 1905 Bulley was full of ambitious ideas. In the safety of his armchair at Ness, he probably never thought what risks he was demanding of his plant collector. His eye was on the goal of plants for his nursery. When Forrest, at the China Inland Mission in Tali (Dali), received Bulley's suggestions, his foremost thought was to return to the Catholic mission in Tsekou, to forage for flowers on the surrounding mountains. He wanted to make a really fine collection there. After consulting with Bulley, he even thought of combining this with a grander project further north. He wrote to Balfour:

> I should like to work my way right across from Atuntze, [eastwards over] that vast tract of country which is blank on all the maps and which is intersected by the rivers Yangtze, Li-tang and Yalung. This is one huge plateau or tableland, of 12-16,000 ft, [3,500-5,000m] and as there have never been Europeans on it before, I think I would be almost certain to get hold of some good new things.[1]

All fatigue disappeared from his mind, risks were not mentioned, the new adventure filled his mind in a huge wave of enthusiasm.

But bold plans were to be thrown into disarray. The proposed journey to Tsekou was beset by many risks. This culminated in the most well-known and dangerous incident of Forrest's life, and his daring has to be seen against the background influences that fed insecurity in an outwardly confident character.

First, Forrest fell ill in Tali before he even started. The mission doctor warned him that he had been overdoing it. Yet it was very difficult for Forrest; new demands kept coming and he was anxious to oblige. At the request of the Consul General for Yunnan, W.H. Wilkinson, he had just undertaken a journey of two weeks to Yunnanfu. And there was always the inner urge to collect plant specimens and seeds. A daily routine, when collecting, meant a very long day: up at 4am, off from camp by 6am, then continuous riding until 6pm, with a short break for tiffin. (This Anglo-Indian word was often used by Forrest for a light midday meal.)

Forrest also felt no security in his job, and had concerns at home, so that professional and personal factors made him extra keen to succeed. This led to pressures that were partly in his own imagination. Basically he wanted to prove his worth. He was anxious that Clementina should see the quality of his herbarium specimens and he wanted to prove himself to her mother, Mrs Traill, who was against their betrothal.[2]

Both Balfour and Bulley showed sympathy and support when they learned of Forrest's personal situation.[3] Balfour allowed Forrest's personal letters to Clem to be posted to the Herbarium of the RBGE; her presents (china, a fan, and the curio of ladies shoes for tiny, bound feet) arrived packed in parcels of plants. Bulley wrote sensitively to Balfour:

> I am very glad you are keeping in touch with Forrest. He says he doesn't mind being alone, but Yunnan is a pretty far away spot, especially when you are in love. I am not interfering in this matter, save that I have written to Mrs Traill, saying what a high opinion I have of Forrest. A man sh' [should] win his wife by himself. If you sh' [should] happen to find that Miss Traill is being unendurably persecuted, I cd' [could] probably find work for her in the nursery here. But I don't want her to leave, unless badly pressed.[4]

Balfour replied:

> Mrs Traill is I am afraid rather foolish, and should have learned by now that no other reply than that you have given is possible from those who know Forrest. I do not think Miss Traill is now so unhappy – the subject is become 'taboo' at home.[5]

Balfour's encouragement

Forrest was fortunate that Balfour was sensitive to his ups and downs and gave him most enthusiastic encouragement and support. On receiving a case of Forrest's dried specimens, Balfour wrote:

> …what a treat you have given me! I know something of the difficulties of collecting, but my experience of obstacles pales before your description of the conditions under which you have had to work. Yet what a result! Your specimens are splendid and their interest botanically intense…They have arrived in excellent condition. Beautifully packed and unharmed in transit.

Balfour was exultant and went on to list five primulas that Forrest had sent:

> The gem is the fifth. I believe a new one. It has bluish flowers arranged in a short spike at the end of a long stalk and the flowers droop like those of a grape hyacinth (*Muscari*). I should call it *P. muscarioides* were I describing it. It is a lovely thing, and oh! If you have got seeds it will indeed be an addition to horticulture.[6]

That was exactly the news Forrest needed and he duly introduced it to cultivation that year (Plate 39).

On receiving a second batch of Forrest's plants, Balfour concentrated on the names of fifteen plants of the saxifrage family and when Forrest received the list of preliminary identifications he whooped for joy. He wrote home:

> Rejoice with me oh my friends, I am at last assured that I have discovered something new…If the average is kept up through the rest of the natural orders contained in my collections I am a made man as far as the botanical work goes for life.

Then doubt took over: 'However, that would be "ower guid luck". You see I am sceptical even yet'. But Balfour had great faith in him:

> Your work ought to bring you some reputation as it will certainly increase your knowledge of plants. What I hope may be possible is that your collection of dried plants may make you known in the botanical world.

Balfour set about systematically describing Forrest's plants in Edinburgh while encouraging him in a most kindly, avuncular way:

> You must take care of your health. I don't like to hear of your having fever such as you describe. Wishing you continued success and thanking you most warmly for all you have done and for your interesting letters.[7]

Danger!

Forrest regained his health and set off from Tali for Tsekou (Plate 38). On arrival at the end of April he wrote:

> I have had a terribly trying journey… I lost a mule… it fell over a precipice breaking its back in three places, the two cases which it carried were smashed to atoms.[8]

Despite warnings of brigands and deep snow, Forrest had tried to cross the Wei Hsi pass between the Yangtze and Mekong rivers, and this mule had slipped in the snow. His men refused to go on. Forrest was left with the problem of how to carry his baggage over the mountainous watershed. He got out of this predicament, as was

Plate 39. *Primula muscarioides,* first introduced by Forrest in 1905 and one of his first discoveries to be published.

to be his trademark, by befriending the next people who came along. A party of Lissoos approached:

> Wild-looking fellows they were, dressed as the Tibetans are, and armed with swords, guns, crossbows and the hated poisoned arrows. (See Plate 50.) They saw the fix I was in, and on my asking them for their assistance, readily consented to help me.[9]

He had already heard dramatic Chinese stories of these people, whose arrows caused 'death on the slightest scratch' and who had the reputation as robbers on this range, having sent a mandarin on his way with 'nothing on but his breeches.'[10] Yet they helped him carry loads weighing 80lbs (36kg) through deep snow. Occasionally a man and his load would disappear and then all hands had to turn to dig him out.

Forrest put up at a headman's house and was visited by a French priest of the Mission Apostolique, Père Bourdonnec, who could not speak English. Fearful news poured out and Forrest got the gist of it. Thousands of lamas from further north up the Mekong valley were on the warpath and only three days from Tsekou. They had already murdered Chinese soldiers, native Christians and a French missionary, Père Mussot.

Forrest arrived at Tsekou to find it 'practically in a state of siege', low in food and

Right:
Plate 40. *Nomocharis saluenensis,* first collected by Soulié near Tsekou and later found several times by Forrest. This is one of the handsomest of colour forms.

Opposite:
Plate 41. *Rhododendron forrestii,* discovered by Forrest in Yunnan before he was nearly killed by lamas in 1905. It has been much used in hybridisation programmes.

L.Snelling del et lith.

daily expecting a visit from the lamas. He heard that Consul Litton was on his way with one hundred Indian troops and wrote unconvincingly to Balfour, 'We will feel much safer after his arrival'. Balfour was filled with grave anxiety.

Later, Forrest heard that the French medical missionary, Jean André Soulié, aged forty-seven, had been tortured and shot at Yaragong, on the Yangtze. From 1886 he had been stationed further north in the Tibetan border regions, making many dangerous journeys in the troubled Tibetan borderland to collect over 7,000 dried specimens for the Paris Museum. It was he who discovered *Nomocharis saluensis* (Plate 40) and introduced the 'butterfly bush', *Buddleja davidii*. His murderers were dangerously at large in the mountains and likely to cause more trouble.

Amidst all the fear and rumours, Forrest collected as many plants as possible and had two men collecting for him. In May he happily told Balfour, 'I have now nearly 300 species for you, and have located some fairly good things for Mr. Bulley…' (Plate 41).[11] As the weather improved in June, he was even busier collecting. He now employed four men and from morning till evening they scoured the mountains, 'minus tracks of any sort", from 10-15,000ft. (3,000-4,500m).

In poorer weather he developed his photographs and wrote notes about his dried specimens, numbering and describing each plant, its habitat and altitude on a slip of paper inserted with each specimen. In addition, there were always letters; in early

2

4

5

3

1

L.Snelling del.et lith.

July he had eighteen to write. Letters were a solace in his solitude, a tonic and inspiration when they brought good news. His family was very attentive, especially his sisters, Grace and Isabella ('Isa'), and when the latter enclosed a celandine 'It was like a breath from the Scotch hills'.[12] He was delighted that his family had invited Clem to spend a weekend with them, 'Many, many, thanks to you all for being so kind to her'. He had also heard that his brother was renting a house, 'Springbank', in Lasswade, for his mother and sisters to move into, and Forrest showed concern that they settled happily there.

In his business letters he had good news from Bulley, who now had a new and expert foreman from the nursery of Veitch and Co. He reported very favourably on the packing and condition of Forrest's seeds. Forrest was relieved and told him of recent finds, hoping that his seeds would germinate to produce new plants 'fit to be introduced to the gardening fraternity'. That was the final test he had to pass.

Meanwhile morale had deteriorated at the Tsekou mission. Forrest and Litton had seen it at its best in the cold dry season. Now, in the heat, Forrest was disgusted by the filth, the food and the stinking refuse. He tired of 'pork and slops' and shared his tins of sardines until the supply ran out. As for the lice and fleas: 'Oh! How they smell when we crack 'em. Kohn's [merchant at Bhamo] extra strong insect powder is useless, they thrive on it as a side dish, sort of curried man feed.'[13]

By early July the lamas still had not come, but Forrest and the missionaries remained defiant. He wrote home:

> We are all rather humpy with the continued strain we have undergone for the past two months. The want of reliable news tells on us more than anything…Whatever happens we mean to stick here to the last…even supposing…I have to take to the hills…

The previous year Forrest had promised to his family that he would not take unnecessary risks, but now he resolved to risk staying in the area:

> By going south now I should lose practically the whole season. In any case I might as well be scuppered as go home a failure. That is always the logic I have in front of me.[14]

A mixture of pride and desperation meant, to him, that staying had become a necessary risk, in order to achieve success in his collecting. Besides, there was probably a grim satisfaction in the daring, with prospects of discoveries. He suppressed his anxiety and spent a week collecting in the mountains about twelve miles (19km) north-west of Tsekou. He showed incredible dedication:

> For three nights I slept in a bog with split pine boards for my bed, my clothes for blankets and a log for a pillow. Thunderstorms, rain, hail and snow, struggling over avalanches and glaciers…Oh! The game is not worth the candle I can tell you at least not at £100 [about £5,500 today] per year.[15]

Rumours and counter rumours of approaching lamas continued to fill the air. The French missionaries at Tsekou doubled their sentries at the rope bridges across the Mekong River. Yet on 13 July Forrest was thrilled with finding rhododendrons, primulas, lilies and azaleas and was writing in jubilant frame of his discovery of large quantities of the beautiful yellow poppywort, *Meconopsis integrifolia*. This was the flower that the nursery firm of Veitch had dispatched E.H. Wilson to find in 1903, and here was a new locality hundreds of miles from Wilson's. Forrest keenly described the habitat in detail. All his difficulties were not without reward. The find gave him a competitive thrill:

> If I am not the first to send home seed of this species, I hope to be the first to send home photos of it taken *in situ*. I hope to be able to send you a print by next mail.[16]

Bulley was currently selling this flower for the expensive sum of 10s.6d. (the cost of a good pair of shoes), so more seed would be very welcome, and a photograph would be a good advertisement.

Forrest planned to be home in May or June 1906: 'That is my present plan but you know 'the plans o' mice an' men'' and there is no knowing how or by what this may be changed, so don't count on it.'[17] This turned out to be dreadfully true.

Suddenly – out of the blue – Balfour received news from the Foreign Office. Mr Litton, His Majesty's Consul at Tengyueh, had telegraphed:

> … There seems unfortunately little doubt that an Englishman, named Forrest, was murdered on July 21, in the course of the disturbances which have lately occurred in the region of the Upper Mekong (Plate 42).[18]

Balfour broke the tragic news to Clementina and to Forrest's mother before writing to Forrest's patron, A.K.Bulley:

> Dear Mr. Bulley,
>
> You will doubtless have heard through the Foreign Office from Mr. Litton that there is little doubt that Forrest has been murdered.
>
> His last letter to me written at Tsekou on 27th May told of the troubles around him – of the murder of French Missionaries and the scarcity of food – but though anxious he seemed to be confident that he would come through all right. The date of the murder 21st July …shows that for about two months after his letter no crisis had come. He was not a man to yield and unless there was treachery he would die fighting as I sincerely hope he did.
>
> You will be as we are all here deeply grieved by the catastrophe. He seemed to me to be showing himself a born collector. The dried plants he sent home were in perfect condition, and I gather that you were pleased with the seeds that reached you from him. It was unlucky that he should go up to Tsekou again just at the moment when the disturbances broke out for apparently that is a centre of a wealth of new vegetation and from which you might have obtained a splendid instalment of good things…
>
> We have lost a really good man from whom I had looked for great horticultural prizes,
>   Yours very truly,
>   (Sgd.) Isaac Bayley Balfour[19]

Bulley replied:

> I feel very sick. The vile feeling is that this fine young fellow was working for pay for me; that he had to do it because he was poor; and that he lost his life in the endeavour to earn my beastly money.
>
> I had frequently told him that safety must be his first consideration, and not flowers. And as soon as I got his last letter, I wrote again urging him to run no risks…Of course it never reached him.
>
> I cherish no hope of his being alive. He was too full of pluck.[20]

Incredibly, within thirty-six hours, Balfour received a telegram from the Foreign Office that brought great joy and relief to everyone: 'Further telegram received from Consul [in] Yunnan stating Forrest is alive and safe. Gorst.'[21] Telegraph wires were humming with the happy news. Forrest's family in Lasswade replied, 'Overjoyed to have good news many many thanks'.

Bulley, the relieved paymaster, ended his next letter to Forrest with very firm admonitions: 'Safety must at all times be your first consideration, absolute, undoubted, safety. Only after that is assured are you to trouble your head about flowers.'[22]

In Yunnan, Litton shared in the family's happy relief, for he and Forrest were close friends after their travels together. He wrote immediately to Forrest, to welcome him to the C.I.M. (China Inland Mission) in Tali.

Tengyueh, August 19th, 1905

My dear Forrest,

I am more glad than I can tell you to hear of your escape. We had all given you up so numerous and so circumstantial were the accounts of your death both official and unofficial including eye witnesses!! I had telegraphed to the Foreign Office 'almost certain' you had been killed and had written privately to Professor Balfour and Bulley. Needless to say I have wired the good news of your escape to London so that your people…will not be long in suspense. You must have escaped by a miracle and I shall be eager to hear all about it. You must have a good rest and get fit at the C.I.M. at Tali under Dr Clark's care and I will be along very soon and you can come down here with me…Unless you are an experienced journalist write no account home, as I know a little about the job and could help you dish up an account wh. [which] ought to bring you in many dollars wh. are always a consideration − I shall bring a shirt or two and things wh. may be useful to you…get back your strength as quick as you can − and believe me always yrs. sincerely

G.Litton

p.s. I don't know though − Such a mighty person as the CONSUL GENERAL having reported you as dead, can you officially speaking be alive? I doubt it…Had you better not pretend to be a ghost… G.L.[23]

Months passed before the family could piece together what had happened. Litton first confirmed that 'Forrest by some miracle has escaped …safe … after "horrible experiences". Thank God for that.'[24] A letter from a missionary at Tali, dated 17 August, told the good news that Forrest was on his way there:

He says he escaped after a fearful experience lasting for 21 days, being hunted like a mad dog for nine days on the hills, suffering terrible privation − then fell in with some friendly people who brought him on his way… Two of the French Priests he says have been massacred…Rest assured we will look after him well when he is here, and we thank God for thus delivering him.[25]

Twelve days later Forrest felt well enough to write to Balfour:

I have just passed thro' [through] the worst experience of my life and I sincerely hope I will never be called upon to suffer the like again…I am in a very weak and nervous condition now that the strain is off me. I did not feel so bad on my arrival here but 2 days later was thoroughly prostrated, and as yet Dr Clark prohibits me exerting myself in the slightest, or doing anything that will bring my late experience too vividly to mind. Even this is written contrary to his orders.

Dr Clark was still treating Forrest's feet, which were in a terrible condition after he had gone eighteen days barefoot. Forrest continued:

About 20 natives were killed, and a great number more captured and taken into slavery. The heads and hearts were taken north to Atunze [sic] …but [I] was lucky and skilful enough to beat them on their own ground and at their own game. Several times I was surrounded, but always managed to break away."

He was thankful to have escaped, but desolate about all he had lost:

In the sack of Tsekou, I have lost everything, 700 species of dried specimens, 70 species of plants' seeds, my camera and over 50 negatives of plants, all my stores, bed, bedding, tents, all letters, papers, books, including those which you so kindly sent me, and nearly Tls. [taels]

300 in silver, in fact everything in the fullest sense of the word, with the exception of my rifle and revolver and a belt of cartridges for each.

Worst of all I have lost the greater part of the season and this grieves me more than anything. After all my recent success apparently I am to end in failure. You can perhaps imagine the state of mind I am in. At times I feel that it would almost have been better had I been killed.

But Forrest was a resilient and determined fellow. He ended this letter on a very positive note, 'As soon as I regain my strength I shall recommence work on the Tsan Shan range [Cang Shan] … and do my best to make up for lost time'.

In early October, having been taken by Litton to the relative luxury of the Consulate in Tengyueh, Forrest relaxed and wrote a thirteen page letter to Clementina, 'My own sweet pet Clem'. He described events in graphic detail and

Plate 42. The upper Mekong valley near Deqen (Atuntze). The lamas came down this valley to Tsekou to ransack, torture and kill the missionaries.

Plate 43. Père
Bourdonnec (left) with
Père Dubernard (right),
the Superior of the
mission station at
Tsekou. Forrest stayed in
their house, then fled
with them when it was
burned down by lamas in
July 1905. Both French
missionaries were
murdered.

how difficult it had been to sift through conflicting rumours. He saw in retrospect
that a traitor had given him and the Fathers false assurances of their safety. Great
anxiety, uncertainty and delays mounted over three critical days. On 17 July, at 2am,
Père Dubernard awoke Forrest with the news that Atuntze had been surrounded and
was likely to fall. Tsekou would be next. Consternation and confusion followed.
Forrest had a close friendship with Père Dubernard and, as Litton had guessed,
Forrest had felt a loyalty to stand by the old man as he plunged into extreme grief
and agitation. Père Bourdonnec wanted to 'remain and fight', causing fateful delays,
whilst Forrest fruitlessly made large offers of silver to anyone who would carry some
of his effects to the south, fearing that all his collections of plants and butterflies would
be lost. 'It simply maddened me to see my seeds and specimens lying around in their
cases, with the knowledge that I had to lose them all.' On 19 July, at 5pm, a runner
brought the news that Atuntze had fallen. Everyone knew the mission would be next.
At 7pm they fled. The two elderly priests mounted horses and, heavily armed, they
all headed southwards along the west bank of the Mekong River, abandoning the
French Catholic Mission and all Forrest's collections (Plate 43).

The path was rough and the going slow and after only two hours a peculiar Tibetan
cry had gone across the river intimating their flight. Forrest advised the priests that
any delay would be deadly, yet the priests insisted on stopping for a cup of tea, and
when they heard that it would be necessary to elude capture by taking a mountainous
route, the elderly priests seemed, to Forrest, to give up hope. He was in a dilemma,
being strongly inclined to go on alone. Loyalty kept him with them as they clambered
to the summit of a range, only to see a large column of smoke ascending to the north.
Tsekou had been burned, and the lamas were probably pursuing them.

Forrest continued:

> Here I made my last attempt to hasten the movements of the Fathers, but without avail.
> Both seemed to have entirely given up hope. When I saw my efforts were useless, I
> pushed on ahead with one of my servants, Anton.

The Fathers followed at a distance but, whereas Forrest and Anton crossed the fast moving stream using a log as a bridge, the Fathers stopped the other side for tiffin, instead of hurrying on. Over a week later Forrest learned that both priests had been murdered, and in his letter to Clementina he spared her no horrors:

It appears that Père Bourdonnec was cornered some time on the second day, shot down, and whilst still alive cut open and his heart torn out. Père Dubernard managed to elude his pursuers until the fourth or fifth day when he was captured. The lamas broke both his arms, tied his hands behind his back and then led him off in the direction of Tsekou. However, he became so exhausted that he begged them to kill him at once, on which one of them struck him down with a sword. He was then cut open and his heart extracted before death. Both bodies were beheaded and all the parts taken north. It is the custom of the natives to eat the heart and brain, and partake of the blood of their enemies (raw of course) if they have died fighting or if they are Christians. It is said to impart bravery. Such would have been my fate had I fallen into their hands (Plate 44).

Forrest had been hiding by day and active at night in his search of a safe escape route. The main hindrance was the lamas' line of sentries along the crest of a ridge, forming a cordon blocking all attempts to go south. When he found that his footsteps were being followed, he discarded and buried his boots, waded in a stream and continued barefoot. After the third night 'on the run', he found on the ground a 'score or so' of ears of wheat. They proved to be the only food he had for eight days. And the narrowness of his escape during that time is shown by his account:

Once, whilst lying asleep, behind a log in the bed of the stream, I was awakened by a sound of laughing and talking, and on looking up I discovered thirty of them in the act of crossing the stream about fifty yards above my hiding place. It was a very near squeak, both for them and for me.

By the end of the eighth day Forrest was so weak, hungry and exhausted that he could scarcely stand. Desperate, he headed for a small Lissoo village to beg for food. He entered a hut, murmured 'Tsampa' and collapsed. Fortunately he had fallen amongst friends who boiled some dough made of Tibetan wheat in water and gave it to him. He knew it was dangerous to suddenly eat this after days without food, but he was so hungry that he gorged himself and suffered painful agonies and diarrhoea for nearly three months afterwards. He rested there for three days, but his trials were not over. The next day he went into hiding when hearing that thirty lamas were searching for him and then two guides accompanied him on a circuitous mountain route to Yeh Chih. They cut their way through rhododendrons and cane breaks to the summit of the Mekong-Salween divide and spent two days between '14,000 ft and 17,000 ft [4,000 and 5,000m] over snow, ice and wind swept tip-tilted strata' that tore his feet to shreds.[26] They had no cover from the bitter cold at night, and not even a fire when it rained too heavily for this, and they existed on tsampa and Tibetan tea, catching rain-water in pieces of bark.

It was ironic that Forrest was suffering such hardships in a beautiful mountain range among magnificent flowers. He told Clem of the sights he saw as they had pressed on with no time to dally. There were:

several species of meconopsis all of them surpassingly lovely, miles of rhododendrons, and acres of primulas of which I counted over a dozen species in flower, many of which I had never seen before…Those mountains have, rightly in my opinion, been called the flower garden of the world.

He had even picked a few flowers, pressed them in his pocketbook and later sent them to Balfour. No wonder Balfour was to call him 'a born collector'.

Plate 44. *Primula dubernardiana*. A plant of cushion habit, first discovered by Forrest in 1904 on limestone cliffs near Tsekou, and named in honour of the murdered Père Dubernard.

L. Snelling del. et lith.

Forrest followed one of the ridges until he reached a spur overlooking the Mekong directly opposite Yeh Chih. It must have seemed like the 'Promised Land'. Chinese officials came to his every need. He found quarters in a house and the representative of Lichiang-Fu, who was camped for the emergency by the river, brought him a blanket and a supply of food, Chinese cakes, fowls, eggs, arrack. Forrest was also brought a change of clothing (Chinese garb for his disguise) and had his beard shaved. He was given guides to take him to Hsia Wei Hsi and crossed over the Mekong by a rope bridge. He was overjoyed to find Père Monbeig there, who received Forrest as one returned from the dead. They were offered escorts of soldiers, mules, food and more clothing. Forrest could hardly believe his transformation:

> I was quite richly and gaily attired in a gown of bright blue flowered silk, thick blue cloth jacket, lined silk, and Chinese-trousers of the same material. Blue shoes, white socks (linen) and a black satin cap with red silk button completed my costume. (Plate 45.)

The two men started for Tali on 13 August, twenty-five nerve-jangling days after the day of destruction of Tsekou. They were given sedan chairs for the last part of the journey and the missionaries at Tali came out to meet them. They arrived safely on 25 August. Forrest's costume covered a thoroughly run-down and weary body, but at least he could now rest under the watchful eye of a medical missionary. In particular, during his escape, he had stepped on a sharp and fire-hardened bamboo spike that had pierced agonisingly between the bones of his foot, protruding a

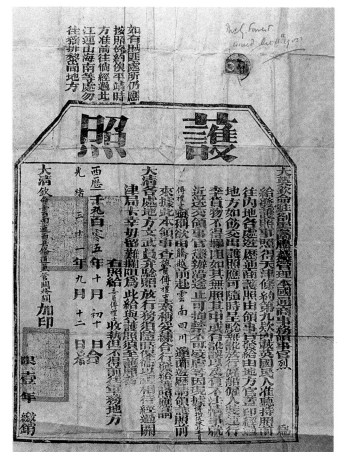

couple of inches above the upper surface.[27] The wound took months to heal and Forrest was very fortunate that Dr W.T. Clark had been posted to Tali in 1902 and serviced a busy dispensary there.[28] Medical missionaries were in short supply in China and Tali was the only C.I.M. medical station in north-west Yunnan.

He described to Clementina his condition on arrival at Tali:

> I was really ill, completely worn out. It was a thorough nervous collapse. I was as jumpy as a young woman and really horrible to look at, hollow cheeks, eyes sunken in regular caves and black for inches beneath, and my whole features drawn and careworn. I shall carry the marks of what I have come through till the day of my death. I am utterly changed…However, I have got off with life…

And life, for Forrest, was never quiet for long. He and Litton were already hatching plans for another adventure.

On 11 September – less than three weeks after Forrest's return to Tali – he wrote a bright letter to Balfour, 'I have decided on joining Mr Litton on a journey which he proposes making up the Salween-Irrawaddi divide'. They were to be far away from lamas and yet venture into entirely untouched country, where Forrest hoped to secure 'many new things'. Only a man of exceptional zeal and energy could have countenanced another exploit so soon. Maybe, for him, it seemed the best antidote. He was delighted, excited and curious to visit a new area, and travelling with his lively and trusted friend would help make a fresh start.

On 11 October Litton issued him with a new Chinese passport (Plate 46) to be shown at all checkpoints in Yunnan and Szechwan (Sichuan). He was given a new title, 'Flower collector of the Museum' and he could employ local labour for his work. Appropriately, at the top of the passport were the words of the Treaty advising the holder to go only in peacetime. The next day the two men set off to explore part of the upper Salween valley where no European had been before.

Above left:
Plate 45. George Forrest at the China Inland Mission, Tali, immediately after his escape.

Above right:
Plate 46. George Forrest's provincial passport of 11 October 1905. It was valid for one year and measured about 16in. x 28in. (40cm x 70cm).

The Land of the Crossbow

The unmapped area of the upper Salween was inviting exploration. Litton obtained special permission to go, his object being both political and geographical. First, he wanted to discover whether the western watershed of the Salween valley formed a distinct geographical and ethnographical boundary between north-west Yunnan and Upper Burma. Secondly he aimed to explore the Salween valley between 26° and 27°30'N. lat., observing its physical form and its people, their customs, agriculture and trade, organisation and prosperity, with a view to reading a paper to the Royal Geographical Society in London.

The two men set off from Tengyueh, Forrest as Litton's assistant, plant collector and photographer. They were well armed and had an escort of two Lissoo sepoys from the Burmese frontier (Plate 22). They took servants, baggage animals and a pointer dog. They headed due north towards the source of the Shweli river and the Lissoo hamlet of Ta-chu-pa. From here onwards they were among the Lissoo people, often with some Chinese blood in them. No one spoke English and even in the south of the valley only the chiefs and their families could speak any Chinese. The men dressed in Chinese fashion, but the women, while adopting Chinese cotton cloth, often wore their own characteristic decorations on the head, neck and arms (Plates 47 and 48). Here Forrest and Litton were supplied with porters who, even in difficult country, carried a weight of 70lbs (32kg) on their backs for six to eight hours. The loads were mainly reserve supplies of rice.

They were unlucky with the weather. In days of downpours of rain they trekked through the desolate, dripping forest of the N'Mai Kha-Shweli dividing range to the watershed-frontier with Burma, finding swollen streams, landslips and broken bridges on their way. They camped or took refuge in smoky and verminous Lissoo huts and lost a mule with its bundle of Forrest's plant specimens. They turned east over the lonely, but beautiful Pien-ma pass at 10,500ft. (3,200m) and descended to the village of Lu-chang, at approximately 6,400ft. (2,000m) and latitude 26°N. Here they were some 3,000ft. (900m) above the Salween River, and this was to be their base for exploring further north. They sent back their baggage animals and were glad to establish friendly relations with the people: a boy chief asked them for sweets while his mother gave them a large capon.

Later, when Forrest related their journey in an article in the *Geographical Journal,*[29] he described the march north as 'a trial of strength to the traveller's legs'. On the higher slopes they saw limestone crags where the strata were tipped up and pointing to the sky, while their path led up and down over an endless succession of steep ridges that descended from the mountainous watersheds on either side of the Salween river valley. Walking was physically tough and in some places, 'we had to haul ourselves over boulders by pendant branches, or scramble along the face of cliffs by notches in the rocks, more suitable for monkeys'.

But the men were in no doubt that their efforts were worth while. The narrowness of the valley meant that they could see the mountains on either side and, as the autumn rains gave way to wintry sunshine, they thought the natural beauty exceeded that of the valleys of the Yangtze, the Mekong and Irrawaddy rivers. They were captivated:

> The great variety of rock formation, the abundant forests and vegetation, and the diversity of light effects between the summits of the ranges (at 10,000 to 13,000 feet [3,000 to 4,000m]) and the abyss in which the river flows produce a vast panorama of ever-changing beauty. In the morning the sun, as it touches the top of the Mekong divide, sends wide shafts of turquoise light down the side gullies to the river, which seems to be transformed into silver. The pines along the top of the ridges stand out as if limned by the hand of a Japanese artist. In the evening all the wide slopes of the Mekong side are flooded with red and orange lights, which defy photography and would be the despair of Turner.[30]

Above:
Plate 47. Lissoo people of the Ming Kwong valley, a tributary of the Shweli river.

Right:
Plate 48. Three Lissoo girls of the Ming Kwong valley, 1905.

Plate 49. Consul Litton with Lissoo people and their crossbows in the Salween valley, 1905.

Litton and Forrest found a sparse and poor population living in scattered villages on the higher ground above the river, between 5,000 and 7,000 feet (1,500 and 2,000m). To the north there was no form of government and almost no Chinese influence; rice was a luxury and coarsely ground maize, buckwheat and wild honey were the staple foods. Cloth was much in demand and when the travellers themselves became short of food one Lissoo suggested bartering their breeches for a bag of rice. These breeches were not on offer, but a Chinese coolie in the party did a deal, bartering his ragged and lousy jacket for some maize and salt.

They were relieved when they came to an area where fowls and eggs were available; they were offered a goat or pig for sale and there was sufficient game to add six brace of pheasants to their larder. At one village there were fruit trees, and

> the picturesque inhabitants, with their beads, cowries, silver ornaments, and long hempen garments came out *en masse* to welcome us, and several of the village elders brought trays of rice, eggs, vegetables, etc., which they offered on their knees.

Nevertheless, at one point they were confronted by warriors armed with huge crossbows. When these men were shown the firing of a twelve-shot repeating Winchester rifle, they decided to be friendly and Forrest took photographs of them (Plate 49). Progress was slow through wild country with towering limestone peaks, but the rewards included forests rich in orchids, and a camp on a sandbank where beautiful crinum lilies bloomed amongst the boulders.

All was not so serene when the party of thirty-five persons and a dog came to a single rope bridge across the Salween river. There was a feud between the villagers on either side of the river. Both claimed that the right and profit of assisting travellers across belonged to them alone. Offers of bead necklaces would not placate them. The single rope bridges across the Salween were far more difficult to cross than the double rope bridges of the Mekong. After being trussed by cords on to a wooden runner, with face to the sky and back to the water, each person had to haul himself across hand over hand, hoping the rope would not break and risking hands full of painful splinters.

The villagers of the left bank crossed over and began to tie up one of the loads, whereupon the leader of the right bank whipped out a poisoned arrow and shot it over the heads of Litton's party into the river. He was about to draw his bow again, when Litton and Forrest rushed at him and Forrest fired several shots from his

Plate 50. Arms of the 'Black Lissoo', Salween valley, given by George Forrest to the (now) National Museums of Scotland. The crossbow has a bow of wild mulberry, stock of wild plum and a string of native hemp. The shoulder strap and quiver are of black bearskin, the latter strengthened by cane lashed with rattan. Arrows are of split bamboo, pared with a knife, fledged with bamboo leaf and coated with *Aconitum* poison.

Winchester repeater ('the gun that won the West'). The bullets smashed against a stone on the other side of the river and the men were told, through an interpreter, that if they made a show of stringing their bows again, 'the next bullet would find a resting-place in some of their carcasses'. There was an awe-struck silence. All the party was safely hauled across the rope while Litton and Forrest stood on guard, giving several more exhibitions of their marksmanship and the power of their weapons.

Litton and Forrest found that nearly all the villages were at war with one another and suspicion and rumour reigned. This made it very difficult to find a guide and impossible to get any accurate information about routes or distances. None the less, they established that there was no plain or open valley in the section they explored, and by climbing to the western, Chi-mi-li pass, at 13,000ft. (4,000m), they saw it was too wild and difficult to be a regular line of communication across the watershed to Burma. On the opposite side of the valley they also climbed the Salween-Mekong divide to 12,300ft. (3,750m) and were rewarded with a wonderful panoramic view, westwards across the Salween valley and beyond. The great Salween-Irrawaddy dividing range was spread out before them like a vast limestone wall separating Yunnan from Burma. In the distance were dazzling snow-peaks. It was easy to see why this mountain barrier was an ethnographical boundary between the Lissoo and Kachin peoples. On looking east, across the Mekong, they also had a superb view across north-western Yunnan to the dominating and glittering snow-mountain west of Lichiang (Yulong Shan).

In private, Forrest summarised this previously unexplored area as 'No roads, frightful travelling, people complete savages and the most barren country I have yet passed through'.[31] Although he considered the botanical results disappointing, he sent to Edinburgh 360 plant specimens and seeds of about one hundred species. He used his photographic skills to record the people and returned to Britain with a dramatic armoury: two double-handed swords and their scabbards and two wooden hunting crossbows complete with their accompanying quivers of poison arrows (Plate 50). He suggested that a suitable title for a book on the upper Salween would be 'The Land of the Crossbow' and his fascination with these 'diabolical' weapons is indicated by his detailed descriptions of them in a later article.[32] He described the woods used, how the poison was made and placed in the arrow, and the terrible power of the poison to kill a cart-horse. An arrow from a war bow pierced an inch (2.5cm) thick deal board at 70 or 80 yards (about 70m). Forrest's collection of weapons is kept today in the National Museums of Scotland.

Litton described Forrest as 'done up' after the physically demanding journey, which had followed perhaps too quickly after his traumas in the Mekong. But the resulting articles and collections form a valuable and lasting record of the people, plants and places that they found in the upper Salween valley, before it was even mapped.

Death intrudes

On their return in mid-December, Litton insisted on Forrest taking a complete rest for some weeks in readiness for further collecting in the spring.[33] Forrest had already negotiated with Bulley to stay an extra year. Earlier he had favoured returning, as planned, after two years away from home and Clementina. Probably the loss of so many of his collections persuaded him to stay and do more to make his expedition a success. Part of him desperately wanted to return to the Mekong divide and other plateaux at 10,000-13,000ft. (3,000-4,000m), to make good his losses. The lamas had dispersed, the missionaries had already returned and Litton could see no reason why Forrest should not try. For a while Forrest found it difficult to decide, the obvious risks vying in his mind with his competitive urge: 'I simply cannot leave those flowers to be discovered by and named after Frenchmen'.[34] Inevitably the competitive urge won. Forrest determined to try and return to the Mekong area.

Balfour had immense respect for Forrest's field work. He had written to Litton, 'His collections are indeed marvellous for their perfection. What he has already done is great and gives promise of even greater things in the future'.[35] To encourage a fresh start, Balfour sent him a new camera to replace the one that was lost, a number of ¼ glass plates, a box of photo chemicals, printing paper, drying paper, all seven volumes of Hooker's *Flora of British India* and the *Flora of China*. At Forrest's request his brother, James, also sent him a replacement copy of Bentley's *Manual of Botany,* a volume of about 900 pages, the size of *The Concise Oxford Dictionary,* full of information about the classification and structure of plants. Forrest had had an old copy of this book at home and he was obviously very familiar with it, possibly since his days working in the pharmacy. He looked upon it as a 'perfect godsend' in Yunnan.

Armed with his new supply of books and photographic equipment, Forrest felt more positive, though Balfour's kindness perversely embarrassed him and heightened feelings of inadequacy and indebtedness. On the last day of 1905, with his strength probably still at a low ebb, his old doubts resurfaced. He told his brother:

> I feel so horribly incompetent at times that I look on praise from a man of Prof. Balfour's position more as sarcasm. To say this, after all he has done and is doing for me, I know must sound most ungrateful but I cannot help it. Just the nature of the animal, and I cannot shake it off. I wish I had the confidence of some people.

Forrest ended this letter:

> I hope to God nothing will come in my way this year…if all goes well this time next year I shall be on my way home. All the same I expect my cursed bad luck will follow me.[36]

It was just as well that he did not know the devastating news that would break in only two weeks' time.

The New Year 1906 started with Forrest temporarily elevated to standing in for Litton at the Consulate in Tengyueh. Litton was suddenly called away on business to the Burmese frontier and Forrest now spoke and understood Chinese. Moreover, he found that visiting travellers had heard of his exploits and were keen for his company. One visitor, Mr Crowley, was a mountaineer and member of the Alpine Club who had attempted unsuccessfully to gain the summit of Kanchenjunga, with four of his party killed in the attempt. He failed to persuade Forrest to be a botanist attached to his next expedition there.

Then the entirely unexpected happened and completely shattered Forrest. He had faced dangers and frustrations stoically and endured privations and suffering, but this seemed more than he could bear. Litton died.

The Consulate
Teng-Yueh,
Yunnan
13.1.06

Dear James,
Have just passed thro' [through] another ordeal which has tried me more than any. Litton died very suddenly, on his way up from the frontier…

..he intended to be at Teng-Yueh on the 11th…on the evening of the 10th a runner came up and said he was very ill, but still struggling on. This was about 10pm. I left at once with the native Dr [doctor] here, travelled as quickly as poss. [possible]…but too late. He had died at midday the previous day. Escorted the body tied on a chair to Teng-Yueh, where, as no-one would have anything to do with it in case of infection I had to strip and lay out the body myself. It was so stiff that I had to cut off the clothing and

Plate 51. Consul Ottewill on an official visit to the Taotai in Tengyueh. Note the State chair and bearers.

so long exposed that it had gone quite black. The Dr., a Bengali and most incompetent could give the disease no name.

I have had such a shock that at present I cannot write more so pray excuse me.

I have lost the best friend ever I had and one that I shall never be able to replace.

Your loving bro.[brother]

George Forrest[37]

This letter was written the day before Forrest and Litton had planned to leave Tengyueh together for Tali. It was a tragedy that a young and strong man should be laid low and, as Forrest realised keenly, he had lost not only a friend, but an experienced guide, fellow explorer and companion.

Litton was only thirty-six and the immediate cause of death was said to be erysipelas, but his successor put it down to four years of the continual excessive strain of travelling and working late into the night on reports (Litton was due for home leave in the spring of 1906).[38] He was buried south of Tengyueh on the slopes of Laifeng Shan. Afterwards Forrest stayed in the town, helping Napier, the Commissioner of Customs, to deal with Litton's private papers. The new Consul, H.A. Ottewill, arrived in early February, just under a month after Litton died (Plates 51 and 52). Forrest helped him, too, with Litton's affairs, but the loss of Litton was a piercing sadness. He felt sickened and depressed and almost as much run down as he had the previous August when he reached Tali after his escape:

We were very close friends, none greater, and I have not only lost one whom I shall never replace, but I fear that with him goes all chance of my indemnity…the whole fabric of my plans has fallen to the ground…my nerve is completely gone and I cannot give battle as I used to.[39]

This was a cruel blow – only six months after the dreadful deaths of his French friends and his own horrific experiences. His mind could not cope with it all and it was to take him a long time to recover fully.

Fortunately, one of the next visitors to the Consulate was Colonel G.C. Rippon, an avid bird collector on leave from a Burmese regiment. He was a member of the British Ornithologists' Club and his reports, and even exhibits, of new bird species of Burma and China were sent to their London meetings. A new species had been named after him the previous year and he was currently collecting for the British Museum. (He was to amass a collection of more than 2,800 skins from Burma, China and India.) He stayed with Forrest for a week and was most anxious that they should travel together. An earlier plan had been that Rippon might travel with Litton and Forrest to the Chungtien plateau and Rippon still hoped that something of this plan might be retrieved. He went on ahead to Tali to await Forrest's arrival. This bucked Forrest up and he realised that he was the 'right side up yet', though it was 'a darned hard life'.[40]

Forrest's mail also brought kind, supportive and loving letters from his family, and good news. On Monday 6 November 1905 the *Scotsman* had published Forrest's article headed 'Lama disturbances in Northwest Yunnan: Destruction of a French Mission. A Scotsman's personal narrative'. Now he received a cheque for two guineas (over £100 today). He was thrilled, and the money was divided between Clem and the family, as a 'wee treat for Easter', with the request that they should all toast to his future success in the writing line.[41] He had always hoped to supplement his income by writing, but this was his first success. Earlier on, when his family admitted that his diary had not been published, he had replied, 'Another paving stone. Wish we had some of them out here for the roads'. The mention of paving stones was turned into a quip, but probably alluded to the road to hell being paved with good intentions. No wonder he was happy to have an article published now. It was a small but well-timed spur to carry on.

Forrest's contract was for one more year in Yunnan and it was not in him to give up, however difficult the circumstances. The previous year's losses had to be replaced. He didn't know whether he would ever have another chance and he was a person who needed to achieve. A strong sense of duty and diligence was also intrinsic to him, as if he were deeply imbued, in his strict Christian upbringing, with exhortations to industry and honest toil for the common good. Forrest implored his brother not to work so hard for the Church, at the same time pushing himself to his limits. As soon as he could get away from Tengyueh, he set off for Tali, to catch up with Rippon and prepare to head 'for the north' in the spring.

'Our Mr Forrest'

At Tali the European missionaries of the C.I.M. were a helpful and steadying influence. During 1906-7 Forrest came to know Mr J.W. Hanna and Mrs Hanna (née Roxie Wood) particularly well. Having met as missionaries in Yunnanfu, the Hannas had only recently been married[42] and were to be firm friends of Forrest in the future. Feeling welcome, Forrest settled to writing up his account of his recent travels with Litton, tried out his new camera and was given space for drying plants.

He kept in touch with Chinese officialdom in the hope of returning to the Mekong valley, but conditions there were so chaotic that the possibility was officially closed to him. Maybe this was merciful. Details of the deaths of Dubernard and Bourdonnec still came to haunt him:

> They are much too gruesome to relate and when I think of what I escaped my blood runs cold. They must have suffered terribly. Castration was one of the least of the brutalities practised on them…[43]

As spring approached Forrest covered his grief by tackling his collecting with huge

Plate 52. The Taotai of Tengyueh, the chief civil official.

Plate 53. *Primula forrestii*. Forrest's gardening advice in 1909 was 'It <u>will not</u> do with damp. The most sunny and dry situations are what you should try, and do not forget to give it plenty of lime. The situations in which I found the species in greatest luxuriance, were the crevices and ledges of <u>dry</u> limestone cliffs.'

Right:
Plate 54. Herbarium specimen of *Primula forrestii* collected by Forrest in 1910, with his handwriting. It shows a characteristic rootstock of a wild plant.

resolve and organisation. He planned his use of collectors so that both the Tali Range (Cang Shan) and the Lichiang Range (Yulong Shan) could be scoured for plants and seed at the same time. We don't know exactly how many people he engaged, but in 1905-6 he trained local Nakhi (Naxi) people from U-lu-kay (Snow Mountain Village), north of their ancient capital, Lichiang-Fu. They formed the core of his collectors on all his subsequent expeditions.[44] In 1906 he also trained three Minchia (Minghai) women, introduced to him by missionaries at Talifu (Plate 56). They lived on the Tali plain, and Forrest described their toughness and practicality for their new task: 'The Minchia women have natural feet, manage boats, carry loads, do masons' and bricklayers' work and even occasionally act as muleteers.'[45] The contrast with Chinese women was very striking, for foot binding was still practised in Yunnan, often reducing their feet to only four inches (10cm) long. When Forrest first saw this, he found it painful to see them tottering along on a couple of stumps. 'Some of them are to be seen with feet, well, I wouldn't call them feet at all, they are simply an ankle bone and a big toe.'[46]

Forrest's zest and industry and the scale of his ambition flow breathtakingly from his letters. In mid-April he reported from Tali that he had:

engaged two native collectors who are to work the Tsan Shan (Cang Shan) range West of this city, during my absence in the north...I am leaving one of my boys ...in charge of them, and if, during my absence, they work as well as they are doing now, I hope to obtain from this district perhaps 2,000 species. Already I have 10 presses going, over 100 species dried, and another 100 well on the way... they will also collect seed.[47]

Looking at Forrest's 1906 collection of primulas alone gives us a good idea of the extent and thoroughness of his collecting that year. Collections were made from the lower slopes to the summit of the Tali Range (Cang Shan), and from the pine forests to the mountain pastures and crags of the Lichiang Range (Yulong Shan) (Plate 57). Collecting continued into October. In April he was finding the familiar, blue, Sino-himalayan, 'drumstick primula', *Primula denticulata*, in the pasture-land of the lower slopes. By May he was on the eastern flank of the Lichiang Range, seeing the flowers of *Primula nivalis* pushing up along the snow line, together with the blue high-level alpine flowers of *Primula sonchifolia*. He described the latter as being one of the first flowers to show on the disappearance of the snow:

> In many instances I found specimens which had actually forced their way through the snow. In such cases the surrounding white showed to the greatest advantage the rich blue of the flowers.

Forrest was in his element, lost in wonder and delight. Further, as he explored the dry, shady crevices of the limestone cliffs, they revealed one of their long-held secrets, the deep yellow flowers of a primula not found by a westerner before. This plant had a woody rootstock that caused Forrest to ponder on its possible great age. It was later named after him, *Primula forrestii* (Plates 53 and 54), and has become one of the best known species that bears his name.[48]

Plate 55. Forrest named this flower *Primula littoniana* (now *P. vialii*) to commemorate his friend Consul Litton. When shown by Bees' nursery in 1909 it received a First Class Certificate.

Plate 56. Minchia women of the Tali plain who collected for George Forrest. Note their characteristic black cloth caps. Taken in Sept 1906 in the courtyard of the China Inland Mission, Tali.

As May turned to June, another lovely surprise awaited Forrest on the Lichiang Range, for as he walked on the moist mountain meadows he came across tall flower stems with distinctive whorls of deep golden to pale orange flowers that he had never seen before. He picked a stem and numbered it, F.2,440, and later affirmed that it was a new species which he 'named in honour of Mr. A.K. Bulley of Ness, Neston, Cheshire, for whom I collected.'[49] In the years to come this was to be a success story in our gardens and Bulley was so pleased that this beautiful new species was named after him that he would introduce himself: 'I am *Primula bulleyana*' (see Plate 62).

In August Forrest collected from the open mountain meadows east of Lichiang, again finding an attractive plant that was totally new to him. There were blue and red spires of flowers crowded together so that, like a red-hot poker (*Kniphofia*), the spire had a striking red apex. Forrest photographed it and movingly named it *Primula littoniana* after his close friend, 'to commemorate the late Consul Litton of Tengyueh, to whom I was much indebted for valuable assistance during my stay in China'.[50] Smith and Fletcher showed later that Delavay had previously called it *P. vialii*, so, according to the rules of nomenclature, this name has to be used today. It is sad that Litton, whose friendship meant so much to Forrest, is no longer commemorated in the name of any flower that Forrest collected, but *P. vialii* remains a fitting tribute to a great friend and it is one of Forrest's finest and most popular introductions (Plate 55).

Delavay had been a leading figure, collecting many of the plants growing in this area of Yunnan, but Forrest showed, in 1906, that there were still more novelties to be found. Of all the primulas that he collected on the three-year expedition, forty per cent of the primula species he identified were new to science.

Sadly, there was a price to pay. On 1 September Forrest admitted 'I am sorry to have to tell you I have broken down, temporarily, and have had to return to Talifu…collapsed'. He claimed that he was 'picking up wonderfully', but we don't know how far that was an optimistic estimate. In November Balfour reported him as only 'nearly right again now'. But Forrest's excellent organisation meant that collecting did not come to a halt when he was ill: he left his three best collectors behind in the Lichiang area. And even at the beginning of September, with more harvesting to come, he was thrilled by the results of his team's work. He reckoned that nearly 900 species had been collected from the Lichiang Range, and those based in Tali had secured nearly 1,200 species. 'If all goes well I hope to bring home… about 3,000 species, mostly from 9-15,000 feet [2,750-4,500m]'.[51]

Meanwhile, Bulley's nursery, The Co-operative Bees Ltd, was busy raising plants from Forrest's seeds. Pride in Forrest was shown by the manager referring to him as 'our Mr Forrest', and herbarium sheets in Edinburgh already had special labels announcing that Forrest was the 'Collector for A.K. Bulley of Ness, Neston, Cheshire'. The sheer size of Forrest's collections meant that taxonomists would be working on them for years to come. In the course of the three-year expedition approximately 5,500 specimens of plants were numbered, pressed and dried, ready for identification.

The flora of north-west Yunnan captivated Forrest. Like the miners at Klondike, he had struck a rich seam. And he'd done his very best to extract a good haul from it, whatever the dangers and difficulties. Would he be returning for more? At this point he had absolutely no idea.

By January 1907 Forrest, still run down and ill, was looking forward to being home again. As soon as the ship docked, he would send his brother and Clem a

Plate 57. George Forrest's camp at 11,000ft. (3,350m) in the Lichiang Range (Yulong Shan) on his first expedition. Note the piles of drying paper in the right foreground, and boulders pressing plants between the papers.

wire. During his nearly three years away Clem had written weekly to Forrest, showing her supportive, utterly reliable love, and he had replied with lengthy descriptive letters (up to fifty pages of A5), telling her of his travels and expressing his longing to see her again. He wanted a reunion with Clem in privacy, without the curious eyes of people from the Botanic Garden, and soon they would be wed.

Primula forrestii

Eve Reid Bennett

CHAPTER FIVE

An Uncertain Future

There is nothing certain but uncertainty,
nothing more miserable and more proud than man.

Pliny

When Forrest came back to Scotland after his successful first expedition, it was still not clear whether he would be able to make plant hunting his career. There were to be many struggles over the next four years before his future would open out satisfyingly. During these difficult years, Forrest's reactions to his experiences reveal the different sides of his character.

The honeymoon period

Forrest received a heartfelt, quiet and informal welcome on his return to Scotland in early April 1907. Clem was given leave from the Herbarium to meet him, Balfour sent a telegram of good wishes and Forrest joined his mother and sisters at their new family home, 'Springbank', Lasswade.

There was no basking in the limelight of a hero. Work and marriage were Forrest's urgent priorities and they were closely linked. In tune with the middle classes of those days, once he and Clem got married, Forrest would be the bread-winner.

Balfour arranged for Forrest to have a job in the Herbarium at the Royal Botanic Garden Edinburgh at the rate of £2 a week (the equivalent of about £105 nowadays). With his collections and knowledge of the Chinese flora, Forrest was worth more than that to the RBGE, but that was the only money they had available.[1] As part of the deal, Balfour allowed Forrest the time necessary to write up some of his collections for publications. The Regius Keeper considered that this was only a just return for a collector who had risked so much.[2]

Forrest's first assignment was to study his collections of the gentian family, in which he discovered nine new species. Balfour assisted Forrest in the plant descriptions and Forrest was enormously grateful for his help. He was keenly aware of Balfour's

Opposite:
Plate 58. *Primula forrestii.*
A botanical drawing by
Eve Reid Bennett.

Left:
Plate 59. Rosslyn Chapel
where George Forrest and
Clementina Traill were
married on 15 July 1907.

guidance, since he first gave him a job at the RBGE. He wrote to Balfour:

> I feel your kindness to me more than I can tell, and I shall always be deeply grateful to you for the manner in which you have assisted and advanced me. In the future, as in the past, so far as lies in my power, I shall strive to merit the good opinion you have of me.[3]

Balfour was a person who instilled Forrest's loyalty and encouraged his utmost hard work. As we shall see, this did not prevent some clashes of opinion, but their close collaboration was to be of great value in the working up of Forrest's collections for many years to come, the young collector observing and recording features of the plants in the field, the older man being a more experienced taxonomist.

Balfour also suggested that Forrest should write a series of notes for the gardening press on the new plants he was introducing to cultivation, and include a photograph of each plant to give publicity to his work.

Photographs had generally replaced botanical artists' drawings as field records of plants in the wild. Missionary collectors had not had cameras, of course, so Forrest was able to photograph many wild flowers of Yunnan for the first time. Not that this was an easy task. His cumbersome camera equipment, chemicals and wooden boxes of fragile glass plates had to be carried by mule through monsoon downpours, over mountain ranges and hauled up steep slopes to reach the perilous positions where Forrest would take his photographs. With patience and resourcefulness he developed the negatives in the field. Disappointments were common, such as when the plates were spoiled by damp or were lost *en route*, but now in Edinburgh Forrest was eager to make and enlarge his prints for publication and to show Balfour how the plants looked *in situ*.

Bulley was relieved that Forrest was back safely and that his seeds were growing well at Bees Ltd. While looking forward, himself, to profits, Bulley also hoped that Forrest would benefit from their collaboration, and 'get a good boom out of his expedition'.[4]

The future looked bright as George Forrest married Harriet Clementina Mary Wallace Traill on 15 July 1907 in the beautiful and ancient Rosslyn Chapel, which is poised above the richly wooded gorge of Rosslyn Glen (Plate 59). He was certain he would never lose her love and was already convinced that she had 'changed him for the better'. For a long time he had looked forward to them setting up home together; two years earlier, when in Yunnan, he wanted to buy a 'tremendous sword, decorated with cornelians and turquoises as large as hedge sparrows' eggs' as an ornament for their future home.[5] Now the happy couple rented Glenkevock House, Lasswade,[6] formerly the home of the manager of the local paper mill (Plate 10).[7] The detached house was spacious yet homely, with French windows opening on to a walled garden and rich alluvial soils for growing vegetables and flowers. Forrest looked forward to experimenting with plants grown from his Yunnan seed. Clem had a local teenager, Annie Bowman, 'in service', and Annie thought of Clem as 'a right lady', kind and sharing.[8] The household was contented and the newly weds were devoted to each other. When the reprints of his 'gentian' paper arrived Forrest's pride in his first publication was shared with Clem. She saw he had named two plant species 'Trailliana' and he wrote inside 'With fondest love to my darling wife Clem. George'.

Frustrations take hold

Forrest found it extremely difficult to settle back into work at the Botanic Garden after three years away from its autocratic organisation and its strict regulations. He had become used to a completely different way of life and on his return he needed to make massive readjustments.

In China he had personal independence and authority; he had become used to getting his own way ultimately by having a 'blazing row' if necessary, or displaying his prowess with the gun. In the RBGE he had to be more circumspect. In Yunnan he employed collectors and stood out in a crowd; once he reported that up to one hundred curious people followed him to a post office. At the RBGE he was just one of the many workers. He received a weekly pay packet and was expected to accept what now seemed to him to be very petty regulations of a hierarchical, authoritarian institution.

One difficulty was the RBGE's strict attitude to time, often compounded by Forrest's problems of health that resulted from his run-down state on his return from Yunnan. In Yunnan Forrest's hours of fieldwork were varied and flexible according to the weather and the season, and he made his own decisions within this framework. In Britain everything was measured by the exact hour and minute of the clock. At the RBGE the timepiece was a symbol of centralised authority and the hours of work were rigid: no flexi-time in those days. Normally Forrest walked the six miles to work as before, but his expedition had weakened him and he was prone to colds, flu and malarial fever. In his first winter back he asked to use the trains, suggesting that, if late, he would work part of the lunch hour. But as the train timetables from Bonnyrigg and Lasswade did not fit in exactly with the timetable of the Garden, the answer was plain 'No!' His initiative was squashed and his independent spirit rebelled.

The Herbarium provided an odd blend of the comfortingly familiar and increased irritations. He did not get on well with the senior person there, John F. Jeffrey (Plate 13), and Clem was no longer in the Herbarium to mollify Forrest. Nevertheless, Forrest toiled meticulously, with Balfour's help, to name and describe his primula collection. He used the pioneering monograph of Professor Pax and produced a substantial paper for the Garden's publication *Notes from the Royal Botanic Garden Edinburgh,* with his own photographs of plants in the wild.[9]

However, even Forrest's relationship with Balfour was subtly changing, and this was a warning sign. Relationships were very important to Forrest, especially with those whom he respected. His letters from Yunnan used to please and excite the Regius Keeper and his industry had been admirable, but he was becoming a difficult employee who resented having to ask permission to photograph a plant or use the lantern to look at his slides. What might be regarded as small problems seemed to mount up and become bigger ones. Forrest became dissatisfied and critical.

Although Forrest had never been ill in his eight months in the Herbarium before he went to Yunnan, he now sometimes needed days off on sick leave. As he could not use the trains, and was unhappy in the Herbarium, he asked, unsuccessfully, if he could work at home. His family realised that he was deeply unsettled and not his usual self, and in March 1908 his sister Grace wrote confidentially to Balfour about him, asking that he be treated leniently.[10] In May and early June 1908 Forrest took a month off work to recover, half as holiday, half as unpaid leave. He excused himself from reading his paper to the Royal Geographical Society in London on 15 June 1908.[11] As far as we know, he had never given a public lecture before and at that stage of his life Forrest would have felt an 'outsider' in the company of the Establishment, especially without the support of the late Consul Litton. Probably anxious and lacking confidence in public speaking, it seems that he just could not manage it.

A long-term problem that caused Forrest much anxiety was how his thousands of specimens were to be named. He could not possibly work up all the specimens without specialists' help and Balfour was an extremely busy man, with responsibilities of administration and teaching. For Forrest a period of frustrated waiting was inevitable and this was difficult for a man who was a 'doer' and liked to get on with tasks and who had risked his life while collecting these plants. He longed to know exactly what he had found, how many were new to science – and he did not want to be forestalled by anyone else. Forrest did all he could to hasten the process and gradually, but too slowly for Forrest's liking, selected specimens were sent for study to other specialists at Kew and across the Continent.

Another basic problem had been simmering away since Forrest returned from Yunnan: who owned the thousands of dried herbarium specimens that he had collected? It seems that originally Bulley had simply written a letter to Forrest, offering to pay him to collect seeds for Bees' nursery. It had all happened in rather a hurry. There was no written contract and no detailed stipulations as to how the dried specimens should be subdivided; just an understanding that they would be mainly sent to the RBGE for description and naming. We have to remember that for Bulley, Balfour and Forrest this was their first experience of being involved directly in a plant hunting expedition. With no written rules there was room for different interpretations concerning the ownership of the dried specimens.

For more than eighteen months Forrest spent hours and hours each day, at home and in the Herbarium, simply sorting and labelling the dried specimens. In view of his hard work in Yunnan and at home, and all that he had endured, he thought that he would be entitled to keep some dried specimens. He took seeds from them for his garden and made up sets to sell. On the other hand, the Garden had paid for their transport and when Balfour eventually realised what was happening he wanted all the dried specimens in the Herbarium. There was an honest difference of opinion which resulted from a lack of clarity in the first place. Balfour was not a man to be trifled with and Forrest had the makings of a good trade unionist in asserting what he saw as his rights. But Forrest's stubbornness was nearly his downfall.

The problem came to a head in the summer of 1908. Balfour was happy for Forrest to keep a set of specimens in the future, but he sent a lorry to collect all the specimens that were currently at Forrest's home, so that they could be sorted in the Herbarium. Annoyed and angry, and already resentful that Jeffrey, in the Herbarium, did not trust him over sick leave, Forrest insisted that first he would have to stay at home for a few days to extract one of each species for himself.[12] He refused further discussion and on 14 August 1908 he offered his resignation, which Balfour accepted. When upset and defiant, Forrest could be as prickly as the thistle that is Scotland's emblem.

Balfour was baffled:

> You were taken on the staff of the Garden to work up these collections in our Herbarium…It appears now, however, that you have at Lasswade a large proportion of these collections…from which as I understand you propose to let us 'have specimens of each species'… Do I understand from this that you regard the collections as your own property to deal with as you choose?[13]

Forrest replied with characteristic directness:

> I most certainly wish you to understand that the portion of my last collection … which I have in hand, I consider to be my own to dispose of as I choose. Any indebtedness which may have been due the Garden by me I consider to be more than repaid by the collections I have already presented.

Forrest worked at home and continued to send lists of identifications to Balfour. He kept the normal courtesies of 'Dear Sir' and 'Yours sincerely', though he became peremptory almost to the point of rudeness. He forfeited two months of pay before Balfour ended the impasse by inviting Forrest for a frank talk that cleared the air and restored their normal good relations. The warm, good-natured Forrest reappeared. His whole family felt happier and Grace wrote to Balfour expressing their relief. Forrest was rescued from the corner into which he had boxed himself and Balfour was learning how to handle his protégé; in modern terms, he gave him more 'space' in which to operate. Forrest never forgot how Balfour helped him at this critical stage of his career. From then on their friendship was sustained by mutual respect and affection and the future of Forrest's plant specimens was made clear before each expedition.

Meanwhile, Forrest's mind kept returning restlessly to the prospects of going back to Yunnan. In a memo to Balfour, written only fifteen days after his wedding, he considered the possibility of a three-year expedition on the Mekong-Salween divide. But it seemed impossible to raise the money as he estimated the cost at between £1,800 and £2,000, including salary and travelling expenses. However, twelve days after Forrest's resignation, the tension was relieved by unexpected news: a visitor at the RBGE was looking for a plant collector.

An American Offer

26 August 1908

Dear Mr Forrest,
    ...Prof. Sargent from America was here today, and I gave him your name and told him of your desire to go out again to China. Probably you may hear from him...he wants someone for this work.
                Yours truly,
                I.B. Balfour[14]

Charles Sprague Sargent was an ambitious, energetic and wealthy sixty-seven year old who directed the Arnold Arboretum of Harvard University, Massachusetts. He had his eye on Eastern Asia as a source of horticultural novelties[15] and was currently employing Ernest H. Wilson as his collector in China. This was a real coup, as Wilson had made two very successful expeditions to Western China for the nursery firm of Veitch. Not yet satisfied, Sargent was on the lookout for another British plant collector and Forrest sounded ideal. After visiting Edinburgh, Sargent wrote to Balfour from the Burlington Hotel in London:

Can you arrange for George Forrest to meet me at the Veitch's Nursery, King's Road, Chelsea, on Tuesday Sept. 15, at four o'clock?
    I have been talking over with Mr. Veitch the possibility of employing Forrest for a journey to Northern China, and if Forrest wants to consider such a proposition I should like to see him before I return home.[16]

After deliberation, Forrest went to see Sargent and Veitch. It was a meeting of determined men and they came to no agreement. Forrest wanted, above all, to return to Yunnan, where he believed he would find many new plants. But, much to his chagrin, Sargent would not even consider the proposition. Sargent thought it was too warm a region and 'useless' for their purposes.[17] Forrest also wanted better pay, so Sargent made him an improved offer, but only to go to northern China. (Previously Sargent had increased his offer to Wilson, who then accepted.) Canny as ever, Forrest was not so easily captured, especially as Yunnan was his stated preference. He asked for time to think about it and checked with Balfour what salary Wilson had received.

Balfour advised Forrest to accept Sargent's improved offer of £300 per annum salary and £400 travelling allowance to go to northern China. Life as an explorer and collector suited Forrest and success in northern China should assure his career. But Forrest was still drawn to those wonderful flowers on the Mekong-Salween divide in Yunnan which had 'eclipsed everything I saw during my three year's sojourn in the country'.[18]

In the end the decision was conveniently made for him. According to Forrest, Sargent suddenly wanted him to set off in January 1909, although he had previously agreed to some time after March. Clem was expecting their first child in March and, as Forrest explained to Balfour, 'You can readily understand that I cannot well leave her until I see her safely through this'.[19] Fatherhood came first, and no amount of persuasion would change his mind.

George Forrest jnr. was born on 26 March 1909. He was a welcome son and heir, but his father's future as a plant collector was still only a dream. News that Sargent and Veitch were to send a Kew man, Purdom, to northern China, emphasised that Forrest had no definite sponsor. Knowing that Wilson was completing his third expedition in China cannot have made his position easier. His only hope rested on Bulley, who would give no promise: 'It is quite impossible for me to say whether I shall be able to commission you for a Yunnan expedition next winter'. That decision depended on the prosperity of his nursery business, which he might not know until November: 'I most emphatically urge you not to bank on this uncertainty…I think the only safe plan is not to take it into your reckoning until it occurs.'[20]

Forrest's immediate future hung on the horticultural success of his flowers at Bees Ltd. Sargent had recognised Forrest's worth as a collector, so who else might finance him to go to Yunnan? How could he ensure that more people heard of his talent for collecting? There was an urgent need to publicise his work to a wider world. Publicity was also in the interests of Bees Ltd and soon the names of Forrest and Bees Ltd were frequently mentioned in the horticultural press and came to the attention of another American.

News spreads

In November 1908 the popular, weekly *Gardeners' Chronicle* began reporting the results of Forrest's expedition. At a fortnightly meeting of the Royal Horticultural Society (RHS), *Primula malacoides* was shown by Messrs Bees Ltd and given an Award of Merit. 'This new species has been raised from seeds gathered by Mr George Forrest in the high alps (9,000ft. [2,750m]) of Yunnan, China.' In December Balfour submitted a drawing and a photograph of *Primula malacoides*, referred to Forrest as an 'excellent collector' and rightly predicted that this Primula would become a general favourite. It was one of Forrest's most important early introductions (Plate 60).[21] In the spring of 1909 its name was splashed across Bees' catalogue in large bold letters, together with descriptions of this 'splendid acquisition', a floriferous, winter blooming plant for the greenhouse. This was a great beginning for Forrest's flowers: an arable weed from Yunnan was acclaimed in British horticulture and subsequent plant selection produced many spectacular strains. In the 1950s it was reckoned that all cultivated material of *P. malacoides* outside China was probably derived from the first seeds Forrest sent to Bees.

1909 was a bumper year for publicity of Forrest's newly introduced plants. Balfour, Bulley and Forrest made a concerted effort to bring the flowers to people's attention. Three new species of primula, *P. bulleyana, P. forrestii* and *P. littoniana (vialii)* were all shown at RHS Shows by Bees Ltd, gaining First Class Certificates. Well-illustrated articles appeared in the *Gardeners' Magazine*, and the *Gardeners' Chronicle*. In May

Balfour wrote joyfully of *Primula forrestii* (Plates 58 and 62):

> It whets the appetite for more of the novelties which the enterprise of Mr Bulley and the skilful exploration of Mr Forrest have brought to this country.[22]

In July there were three illustrations each of *Primula bulleyana* and *P. littoniana* (*vialii*) and Balfour reported that the colours of *P. littoniana* (Plate 55) 'makes this the most extraordinary of all known Primulas'.[23] In November and December two whole pages of *The Gardeners' Chronicle* were filled with Forrest's photographs of three different primulas[24] and two striking Chinese orchids, *Cypripedium tibeticum* and *C. margaritaceum.*

Regular readers were left in no doubt that Forrest's plants were worth obtaining and the RBGE sent Forrest's primulas to keen gardeners across the land from Aberdeen to Bristol and the Botanic Gardens of Kew and Glasnevin (Dublin). Bees' and Forrest's names were becoming well known and interest in Forrest's credentials as a plant collector and photographer continued to mount in the coming months and years as the columns of the *Gardeners' Chronicle* frequently featured his plant photographs to striking effect, with Forrest now providing accompanying notes.

News of Forrest spread to America for a second time, this time to the United States Department of Agriculture where an enthusiastic American botanist, David Fairchild, was in charge of Plant Introduction. He was a correspondent of Bulley and, in the summer of 1909, visited him at Ness, where part of Bulley's garden was devoted to his commercial nursery. Fairchild was amazed by the array of Chinese

Plate 60. A photograph of *Primula malacoides* taken *in situ* by George Forrest, and used by Bulley as an advertisement in Bees' catalogue.

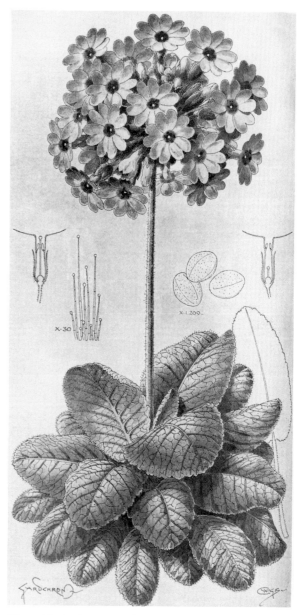

Plate 61. *Primula bulleyana*. Forrest found this beautiful primula covering several acres of the Yulong Shan. He named it after his first sponsor and collected several pounds of seed. Drifts of the richly coloured flowers now enhance many stream-side gardens in Britain.

Plate 62. A drawing of *Primula forrestii* published in 1909. Forrest commented, 'Did you ever see such a freak as the drawing in the G.C.?... the person... should be on the staff of a ladies' periodical drawing floral designs for teacloths.'

plants grown from Forrest's seeds. In Yunnan Forrest had collected as much as 4lbs (1.8kg) of hand-cleaned seed of some Primulas such as *P. bulleyana* (Plate 61), *P. littoniana* (*vialii*) and *P. forrestii*, enabling Bees Ltd to establish a good stock. Forrest, ever the perfectionist, had previously complained that many of Bees' new plants were 'butchered in the growing', but Fairchild painted a much rosier picture, describing what he saw as 'one of the largest collections of Chinese ornamental plants in Great Britain'.[25]

Bulley introduced Forrest to Fairchild and the two men immediately developed a good rapport. Forrest was delighted to tell the interested and friendly Fairchild about his collecting in Yunnan and Fairchild was impressed and charmed by him:

He is a man of exceptionally pleasing personality, a good talker, an unusual photographer, a trained botanist and a real explorer.[26]

PRIMULA FORRESTII.

Glorious golden yellow rock plant, leaves and flowers fragrant of ripe fruit.

Plate 63. *Primula forrestii* proudly displayed in the letter heading of Bees Ltd.

Forrest had the skills and enthusiasm that Fairchild was looking for and he realised that Forrest could be useful for plant introduction to the U.S. He even wondered whether Forrest could be hired for research into the problem of the introduction of American corn into China; he decided to keep an eye on Forrest.

Fairchild's visit heralded new prospects for Forrest, whose talents and success were being recognised beyond the shores of Britain. Bulley felt more confident, too. On top of Bees' selling Forrest's new flowers, Bulley's personal income as a cotton broker must have increased with the rising consumption of raw cotton in the U.K. He decided to send Forrest back to Yunnan for one year, extendable to three years. Forrest would have a salary of £200 per annum, plus initial expenses and a travelling allowance of over £650.[27] Forrest had wanted a salary of £300 per annum, as promised by Sargent, but here was his chance to return to his old hunting ground and he accepted the offer.

After reading Forrest's account in the *Geographical Journal* of his travels with Litton up the Salween valley, Fairchild also encouraged Forrest to write more articles. Fairchild was related by marriage to the editor of the *National Geographic Magazine*, Gilbert Grosvenor,[28] and showed him Forrest's photographs of people and places in Yunnan.

Grosvenor liked new ideas for articles, especially dispatches from the back of beyond. He retained twelve of Forrest's photographs for $18, and promised him a further $50 for a 6,000 word article. He hoped that this was only the first of many contributions and he promised to pay $1.50 for each additional photograph they used.[29]

Forrest was delighted: he had found a new outlet for his photographs and a wider readership abroad. He submitted his article to Grosvenor on 20 December 1909, before leaving for China on his second expedition, and he assured Grosvenor that he had already arranged for extensive photographic work of the country and 'the tribes-people' in a practically unexplored area. Moreover, he fully intended to take advantage of Grosvenor's offer to send him more articles.[30] The editor was pleased and asked Forrest to keep the magazine in mind while in the Orient.[31]

Forrest's second expedition

Happiness, for Forrest, was often associated with the pleasure of approaching some goal; and what better goal than returning to Yunnan for a second expedition? The increased activity gave him a 'buzz', and his mind whirred with all the jobs he had to do.

First Forrest requested the help of Balfour and the Foreign Office in procuring an Imperial passport and all the facilities that he might need from the Consuls and other officials in China. He wanted maximum cover in the event of trouble, having received a warning that the country was in a 'most disturbed condition'.[32] The Manchu dynasty was in its last years of declining power. Far from Yunnan, in the seclusion of the Forbidden City and the Summer Palace, the Empress Dowager, Tzu Hsi, died in 1908 and the new Emperor of the Ching dynasty, Pu Yi, was then only two years old.

Forrest was determined to make the very best use of his expedition. He contacted the Natural History Museum in London and offered to collect small mammals for them. He explained:

> It is not altogether a matter of £.s.d. with me, I take a keen interest in collecting, but owing to circumstances I shall only be too glad to add a little to my income by my labours.[33]

Forrest pointed out that he already had some practice in skinning and asked for information on preservative soaps and small labels. In the event no financial deal was forthcoming, but Forrest was eager to make some zoological collections if the opportunity arose.

Balfour gave Forrest a camera and books, including Pax's indispensable monograph on primulas, but in the midst of his preparations Forrest had a totally unexpected blow. Without any prior illness his mother died suddenly on Sunday evening 2 January 1910.[34] She was the head of the family, Forrest was very fond of her and his letters to the family had always begun, 'Dear Mother and all of you'. That was to be no more. After the funeral, upset and in mourning, Forrest finished his packing and his departure for China was far more difficult than before as he took leave of his bereaved siblings and left behind his wife and his son of only nine months old.

Forrest sailed from Liverpool on a ship of the Henderson Line, SS *Irrawaddy (II),* bound for Burma. On approaching Port Said he wrote to Balfour of his continuing sadness:

> I have not yet recovered, nor do I expect to for some time, from the wrench of leaving my wife and child. In all my wanderings I never felt so utterly home-sick as I do now.[35]

He kept himself occupied on the long journey and passed the time writing a two-part article for the *Gardeners' Chronicle* on 'The Perils of Plant-Collecting', which was published a few months later.[36] It was a gripping version of his horrific escape from warring lamas, death and torture in 1905. From the safety of the ship he related the tale like a *Boy's Own* adventure, little knowing what was in store for him.

On arrival at The Royal Hotel, Rangoon, Forrest was aghast to find that Bulley had failed to send him enough money for his expedition. Only £25 awaited him; about enough to pay his train fare and expenses to Bhamo, but leaving nothing to pay for supplies for his expedition. Forrest had no money to buy the tents, saddling, ammunition, bedding and drugs which he needed, or even to pay his hotel expenses in Rangoon, where he had expected to spend a week. He felt 'within an ace of returning home by the same steamer', disillusioned by the seemingly uncaring unreliability of his employer. However, Forrest was a resourceful person: he asked the captain if he could remain on board the ship, until, hopefully, more money arrived.[37] He cabled Bulley, who sent him £150.

Forrest learned later that the lack of funding had been due to a mix-up at Bees' office. But the homesick Forrest was vulnerable in Rangoon, stranded thousands of

Plate 65. A portrait by George Forrest of a Chinese lady in front of painted scrolls dedicated to the Consul's wife.

miles from home and over a thousand miles (1,600km) from his destination. He felt so undermined and let down that he decided he simply could not work with such an employer longer than necessary; he would finish the agreed year of his contract, enough to explore more of the Lichiang Range, but that was all. He could not know that financial problems would be a recurring nightmare on this expedition.

When Forrest reached the Chinese border town of Tengyueh, another promised sum from Bulley had failed to arrive and again Forrest was reliant on the friendship and goodwill of others. He arranged with Consul Rose for a loan. Forrest now wrote to Bulley confirming that he would return home as soon as he had secured the year's harvest. He knew that this might jeopardise his career, but he felt that Bulley was behaving 'in an impossible manner'. Fortunately, Forrest's missionary friends were still in Yunnan – Mr Embery at Tengyueh and Dr Clark in Tali – so he had a warm welcome and support as he gathered together as many of his former collectors as he could. They also stood loyally by him and there was a sympathetic and encouraging letter from Balfour, with a request from the lily expert, Arthur Grove, anxious for seeds or bulbs of *Lilium davidii* and *Lilium oxypetalum*, which were unknown in cultivation. Forrest's balance was restored as he settled to work and his appetite was once again whetted for plant hunting. Social unrest meant that the region of the Salween valley was closed to exploration, which precluded some work for Fairchild. However, 'Delavay's territory' was politically possible and Forrest was keen to search out more of Delavay's discoveries.

On Forrest's arrival at Tali he noticed big changes had occurred in the past three years. The Government had established a garrison of fully 3,000 well-equipped soldiers, drilled by Japanese instructors. At each street crossing there was a sentry box. The city was properly policed, more prosperous, and wages were higher. 'There is no question about the matter', wrote Forrest, 'China is awakening'. But his financial problems had not changed. Forrest was still waiting for money from Bulley and now had only £30 left, enough only to take him to Lichiang-fu and to keep him for a fortnight. He declared himself 'thoroughly sick of the whole affair' and added 'One thing is certain if ever I go anywhere again as a collector it shall never be for Messrs Bees Ltd.'[38]

Importantly, at that particular time, the love of flowers that he and Bulley shared temporarily restored harmony between them. At Tali Forrest received a letter from Bulley, asking if he had ever found *Lithospermum hancockianum*, which he rated as dear as gentians. The plant hunter's instinct came to the fore. Forrest had seen this flower in 1905, just north of Yunnan-fu. He was currently on his way to Lichiang, but left detailed instructions for the collection of its seed with Dr Clark, who was supervising his collectors at Tali.

However, when Forrest heard from his wife that a quarter's salary, due to be paid in advance to her, was five weeks overdue, he was incensed; even his wife and child had now been let down by Bulley. This was the last straw and confirmed his determination to return home in January 1911 and not to work for Bulley again.

It seems ironic that Bulley, who had the enterprise to send Forrest to Yunnan, and gave him a second opportunity to go there, then discouraged him through inefficiency and thoughtlessness. On top of not sending remittances from Bees' office on time, there was also a serious lack of understanding of the personal support needed to bolster a collector in the field, so far from home, and in a country on the verge of civil war. Bulley was proud of his plant hunter: in Bees' catalogues he was still 'Our Mr Forrest' doing great things. But Bulley never realised that showing his appreciation and giving even a little praise would have been like gold dust to Forrest. Only after leaving Bulley's employ did Forrest eventually learn that Bulley actually appreciated his endeavours. In Yunnan Forrest felt increasingly like a servant of commerce. When a new iris was named *Iris forrestii*, Bulley's only comment to Forrest was that it was not showy enough to sell well (Plate 64). Such an outlook, combined with what he saw as low pay, brought a strong reaction from Forrest. He wrote of Bulley as a 'cad of the first order'. He decided never again to work for any nurseryman and railed against them:

> There is a lot said about the meanness of the Scotch but in my time I have met more stingy English than I ever did Scotch, and Bulley and Veitch, the great Sir Harry, are types, extreme types![39]

When Bulley said he was willing to continue 'the speculation' and offered Forrest two more years in Yunnan, it was firmly rejected.

On the other hand, as often in life, the situation was complex. Forrest's particular family situation must have swayed him towards returning home after one year, and he admitted there were faults on his side. On his first expedition he had overcome problems of loneliness and depression and even after Litton's death he had stayed the course. On this second expedition, however, Forrest had a bad start and never had the company of anyone with Litton's zest, who could have made light of the financial let downs and countered them with humour and some slightly mad diversion. Nevertheless, Bulley admitted that it was shocking of him to leave Forrest short of funds and Forrest considered him neither a reliable nor reasonable employer. The problems that Forrest experienced with Bulley rankled him for months after his return to Britain.

In contrast, Balfour offered practical support, even a donation of £25 when hearing of Forrest's financial difficulties. His understanding and sympathy were an emollient and strengthening influence. Forrest expressed his warm gratitude to Balfour and there is no doubt that the excellent relationship that had built up between the two men was fundamental in bringing out the best in Forrest.

A successful outcome

The wealth of bloom that greeted him in May, on the Sung Kwei pass, was a wonderful welcome and recompense for earlier troubles. From the margin of the open pasture that surrounded a small lake, to the tops of the enclosing low hills, a zone of rhododendron forest stretched for about 1,000ft. (300m) altitude. He relished every detail:

> The foreground is occupied by large matted masses of a dwarf species, 1-2 feet [30-60cm], with deep purplish-blue flowers; behind this come groups of *R. yunnanense*, simply showers of bloom, forming a belt of the very palest conceivable shade of rose-lavender, almost white and showing so at a short distance; then a taller species bearing huge and well-formed umbels of beautiful rose-magenta flowers, and, behind all, to the verge of the alpine pasture at the summits, an almost impenetrable forest of tree rhododendrons, from 20-30ft. [6-9m] in height, composed of such species [of Rhododendron] as *bureavii, irroratum, crassum, lacteum, heliolepis,* etc. etc. all in the very perfection of bloom, with a dense undergrowth of dwarf bamboo. Viewed from the pass the surface of this forest appeared almost level; it was an ideal day, and the effect of the brilliant sunshine on the dark glistening sea of foliage, interspersed with masses of colouring, ranging from the almost pure white of *bureauvi* and creamy yellow of *irroratum*, through nearly every shade of lavender-magenta to the deepest crimson, was a sight far beyond my power to describe. To be appreciated such has to be seen. It was with the greatest effort I tore myself away; I think I could have remained for days drinking in the beauty of the scene. Truly our home knowledge of rhododendrons is nil.[40]

Plate 66. *Meconopsis integrifolia*. One of George Forrest's most used photographs, for example in the *Gardeners' Chronicle* (1911), Bees' catalogue (1912) and *Country Life* (1923).

Plate 67. *Meconopsis integrifolia* growing in the wild above Lijiang on the Yulong Shan (Lichiang Range).

Plate 68. *Primula dryadifolia* photographed by Forrest in its natural habitat and published in the *Gardeners' Chronicle* in 1911.

Plate 69. *Primula dryadifolia,* a plant of high, exposed mountain screes and stony ground. This photograph was taken at 4,300m (14,000ft.) on the Beima Shan.

Plate 70. *Rhododendron lacteum* growing on the slopes of the Cang Shan above Dali (Tali). It was introduced to Britain by George Forrest in 1910.

Here we have our first vivid indication of what was to motivate Forrest for many years to come. The range and variety of rhododendrons were weaving their own allure, capturing his curiosity and fuelling his drive to find more. Any rhododendron-lover would savour his description, and we see what drew him to Yunnan, leaving his wife and child. In Britain there was official mourning for King Edward VII who had died at Buckingham Palace and the *Gardeners' Chronicle* had black lines between the columns, but Forrest was entranced by the beautiful flora of Yunnan and he was realising how much more there was to discover.

Forrest strove hard to use the time available in the most productive way. He made his base at the foot of the southern end of the Lichiang Range, camping at about 9,000ft. (3,000m), and again the beauty and interest of the flowers revitalised him. He went into overdrive and, whatever the weather (it was often raining in torrents or blowing a gale), he filled his time fully. Hours were spent on photography. He admitted that he was not the most patient of individuals and photographing plants in the mountains was a severe test in those days of less advanced technology. To secure a photograph of *Primula pinnatifida* he returned to its habitat five times, each journey representing a climb of at least 4,000ft. (1,200m). He exposed a dozen plates, yet all of them were spoilt by the movement of plants in the wind, or the underexposure of plates in the fog. It was heart-breaking and he admitted that in such moments he could 'hurl the camera into space, and have done with it'. He said that it was only his 'Scots dourness' which enabled him to carry on.[41] Sometimes Forrest even developed prints at his campsite and struggled in the damp conditions with poor paper and insufficient chemicals. Yet he produced some winners, including photographs of *Meconopsis integrifolia* (Plates 66 and 67), *Primula dryadifolia* (Plates 68 and 69) and the magnificent rock plant, *Isopyrum grandiflorum*. He was thrilled when photographs turned out better than expected, posting them to Balfour to share his joy.

Forrest was also ambitious in his field observations. He set himself to find as many primulas as possible on the Lichiang Range and on a three-week trek along the range to the north of the Yangtze bend he spent three weary and unsuccessful days 'beating the ground around the base of the great glacier' in search of *P. glacialis* Fr. which Delavay had found there.[42] However, in general he was delighted with the number he found. He carefully searched five miles (8km) of country to find *Primula pulchella* and when he came across acres of it in open alpine pasture it was worth all the toil. He returned to the area where he had found *Primula bulleyana* before, and when he found specimens with 'crushed strawberry' or 'apricot-red' colouring he realised that these must be natural hybrids between *P. bulleyana* and *P. beesiana*. He discovered and introduced *Roscoea humeana* (see Plate 91). And when he hunted in the habitat of *Primula littoniana* (now *P. vialii*), to the east of the valley of Lichiang, he discovered a bonus in a lovely rose-coloured form of *Nomocharis pardanthina* which he had not seen before.

One of the finds of the season was *Primula dryadifolia* (Plates 68 and 69) and, when writing to Balfour one evening, he wrote so vividly that Balfour could easily imagine the plant in its wild, high, mountain home:

> How I wished when I came on it that you were with me. How you would have enjoyed the sight. Its habitat is a cup-shaped, boulder-strewn basin about a mile in extent, almost at the limit of vegetation at an altitude of approximately 15,500ft. [4,700m]. Snow and barren limestone peaks all around, a cutting wind, and moisture everywhere. The centre of the basin was occupied by a small lake of crystal clearness, formed of the melting snows, every depression of any size was filled with heavy snowdrifts, but on the bare intervening prominences, and in every crevice of all the larger boulders capable of retaining a sufficiency of loam and moisture, was *P. dryadifolia*.[43]

One of his most controversial and striking discoveries on this expedition was the growth of rhododendrons on limestone. He observed the conditions carefully and explained to Balfour:

> The soil was composed of peat, disintegrated limestone, with a good admixture of limestone chips, a compost which I cannot get Mr Bulley to believe in, nor yet any member of your staff in the Garden.

As rhododendrons in Britain generally grow best on acidic soils, it was understandable that British gardeners were incredulous at Forrest's report, and it was to be a topic that continued in discussions with Forrest over many years and is still the subject of research today.

On top of all his fieldwork, Forrest maintained a prodigious correspondence, but did not fulfil all the commissions requested, such as articles for the *National Geographic Magazine*. Amongst the many letters he received were ones from Gregory of the Botany School, Cambridge, Dykes of Charterhouse, Palibin of the Museum of the Botanic Garden, St. Petersburg, and Fairchild in the U.S. These letters were testimony to people's appreciation of his work, and the building up of his reputation.

Despite months of wretched weather (in which Forrest saw a man and two bullocks killed by lightning), it was a productive expedition. As an unpaid sideline he did some zoological collecting, donating to the (now) National Museums of Scotland approximately 2,000 insects, mainly from the neighbourhood of Lichiang, and some butterflies from Rangoon. From the Lichiang area he added in a few frogs, leeches, birds and bats, and was particularly keen to send eighteen snakes to the Keeper of Natural History, Mr Eagle Clark. The snakes were preserved in spirit in glass bottles, and needing a special form sanctioning receipt of duty-free spirit. They still form part of the museum's research collections (Plate 72).

Forrest decided not to collect all the commoner plant species, but he despatched several cases of plants, totalling approximately 2,000 herbarium specimens, including type specimens. Through his seed collections he introduced a wide range of plants into cultivation, one being the unusual *Roscoea humeana*, a hardy plant of the largely tropical ginger family (see Plate 91) and another, the beautiful blue autumn gentian, *Gentiana sino-ornata*. (Plate 30). Of rhododendrons, he introduced the compact little shrub *R. impeditum*, type F.5,863 (see Plate 97), and another for small gardens, *R. dichroanthum*. He discovered and introduced *R. oreotrephes*, which Kingdon Ward later recommended for its 'pale rosy-mauve flowers', and *R. lacteum*, with its rounded trusses of yellow flowers that Lionel de Rothschild, at Exbury, later used extensively for hybridising (Plate 70).

Despite Balfour's disappointment that Forrest had returned so soon, he was delighted with Forrest's 'splendid specimens', marvelled at his activity and congratulated him on what he had achieved.

Plate 71. *Pleione grandiflora*. A photograph by Forrest in April 1906 taken on the Cang Shan (Tali Range). This semi-epiphytic orchid has fragrant white flowers with an orange-brown labellum.

Plate 72. On 15 January 1911 Forrest wrote from Rangoon that he had dispatched 'half a dozen bottles of snakes preserved in spirits'. This is one of them, named *Tropidonotus nuchalis* (now *Rhabdophis nuchalis*), and part of the first zoological collection that Forrest presented to the National Museums of Scotland.

CHAPTER SIX
The Third Expedition, 1912-1915

Forrest is unquestionably the finest collector of modern times
I.B. Balfour to A.K. Bulley, 15 April 1912

Arthur K.Bulley made a huge investment in Forrest's first two expeditions: in terms of the present value of the pound (November 2002) it is estimated that he spent £185,000. In return, Bees' nursery was the first to market Forrest's introductions and requested that some new garden plants be named as an advertisement: 'bulleyana', 'beesiana' or 'beesii'. Forrest was convinced that many more species awaited discovery and he set his heart on returning to Yunnan. But who would sponsor him?

Rescued by a Cornishman

As Forrest steamed homeward on S.S. *Amarapoora* in January 1911, he looked forward to being reunited with his family. His son, now a sturdy toddler, would not know him after his year away. Clementina had been loyally 'keeping the home fires burning' in their rather isolated house and in their delight at being together she conceived their second child. But this homely togetherness was to last less than a year. Unknown to them, before Forrest had even left Rangoon, Bulley's networking was leading to new beginnings for Forrest's plant hunting: a different employer, a third expedition, and another professional plant hunter at work on what Forrest had begun to think of as 'his' territory.

Bulley had consulted Balfour about the prospect of replacing Forrest. Balfour recommended Frank Kingdon Ward, a twenty-six year old school master in Shanghai who was longing to go on an expedition. He had taken a Cambridge Tripos in Natural Sciences, had a 'good knowledge of botany and of plants', and he had already travelled by junk and on foot across the breadth of China, collecting birds and animals on an American zoological expedition. When, in January 1911, Bulley offered him an expedition to collect hardy and alpine plants for Bees Ltd, Ward accepted at once, and he was in Tengyueh, Yunnan, by March. He was to hunt for new herbaceous plants in the mountains of Yunnan but, officially, avoiding Forrest's main stamping ground. It was yet to be seen how this would affect Forrest.

Plate 73. Caerhays Castle, Cornwall, the home of J.C. Williams, who sponsored George Forrest from his third expedition onwards.

Bulley was also in touch with J.C. Williams of Caerhays Castle, Cornwall, an eminent gardener who was particularly keen on introducing trees and shrubs and was well informed on the work of E.H. Wilson. He had received his first batch of Wilson's Chinese rhododendrons from Veitch's nursery in 1903, and they were now growing splendidly in the sheltered valley of his Caerhays garden. As Bulley was more interested in growing herbaceous plants, he invited Williams to look over Ness gardens in 1910 and to select all the rhododendrons that seemed worth growing.[1] Williams offered to pay Bulley £300 for all of Forrest's rhododendron and conifer seeds from his 1910 expedition;[2] he was clearly aware of Forrest's collecting abilities.

In spring 1911 J.C. Williams invited Forrest to stay at Caerhays Castle, his castellated mansion on the south Cornish coast (Plate 73). Williams, who was born in Caerhays Castle and educated at Rugby and Trinity Hall, Cambridge, had inherited a large capital sum and his father's landed estate, Caerhays. He had bought Werrington Park on the Devon-Cornwall border and he rented an estate, Strathvaich, in the Scottish Highlands. It was a contrasting world to any that Forrest had inhabited, but the two men shared an enthusiastic love of plants, and an eagerness to introduce new plants from China. Williams wanted to meet Forrest and show him his rhododendrons,[3] as he planned to develop his garden with new species. He had the wealth to employ a plant hunter and admired Forrest's courage, tenacity, and evident success in finding new plants. Williams was the same age as Bulley and, for him, gardening was a pleasurable hobby. He had a generous, sympathetic and considerate nature that appealed to Forrest, while Williams described Forrest as 'a very small compact man with a fine chest on him, built for fatigue. Has done much and can probably do much more'.[4]

As they wandered round the garden at Caerhays they had a stimulating conversation, the collector and grower sharing their expertise on the plants before them. The two men warmed to each other. They were both countrymen with a loathing of the city and a love of fishing and shooting (fly fishing for salmon and trout had been Forrest's chief pastime since he was 'as tall as your walking stick').[5] In the coming months it was as if Williams took Forrest 'under his wing', and Forrest opened up to him as to a new and understanding friend.

Forrest was busy. He presented his zoological and ethnographic collections from N.W. Yunnan to the National Museums of Scotland (Plates 72 and 74). At home he was writing up his plant collections from the second expedition, and he took up some taxonomic work on his primulas and other plants, naming *Dracocephalum isabellae* after his sister (Appendix 8). He began to reinvigorate his garden at Glenkevock House, asking Balfour for a sample of the Yunnan rhododendron seeds that were germinating freely in the Botanic Garden.

In the second half of 1911, at approximately monthly intervals, he submitted notes to the *Gardeners' Chronicle* on eight herbaceous plants of Yunnan, and these were published alongside striking, full-page photographs that showed his photographic skills as well as the plants. It was useful pocket money and the gardening public was also being reminded of George Forrest and the riches of the Chinese flora before he went off again.

By August 1911 Williams and Forrest were discussing plans for Williams to fund an expedition. He offered to increase Forrest's salary from £200 a year to £500 a year (£27,500 today) for three years, and was flexible over where Forrest collected, since much would depend on the political situation in and around Yunnan. He agreed that sets of herbarium specimens and the greater part of the seeds would be shared with the Edinburgh, Kew and Dublin Botanic Gardens, although there also seems to have been agreement that some seeds of herbaceous plants should go to the nursery of Wallace of Colchester.

All augured well and it is interesting to note the conscientiousness with which both men approached the expedition. Williams fed Forrest with all manner of information: the *Journal of the Royal Asiatic Society*, a copy of Wilson's Notes and a set of 700 of Wilson's photographs, Bretschneider's *Notes on Chinese Botany*, and Ward's letters confirming that he had met no untoward trouble in China. Then, for good measure, Williams sent Forrest a water-proof cover to protect his telescope and a box of cuttings for his garden. How quickly Forrest changed from the man who had sometimes felt so desolate on his second expedition. With all this attention and encouragement, Williams was not only rescuing Forrest's career but restoring his enthusiasm and self-esteem.

A happy Forrest began the background reading and detective work that ensured that he was well prepared. Above all, he wanted to update himself on what other collectors had found. He studied Volume I of E.H. Wilson's *Plantae Wilsonianae*. He visited Vilmorin's nursery in Paris to find out what Chinese plants they grew, and spent three days in the Paris Herbarium, where he was thrilled to find fine species of rhododendrons new to him. Carefully he noted their localities, hoping to find them to collect seed. He also spent several days at Kew.[6]

There he had the charming idea of sending the ninety-four year old Sir Joseph Dalton Hooker, formerly Director of Kew, a bloom of a Chinese balsam, *Impatiens delavayi*.[7] One senses that Forrest valued his link with this great man and felt a huge respect for him. In Hooker's younger days he had discovered marvellous rhododendrons in the Sikkim-Himalaya and compiled the classic seven volumes of the *Flora of British India*, with which Forrest was familiar. Balsams were among Hooker's favourite flowers, and their study had become his all-consuming passion. After examining Indian balsams he moved on to study Chinese ones, including some of Forrest's collecting.[8] The old man probably received Forrest's gift of a fresh flower a few weeks before he died.

However, trouble was erupting in China. With a young boy as Emperor, the Manchu dynasty was weak. The revolutionary Sun Yat-sen was exiled but engineered many uprisings from abroad, and on 26 October 1911 a Chinese Republic was proclaimed. Forrest was worried. He feared that isolated Europeans would be threatened by rebel troops, but hoped that conditions would improve by

Plate 75. Forrest's second son, Eric, with Clementina's mother, Phoebe Marshall Traill. The photograph was taken after Forrest had left on his third expedition.

the spring. He suggested making arrangements as usual, and on arrival at Tengyueh he would see whether to use that as his base, or go further north, or even retreat into Burma – though he was reluctant to learn another language, either Kachin or Burmese. He wrote to people in Tengyueh for the latest information and asked Williams to watch the papers for news.

We can only guess at Clementina's thoughts on all these developments. Forrest declined to go to Kew in December because she was expecting to be confined in the middle or end of that month, and he wished 'to be at hand'.[9] But Clementina knew that the proposed expedition would mean that she would be left at home with two young children for three whole years. And there was nothing she could do about it.

Forrest had already prepared a detailed shopping list of items to be bought before he left Britain (Appendix 4).[10] Guns were his most expensive equipment, especially a 12 bore double-barrelled fowling piece and a 12 bore automatic repeating fowling piece, followed by a .45 Colt repeating pistol and a 12 shot Winchester repeating carbine. Boots and other special clothing were costly, including an oilskin coat and sou'wester. Camping equipment was essential, and he listed a camp bed and stout linen, camp table and chair, a pillow and a rubber bath, a medicine chest, and leather cases for mule travel. For field-work he needed two axes and a sharpening stone, sheath knives, and lots of stationery: field notebooks, envelopes for seeds and lined envelopes for forwarding seeds, and 3–5,000 labels. He added in his photographic equipment: reflex camera, wide-angle lens, cases of plates and chemicals. Altogether, with his passage monies to and from Rangoon and other travelling expenses, he reckoned, meticulously, that he would need to spend £166.9s.6d before he got to Burma.

Forrest also sent Williams a list of the articles he would need to buy in Burma, including two canvas tents, a mosquito curtain, a saddle and bridle, his stores and ammunition. Together with his salary and travelling allowance he estimated the initial total outlay for Williams would be over £3,000[11] (£163,000 today). Williams appears not to have quibbled over anything and Forrest started placing his orders.

Forrest had carefully drafted in longhand, on lined foolscap paper embossed with the Royal Coat of Arms, a legal document on the proposed expedition. He undertook to collect 'bulbs and seeds of plants of horticultural value, and botanical specimens' in accessible areas lying on the N.E. frontier of Upper Burmah [sic] and West and N.W. Yunnan, exclusively for J.C. Williams, and subject to conditions of expenditure already agreed.[12] He signed it on 4 December 1911 and sent it to Williams, who accepted and signed the agreement on 23 December, having sent Forrest his first year's salary in advance.

All was set for the expedition. It was just a matter of waiting for the baby to arrive. John Eric Forrest was born on 7 January 1912. By 23 January Forrest reported that Clementina was 'slightly better' and he left her overnight whilst he met Williams.[13] On his return he was pleased to find her 'somewhat better'[14] and in February he left Clementina to cope, with their families near at hand to help, as he boarded S.S. *Martaban* bound for Rangoon.

To the new Republic

Forrest had an uneventful journey to Rangoon and used it to catch up with his work. He wrote up specimens that W. Wright Smith had sent him from the RBGE, and notes on more of his photos for the *Gardeners' Chronicle*. In one article, 'Rhododendrons in China', he expressed his belief that the real 'home' of the genus was in the high alpine regions on the Chino-Tibetan frontier, where many different species were to be found.[15] That was the area that he dearly wished to go to on this third expedition. His hopes of getting there had been thwarted on his second expedition and all would now depend on the state of unrest in China.

On arrival in Rangoon he was cheered on his way by a letter from Balfour with the happy news that some of his orchids, sedums and saxifrages were described in the current *Notes from the RBG Edinburgh*, that Diels' naming of his plants would soon be published, and that Stewart, the propagator, was looking forward to the flowering of Forrest's seedlings. At the same time, the Commissioner of Customs in Tengyueh, E.B. Howell, reported poor prospects of getting into Yunnan.

When Forrest reached Bhamo, there was no definite news from Tengyueh. Instead he heard the most blood-curdling tales circulating among the Europeans, though he realised they might be rumours and attributed them to 'the fecundity of the drink-soddened Bhamo brains'.[16] Sensibly cautious, Forrest crossed quietly into Yunnan, prepared to escape by another route if necessary.

China, an 'active volcano'

When he reached Tengyueh, Forrest compared living in China to camping alongside an active volcano. Brutal murders were rife. Since before the proclamation of a Republic, Tengyueh had been in the hands of revolutionary troops, 'a band of undisciplined ruffians'.[17] Forrest reckoned that 250 people in Tengyueh, out of a population of 5-6,000, had been beheaded without any kind of trial, leading to such revulsion that many people favoured the restoration of the Manchus.

Forrest had to live from month to month in this perilous situation, and travel north to the 'home' of the rhododendrons was impossible. Only four days' travel away, on the Tali road, the town of Yungchang-fu was practically burned down and many people killed. To make matters more complicated, all the silver ingot currency that had been in circulation during the Manchu Dynasty was replaced by a new republican dollar. The rate of exchange was dropping and the price of food was rising rapidly, so Forrest had to pay his collectors and servants more than double the amount he paid them in 1907. During the next few months he had to increase their wages twice, until he was forced to ask Williams for more funds.[18]

He began work in the area around Tengyueh in early May, when some of his previous Nakhi collectors rejoined him from the Lichiang valley and worked as hard as ever for him.[19] They collected freely in local areas and on to the Shweli-Salween Divide, with its rich, semi-tropical forest vegetation, and in less than a month Forrest had thirty-five plant presses going. By July his excitement mounted, as he had fully nine hundred dried species in hand, many of them written up and ready for dispatch, including berberis, buddlejas, clematis, primulas, roses, rhododendrons, 'three superb jasmines' and twenty to thirty epiphytic orchids. He was working hard to make the season a success, even though the British Consul in Tengyueh would not allow him to go further up country. Disorder prevailed over much of the province, with uprisings and stories of people being tortured and burned alive. Forrest himself did not thirst for adventure among such disturbances, feeling that he had already had his share in the past, and didn't 'hanker after another turn'.

Williams sent Forrest new supplies of photographic plates, cuttings from *The Times,* and a book for an 'enjoyable read': *In Forbidden China. The d'Ollone mission, 1906-1909, China-Tibet-Mongolia,* translated from the French.[20] He reported that Forrest's plants were to the fore at the Royal International Horticultural Exhibition at Chelsea in May 1912, being shown by Bees Ltd and Wallace of Colchester. He told Forrest that he was experimenting with his seeds in all three of his gardens, and later in the year he delighted Forrest further by thoughtfully sending Clementina some bulbs.

However, on 31 August Forrest wrote anxiously that Tengyueh was about to be attacked. He might have to leave at any moment. His collection of 1,700 dried species of plants and nearly 100lbs (45kg) of seed were at risk, including some undried rhododendron seed from the Shweli-Salween divide. The thought of losing it all made him feel sick, so he was desperate to get them on the way to Mr Williams as soon as possible. (Williams had agreed to send the specimens and a portion of the seeds on to the RBGE.) Forrest planned to risk sending eight cases of specimens and seeds down to Bhamo, with Chinese wrappings to disguise them as Chinese exports. Moreover, he asked Balfour to tell only one of his staff (W.W. Smith) of this potential trouble, and Mr Smith was not to tell even his wife, for fear that news would reach Clementina and cause her extra anxiety.[21]

Forrest's export plan failed; the road to Bhamo was blocked, so the cases could not be sent along that road. Conditions in Tengyueh deteriorated, Forrest could not go out collecting, and the British Consul refused to take any further responsibility for him or his collections. The only option was for Forrest to take his eight cases of specimens and seeds with him and escape over the mountains to Myitkyina in Burma. He later summarised the journey as, 'Jungle frightful, 9 days out of the twelve, heavy tropical rains, several places had to build bridges'.[22]

He left Tengyueh in torrents of rain on the morning of 4 September, taking with him some of his collectors, on the offchance that they might all return later. He had twelve mules carrying his 'kit of tents, etc.' and thirty coolies. But the mules were 'underfed, undersized creatures' and the coolies were 'opium smokers to a man!' He gave the coolies one tent, and described the sight on peeping inside: 'Door closed, 40 pipes going, and an atmosphere one could have sectioned with a microtome'. Towards the summit of the pass two bearers broke down in the cold and wet, two deserted, and he had to replace them with local Lissoo people. Forrest walked and admitted to Williams that he kept the 'gang' on the move by sheer force of will and 'a display of language which astonished even myself'.

To make matters more difficult, Forrest had promised to take a petrified Customs man and his wife, Mr and Mrs Ross, with him to safety together with their two staff, a wife and three youngsters. They were reliant on Forrest's tents and equipment and part of his stores. Ross rode a mule and his wife had a sedan chair and four bearers. They did not know the dialect, so Forrest translated for them.

Conditions were terrible: 'Rain poured in solid sheets, the valleys were filled, and the mountains swathed in heavy mists and the streams continually rose'. It was a miserable journey, with mules falling, loads slipping, and five large mountain streams to cross. The mules were towed or swam across the water, after their loads were taken off their backs and carried over separately. In places Forrest had to commandeer local Kachin people to build bamboo bridges padded with grass and foliage to prevent slipping. The bridges trembled as they crossed rivers of 'boiling, beer-coloured foam' and one, which Forrest was the last to use, became almost submerged, and a few minutes later was washed away (Plate 76).

After five nights in dripping tents and soaked bedding it was a relief to reach the frontier, with its fort garrison and official rest house. They had a day's rest before the three day journey to Myitkyina, the rail-head in Upper Burmah, and the civil officer heliographed for a strong guard to escort them safely. They crossed the 700 yard (640m) wide Irrawaddy river in a big Burmese dug-out canoe, Forrest's

baggage alone needing four double trips, and Forrest was greatly relieved when his responsibility to Mr and Mrs Ross had been completed. Leaving them in Myitkyina, he continued on by train and river steamer to Bhamo, settled in a bungalow and decided on his next strategy. All his collections were with him and, as he had taken the precaution to varnish the cases, and to seal the joints inside and out with beeswax, the contents were in perfect condition.

Forrest relaxed, met old friends like Captain Medd, the Bhamo agent for the Irrawaddy Flotilla Co., and reflected that China was becoming altogether too nerve-racking. In some ways he felt like 'chucking it in' and going home for the winter, but his conscience would not let him. Williams continued to write encouraging letters. Consul Smith reported that the region around Tengyueh was more peaceful again and Forrest resolved to return to collect seed for the rest of the season. He had 'marked down' in his field notebook those numbered specimens for which he would like seed. He sent his headman, Lao Chao, and four of his best collectors in advance, while he stayed in Bhamo to complete the writing up of his specimens and finish the seed drying. The specimens, seeds and a few butterflies were then packed into cases, ready for dispatch on the Irrawaddy Flotilla Steamer to Rangoon, and Forrest walked back over the mountains, 130 miles (200km), to rejoin his men.

The collectors who had gone ahead to Tengyueh first worked for Forrest in 1906. He had trained them and he trusted them completely. He described his chief collector as a 'jewel' and said that he put more faith in him than he did in himself. 'He has been tried many times now and never failed me.'[23] Forrest's confidence in his collectors was well rewarded. On his arrival in Tengyueh they returned from the

Plate 76. Forrest's photograph of a bridge made of cane and lianas across a tributary of the Salween River.

Plate 77. *Rhododendron sinogrande,* discovered in 1912, is one of Forrest's most dramatic rhododendrons, with leaves up to 2ft.6in. (76cm) long and capsules as 'thick as one's thumb'. In 1934 an immense truss of flowers and leaves, grown at Arisaig, was carried like a magnificent umbrella along Princes Street, Edinburgh, and its owner was almost mobbed.

Shweli-Salween Divide with a mule-load of seed. He could not praise them enough: 'They have worked like Trojans.' When he looked over their dried specimens of plants he found hydrangeas, cotoneasters, vacciniums, a *Pieris* and many rhododendrons. He hoped some were new to science, and one particular 'magnificent species' caught his eye. The specimen had been picked from a tree 20-30ft. (6-9m) high and seems to have been his first sight of *Rhododendron sinogrande,* a wonderful discovery. He described it to Williams:

> The capsules are 2-2⅓in. (5-6cm) long, slightly curved and as thick as your thumb. The foliage runs from 1ft. x 6in. [30cm x 15cm] to as much as 24in. x 10in. [60cm x 25cm], dark green and glossy on the upper surface, ash-coloured beneath. Very handsome![24]

No wonder Forrest was impressed; this rhododendron has the largest leaves of the genus (Plate 77).

Fortunately the area remained peaceful and, to collect as much as possible, Forrest made detailed arrangements as to where each man would go over the coming months. He would have seven men based in Tengyueh all winter to continue collecting while he went to Rangoon to obtain new supplies. Lao Chao would return to his home village near Lichiang to recruit four more men, so that there would be twelve collectors ready to start in the spring. He assured Williams that he hoped to have the same excellent collectors throughout the expedition. 'We thoroughly understand each other', Forrest explained, and Williams could count on him 'doing right by them'.

In a postscript on his last letter of the year, he asked Williams if it would be possible, please, to let 'Mrs Forrest' have the stamps off all his letters and packages. Williams readily agreed. Clementina was the unseen, private and constant figure in Forrest's life; the hidden person in this story. She and Forrest wrote to each other weekly, but few of her letters remain. He involved her in his life by requesting messages and sending her all his photographs of general interest including, it seems, photographs of

the executions in Tengyueh. 'Ghastly subject, I know, but in a sense interesting'. Yet he tried to protect her by asking Williams not to let her know when he was facing increased risks. He would tell her in his own way, as 'There is no call to worry her more than she is now!' Sometimes he didn't tell her: 'Don't give this [bad news] away to anyone in case Mrs Forrest gets it. I'm writing to her just as usual this week. Should anything happen she'll get it through the press soon enough, poor girl.'[25]

Balfour and Williams were very sensitive to Clementina's difficult and important role and they tried to keep her informed and supported. Balfour sent her *Notes from the RBG Edinburgh*, many of which published or reflected Forrest's work. Williams forwarded items from Forrest and sent her little gifts of his own, for which Forrest always returned his deeply grateful thanks. Clementina kept going with admirable resolution.

Expansive ambition

1913 began full of promise for Forrest. A mutiny at Tengyueh was quelled and the Consul predicted a quiet year, so Forrest was free to organise the distribution of his men over a much wider area. He also increased the number of his collectors. Lao Chao, as promised, returned from his home village near Lichiang with three more recruits, and more to come, including his brother, Lao Si. 'I would willingly give him [Lao Chao] treble the salary he has', wrote a grateful Forrest, 'but he is quite contented and I fear to spoil him. I'll give him a big present when finished with him'[26] (Plates 78 and 87).

Forrest's strategy was to have his men ready to collect the spring-time flowers in relatively unexplored areas. He used parties of men as probes, to explore, collect and report back on their findings. In 1913 he planned that four men would go back to the Salween-Shweli divide, two men would 'work' the relatively untouched western flank of the Tali Range (Cang Shan), Forrest and eight men would work the north-west and most northern part of the Lichiang Range (Yulong Shan), and two or four men were to go a further 120 miles (190km) north-west to work the

Plate 78. Forrest's headman, Lao Chao (fifth from right), and nine other collectors with stacks of drying papers roped to wooden saddles ready for mule transport.

Plate 79. The eastern flank of the Lichiang Range (Yulong Shan) with *Stellera chamaejasme* var. *chrysantha* in the foreground.

ranges beyond Chungtien (Zhongdian). They all set off with mules loaded with plant presses and papers in which to preserve their collections.

On Forrest's journey an incident with the army reminds us of the quick thinking audacity that served Forrest so well in the unsettled times in which he did his fieldwork. He knew the regulations that a European had to respect and if he were challenged falsely he stood no nonsense. He now had confidence bred of experience, knew the language, and was determined not to be messed around by anyone. On this occasion he was on the 'road' to Tali, ascending the eastern slope of the Mekong valley, along a very narrow, steep and tortuous path, when he met forty soldiers from Yunnanfu (Kunming). Forrest was ahead of his caravan, with five collectors, each responsible for separate items such as plant presses, camera equipment, and rifles. The officer in command was Japanese, and he and Forrest bowed and greeted one another. 'Then' wrote Forrest afterwards,

> without more palavas he commenced circling round my men, like a mouse round pieces of cheese, examining all they carried. Eventually I got rather incensed and asked him rather abruptly what he wanted. He replied in rather a sarcastic tone that he simply wanted to see what my men's loads consisted of. I got mad at that, my temper isn't the sweetest at the best of times, and turning my back on him I gave the order to march. We left him standing in the centre of the road way.

Forrest's destination was the village of U-lu-kay, or Snow Mountain Village, the home of his collectors. It is about fifteen miles (24km) north of Lichiang (Lijiang) near the southern end of the main range of Jade Dragon Mountain (Yulong Shan), with the main peak towering above (Plate 79). This beautiful spot was to be his base for the season, so he rented a house and lived in the garret (Plate 80) and his renewed delight at plant hunting on the mountains shines from his letters. He found flowers of exceptional beauty and wrote ecstatically, 'It shows we may expect almost anything from the flora of this region'. He marvelled at the range of colour

produced by natural hybrids of *Primula bulleyana* and *P. beesiana*, and asked, 'Can you conceive a plant with the habit and robustness of *P. bulleyana*, carrying the colour of *P. cockburniana*? I cannot. It seems too good to be true, <u>yet it is</u>!' He described himself as being in a 'twitter of excitement' over the possibility of collecting viable seed and taking the world by storm. He found a Buddleja with flowers 'as near blue as possible' and a clematis with flowers almost chocolate colour, 'just the faintest tinge of maroon to throw it out of that colour. I'm not romancing!' Then he came upon large quantities of the beautiful *Paeonia lutea*, 'a magnificent sight, flowers 2-3in. [5-7.5cm] diameter and a pure canary yellow', and he was sad that he had run out of plates for his camera, though he sent Williams a packet of forty-one prints.

Williams was keen to see photographs of plants growing *in situ*. However, as on previous expeditions, Forrest was often working under difficulties, especially while camping in the mountains. He wrote vividly of swarms of flies on very hot days:

> These insects apparently imagined the lens of the camera was a beautiful open eye, and most days, when taking photos…waiting for a lull in the almost incessant wind, trying to keep my eyes clear of those flies, whilst keeping a watch on the plant and defending the lens of the camera against their attacks…I was really driven to the verge of madness with them.

At the end of a long day the photographs had to be developed in a tent after dark,

Plate 80. Forrest's garret, probably in Snow Mountain Village, with packets of seeds hanging from beams low enough for him to bump his head. The end of his camp bed is in the foreground.

Plate 81. *Rhododendron roxieanum*. Forrest named this species after Mrs Roxie Hanna, in gratitude for the kind hospitality that she and her husband gave him at the China Inland Mission, Talifu.

Plate 82. Primula capsules after an October snowfall in Yunnan.

which was about eight o'clock in the summer. Some nights he was busy until the early hours of the morning and, if he then found that a batch had been 'fogged in the changing bag and utterly spoilt', he felt inclined to sit down and weep.[27]

As ever, there were many demands on Forrest's time, and with his collectors based in several places it wasn't easy to supervise them all. His sense of humour came to the rescue and he joked with Williams, 'You couldn't by any means invest in a monoplane for me could you! It would be just <u>the thing</u> for this country! My word! What a haul I'd show you for a season!' However, that time had not come and, as well as relying on trained and trusted local headmen, European friends often substituted for him. On this expedition one was Mr Howell, the Commissioner of Customs at Tengyueh, and stalwarts were Mr and Mrs Hanna, of the China Inland Mission at Tali, who provided supervision and a room for drying plants.

Forrest first met the Hannas when they were newly married in 1906. Although he tended to harbour grievances against some people, he never forgot kindnesses and he received many from the Hannas. Mr Hanna was one of the first people to outline to him the minority groups of N.W. Yunnan and introduced him to potential collectors from the surrounding plain. The Hannas kept an open house that, for an itinerant person like Forrest, was a wonderful thing, especially as the inns were 'filthy beyond conception'. When he returned time and again to Yunnan, the European missionaries who remained at their stations provided invaluable ongoing friendship and support. Forrest was so grateful that he asked Williams for seed of English garden flowers to distribute to missionaries who helped him. He suggested a long list, from laburnum, lilac and broom to dahlias and delphiniums, phlox and hollyhocks, as well as good vegetables. He also named a fine new species after Mrs Roxie Hanna, *Rhododendron roxieanum*, writing in his dedication, 'I take this opportunity of acknowledging my indebtedness for kind hospitality to Mr and Mrs Hanna, of Talifu, by dedicating this plant to the latter' (Plate 81). The Hannas' hospitality was to continue to be a boon. It is notable that when Forrest had three children, and was on his fourth expedition, Mr and Mrs Hanna witnessed his will on 9 May 1918 at the C.I.M. Talifu.

In 1913, it was a happy move for Forrest to settle for the collecting season into Snow Mountain Village, nine miles (15km) north of Lichiang, where most of his collectors lived. It was a change from camping and he got to know his collectors and their families as friends and neighbours. While an 'exile' from his own home and country, he was happier living in that Nakhi community than anywhere else in Burma or China. When he returned there in 1914, the elders of the village came out to meet him and he received many gifts of pork, chickens, eggs, vegetables and delicious honey in the comb. In the village he taught some people English and was sympathetic when villagers were sick. He kept a stock of quinine and when malaria was prevalent in 1914 he had almost two dozen patients on his list. A touching, undated letter from 'Yung' showed appreciation of his medical help: 'Dear Mr Forrest, Many thanks your medicines my son's red eyes is getting better', and he asked for another dose.[28]

On another occasion, when Forrest heard that Lao Chao's father was seriously ill and dying in Snow Mountain Village, he immediately wrote to Tengyueh to tell Lao Chao's brother, Lao Si, so that he could return home, and sent two men to relieve him in Tengyueh. However, it later emerged that Lao Si had returned already, before permission had been given, and when Forrest found out and the man lied to him, and had few seeds as evidence of work done, Forrest promptly discharged him. There is a Scottish saying, 'Better meddle with the devil than the bairns of Falkirk', and it applied uncannily to Forrest. No-one could mess around with him. His strategy depended on the trustworthiness of his collectors and he would brook no laziness or deceit. He was strict and decisive, open and straight, and every one knew where they stood.

If his collectors did not bring in some particular seed that Williams wanted, Forrest simply sent out another search party. He sent two men all the way to Tengyueh to collect seed of *Rhododendron sulfureum*, keeping back half their wages until he had the seed and specimens to hand. In another case, men just back from the Lichiang Range had secured only a few capsules of *Primula dryadifolia*, saying there was eighteen inches (45cm) of snow. 'Snow or no snow, I must have it,' was the reply, and Forrest sent off two more men (Plate 82). He did not shirk from collecting in snowy conditions on the range himself, camping at 12,000ft. (3,600m) with heavy frost at night and several snowfalls, so his men could hardly refuse him. Such is the work of a collector.

One big advantage of Forrest living in Snow Mountain Village was the rapport that he built up with his collectors. By living and working in close contact with his men, they could readily discuss plans and give feedback to one another. When a party of men set off, Forrest showed them a sketch map or demonstrated samples of dried specimens from which he wanted seed. When they returned to the village weeks later, he sorted their haul and directed the drying of seeds in his courtyard.

Plate 83. *Roscoea cautleyoides* was found by Forrest in the spring, growing in pine and oak forest in 'magnificent turfy glades carpeted with *R. cautleyoides, R. purpurea, Cypripedium tibeticum* and *Stellera chamaejasme'*. The plant was introduced through Bees Ltd.

His ambitions became their ambitions, and it was not one man, Forrest, but teams of men who were employed in the effort to obtain the plants and seeds that he and his patron desired. By October 1913 Forrest reckoned that he and his men had scoured an area nearly 100 miles (160km) across (Plate 78).

Forrest was delighted with the total haul and, as he had just received an enthusiastic report from the Edinburgh Garden Propagator, Stewart, giving a glowing account of the 'finer things' that were growing from his seeds, he felt very optimistic. With the good harvest, a sense of triumph filled the air.

Forrest's letters show that working for a sympathetic sponsor made a great difference to him. There is no trace of the depression that sometimes overtook him on his second expedition. He did not forget the past, which came back to him all too readily, occasionally spoiling a glorious moment (as when he found a new *Tsuga* 'of grand proportions' and was reminded that Sargent and Veitch had hurtfully 'pooh-poohed' his idea of such conifers existing in Yunnan).[29] Bees' catalogues were advertising Forrest's 'New Chinese Primulas' but, as he had developed a jaundiced view of Bees' propagators, he was sure that they had 'lost' some of his introductions unnecessarily.[30] Moreover, he resented getting little credit for introductions such as *Roscoea cautleyoides*, from which Bees gained acclaim (Plate 83).

J.C. Williams was generous in pay, words and actions. He was unstinting in the trouble he took to propagate and distribute Forrest's seeds. He wrote so many letters that Forrest sometimes found it difficult to find time to reply. Williams sent

newspaper cuttings and articles, including a report of the 1913 Primula conference on which Forrest commented, 'I don't think I have enjoyed any article so much for a long time'. Indeed, when he read the discussion he must have glowed in his garret in Snow Mountain Village, for Balfour explained the usefulness of collectors' notes to gardeners, 'That is where Mr. Forrest excels; he gives us a lot of detail of the exact habitat, and you can correlate it.'[31]

In return he sent Williams a book of pictographs used by the Nakhi (Plate 74), obtained some ancient bronzes for him, and was effusive in his gratitude:

> I am everlastingly grateful to you, for the painstaking labour you are lavishing on the seed material…if you only realised how much I appreciate your kindness and the incentive it gives to my work you would be amply repaid. It is indeed a pleasure to work for you! You may count on me doing my utmost for you at all times.[32]

However, in November 1913, Forrest had one caveat: "<u>Nothing</u> will ever compensate me for the separation from my wife and children! Nothing! But don't think I grumble in saying so. What needs be must be!'[33]

The tension between wanting to be with his family and yet working in Yunnan, was something Forrest learned to live with. He expressed his feelings openly in regular letters to Clementina and in Yunnan he immersed himself in his job, the beauty and grandeur of the mountains and the changing seasons. At the time of his outburst to Williams, Forrest also wrote a glowing account of the autumn colours. He enjoyed camping in an alpine meadow filled with autumn gentians, and relished the scene of the bare limestone crags of the Lichiang Range powdered with snow against the deep, sapphire blue sky, or by the light of the full moon (Plate 79). Despite his face being chapped in the fierce and cold winds, when more men returned laden with nearly a mule-load of seed he felt 'like whistling that night'. He told his sponsor proudly, 'I have seed enough to sow all Cornwall!' Whereupon he left instructions for his headman in Lichiangfu until the coming spring, and set off for Tali with a caravan of his men and their collections, to find what others had gathered in from the Tali Range (Plate 84).

Plate 84. George Forrest's photograph of the snow-covered Tali Range (Cang Shan) from the back court of the China Inland Mission, Tali (Dali), March 1906.

Approaching Tali on 8 December, Forrest feared the worst. There was gunfire and people fleeing for safety from the city gates told him that the garrison of three regiments had mutinied that morning. Learning that foreigners were not being molested, Forrest entered the north gate and went immediately to the China Inland Mission where he found Hanna tending the wounded. The mission chapel and school-house became temporary hospitals filled with the wounded and dying. Hanna carried out surgery and Forrest nursed the wounded. They were thankful that only three patients in their care died. Two weeks of terror reigned in Tali and no-one dared go on the streets. When troops rescued the city from the rebels, the burned body of the leader was exposed to public view and Forrest took a photograph. Gruesome executions continued, but the affairs of the city settled down.[34] Strained, but very thankful to be alive, Forrest and the Hannas spent Christmas together. Their experience, in the words of Forrest, had been 'too narrow a squeak to joke of'. Reflecting on the help and kindness shown him by Mr Hanna throughout the past year, Forrest suggested that perhaps Williams might give a small donation towards the building of their new chapel, which he was very pleased to do.

The country was in intermittent turmoil and, only six months later, Forrest heard of the murder of his collector friend, Père Monbeig, at Litang. However, once the mutiny at Tali had been quelled, Forrest and his caravan continued safely on to Tengyueh in January 1914. Forrest had a delayed reaction to the traumas of Tali but, after some rest, he continued on to Bhamo to dispatch the collections and procure more stores for the coming season (Plate 85).

Forrest and his men gathered a bumper harvest in 1913; in the eyes of Balfour and Williams, he had established himself as a plant collector of exceptional qualities. He had survived two uprisings unscathed and made the best of the peaceful times. He had organised more men as collectors and distributed them to work over a larger area than ever before. Balfour gave him fulsome praise.

> Forrest's collection is, like all his previous ones, magnificent. He is undoubtedly the prince of collectors. No-one approaches him, alike for the excellence of the specimens, number of specimens, proper selection of forms, and notes upon habitat. There are in this collection naturally many plants which he has obtained in previous years, but there are also many new ones.[35]

Buoyed by a new patron and new hunting grounds, a renascent Forrest was a happy man fulfilling his potential. But what of Forrest's relationship with other plant hunters who came on the scene?

Friends or rivals?
Forrest's work satisfied deep yearnings. At the end of 1913 he admitted

> I have always the intense longing to get into an entirely new area; a sort of new world where everything was new…to have such an opportunity as had Delavay or [Augustine] Henry.[36]

In the mountains of Yunnan, where Delavay had been, the flora was so rich that Forrest was still finding new plants, and he believed there were more to discover on the next mountain or the next. However, with his ambition and competitiveness, it was natural for him to view one more plant hunter as one rival too many. As he said, 'Even the veriest novice might fall on something good', leaving fewer undiscovered treasures for him to find.

No other British plant hunter had worked in north-west Yunnan during Forrest's first two expeditions, but by 1912 that had changed and Forrest found it hard to

adjust. In Tengyueh he found that even the Commissioner of Customs, Mr Howell, was collecting plants for Professor Balfour, if only on an occasional basis. Forrest feared that Howell's collectors might find some new species before he did and he asked Balfour to stop Howell collecting. Balfour was amazed at Forrest's apprehension and was certain they could work in different valleys; the area ought to be large enough for both![37] In the event, Forrest and Howell became good friends, and in 1913 Howell supervised two of Forrest's collectors.

Frank Kingdon Ward, on the other hand, had been collecting for Bees Ltd in Yunnan during 1911 while Forrest was at home. On hearing that Ward had discovered two or three new species of primula, Forrest became anxious, though Balfour assured him that he had nothing to fear as Ward was relatively new to plant collecting. New or not, Forrest was very conscious of an intruder. With Ward's re-appearance in 1913, Forrest was watchful, like a robin guarding its territory, for Ward was a full-time professional, potentially more mobile and thorough than Howell. Forrest gave Ward no clues as to the best hunting areas, his plans, or his route. He learned of Ward's movements from missionaries and then heard, to his amazement, that Ward had been 'playing with a set of instruments' lent by the Royal Geographical Society. The next development was that Forrest was mistakenly named by suspicious authorities as the foreigner making maps of the country, when the culprit was Ward who, according to Forrest, was 'attempting to map country which was surveyed before he went to school'. Forrest was as 'mad as a bag-full of cats' to be caught up in the backwash of Ward's activities, but at least there was no

Plate 85. Packing cases of seeds and specimens collected in 1913, piled up at the China Inland Mission in Tali, ready for dispatch to J.C. Williams in Cornwall. The photograph was probably taken in January 1914 after the Tali mutiny.

Plate 86. Forrest with his missionary friend, Arie Kok from Amsterdam. Forrest signed the birth certificate of Kok's daughter, Elsje Evangeline, in July 1914.

concern over local competition for plants as Ward went north towards Atuntze.[38]

Balfour was so impressed by Forrest's 'army' of collectors in 1913 that he warned one potential 'poacher', Reginald Farrer, against going to Yunnan. 'Yunnan is swept up' was Balfour's vivid phrase, reporting that Forrest was now systematically scouring that rich area with an army of some hundred collectors, and pointing out that Ward was also collecting further north, with Atuntze as his base. As all the trained collectors in the region were likely to be employed by Forrest or Ward, Balfour thought Farrer would have to train his own men if he were to venture into that area of China.[39] Farrer went to North China instead.

As 1913 progressed, Forrest still kept a safety net of secrecy. When he sent Williams a list of his discoveries, he ended with the instructions, 'Keep all this for yourself alone at present. I have no desire for the appearance of poachers on my preserve'. However, as Forrest's confidence grew he realised that other professional European collectors would not necessarily spoil his success. The flora of the region seemed 'almost inexhaustible', and he reckoned that even after ten years in Yunnan, the work would be far from finished. It was just as well, because a German botanist was, in Balfour's words, 'on the warpath'.

In fact, this German made a delicate approach that could not have been better calculated to get the best out of Forrest. In February 1914 Forrest received a most courteous letter from Camillo Schneider,[40] who was collecting in China with an Austrian botanist, Dr Handel-Mazzetti. They planned to come to Lichiangfu later in the year, after travelling through Yungning, and Schneider enquired after Forrest's intentions, sensitively suggesting that Forrest should tell him, if it would be 'better I don't come to Lichiangfu'. A letter from Schneider in May confirmed that they would arrive at Lichiangfu in July.

Was it a coincidence that Forrest made a journey to Yungning before the visitors reached there? Certainly he panicked that Schneider and Handel-Mazzetti might

also discover two primulas that he had found 'right in Schneider's track', and he asked Balfour to publish quickly any new finds of his 1913 collections. Balfour could see no reason for Forrest to panic. He wrote to Williams, 'I think Forrest should now recognise that his position as an explorer of the vegetation of Western China is established for all time on the plane of Henry, Fortune, Delavay, Wilson, to name the giants.'[41] Forrest's reputation did not depend on numbers of new plants alone. 'Surely', wrote Balfour, 'Forrest need not worry his soul over that".

Balfour was overlooking the force of Forrest's ambition. Forrest once admitted that, 'In the compass of the Bend [of the Yangtze] alone there is work sufficient for many years for several Schneiders, Wards and Forrests', but rationality does not always overcome gut reaction.

When Schneider and Handel-Mazzetti arrived at the Pentecostal Mission in Lichiangfu, Forrest had dinner with them and acted as interpreter of the local dialect. Charmingly, too, a six-month old baby brought Forrest and Schneider together in a small ceremony, when they both signed her birth certificate on 26 July 1914. The little girl, Elsje Evangeline, was the daughter of his missionary friend, Arie Kok, and born on 24 January 1914, soon after the mutiny in Tali[42] (Plate 86).

After their meeting in Lichiang, Forrest realised that these visitors were eager to learn about the local mountain flora, first made famous by the collections of

Plate 87. Forrest's caption for this photograph was 'Yours and a crowd'. On the right is Lao Chao. It was taken on 17 August 1914. At this time Forrest was botanising with Camillo Schneider, who may have taken the photograph. Who would have guessed that war had just been declared?

Delavay. Schneider even offered to pay for samples of Forrest's seeds.[43] Both men appreciated Forrest's expertise and he felt he was in control. So much so, that when he heard of their unsatisfactory accommodation in Lichiang, he suggested they stay in a house in Snow Mountain Village. Handel-Mazzetti stayed nine days and then went his own way to collect herbarium specimens and do some surreptitious surveying to update the available maps.[44] Schneider stayed for two months and botanised with Forrest on the Lichiang Range[45] (Plate 87). It was an enjoyable time for they were both plant enthusiasts, of much the same age, experts in their own fields and learning from one another. They shared dreams of venturing to other distant mountains. Schneider 'raved' about the flora of the Andes that Forrest had heard of from his brother-in-law who spent ten years in Western Argentina. He wrote to Williams: 'I think if I get a chance my next choice would be the Argentine and Patagonian Andes'.[46]

Schneider and Forrest were brought closer by the onset of war in Europe and the predicament of being far from home, in China. News of the war trickled in disconcertingly during August 1914 and inevitably brought fear to many Europeans in China. What would happen to their mails? How could they send their collections home safely? What would be the effect on banking arrangements? On 17 August they heard that the Chinese telegraphs would only accept wires worded in English or French, not German. Schneider was anxious because his home, wife and family were in Vienna. Handel-Mazzetti was recalled by the Austrian government.[47]

Their Consuls in Yunnan sent conflicting news. Forrest and Schneider longed for newspapers. Pouring rain added to their woes; collecting and photography came to a standstill. On 20 September Schneider decided to try to leave China to avoid being interned. He promised that when the war was over they would exchange Herbarium specimens and he would send Forrest photographs, including ones of

Plate 88. *Cypripedium tibeticum:* These flowers appear almost immediately on the melting of the snows. Forrest found that on the eastern slopes of the Mekong-Salween Divide 'scarcely an Alpine pasture can be traversed which is not starred with its dark, nodding blooms'. Farrer compared it to 'a malignant Tibetan toad' in *The English Rock Garden!*

Plate 89. *Meconopsis integrifolia* growing on Big Snow Mountain, Da Xue Shan.

him in his house in Snow Mountain Village, for Mrs Forrest to see. He eventually left Shanghai safely and worked at the Arnold Arboretum in Boston, to work on *Plantae Wilsonianae* until the war ended,[48] and he and Forrest kept in contact.

Forrest remained at Lichiang to gather in the seed harvest before sailing to Britain in January 1915. He sent men in diverse directions, including the upper Mekong valley and on to the Beima Shan, and sent to Britain an intermittent stream of small seed packets to prevent bulk losses from German submarines. Fortunately his specimens and seeds arrived safely and, despite the heavy and prolonged rains of 1914, he concluded this expedition with a haul of over 6,000 numbered specimens, the largest total of any of his expeditions. He pocketed some limestone to show to people back home the substrate on which rhododendrons may grow. He expressed moving thanks to Williams for all his support and, as the war intensified and Williams' sons joined up, he sent his sincere good wishes, 'May all of them be kept safely through the course of the war'.

At Rangoon the government commandeered the ship on which he was booked, but Forrest returned safely to Britain on S.S. *Tenasserin*. Exhausted but relieved, he rejoined his family after a gap of three years. The family had moved to a house in Peebles that he had never seen and his second son, whom he last saw as a newly born baby, was now an energetic youngster.

Lilium ochraceum

CHAPTER SEVEN

War and a Syndicate of Gentlemen

This damned war has spoiled everything
G. Forrest to W.W. Smith, 1 February 1918

Letters in the Edinburgh archives show how the life of each person in our story was affected by an event that became known simply as the Great War. Some of these lives were devastated. Others, including Forrest's, were less seriously affected, but none was entirely unscathed.

Within a month of Britain's declaration of war on Germany in August 1914, fifty of the men who worked at the Edinburgh Garden had enlisted. They ranged from garden boy, labourers, time-keeper, hall attendant and lab assistant to an implement keeper and a packer. This threw a particularly heavy burden on Balfour, who wrote to Reginald Farrer a few months later:

> We are…on our beam ends so far as gardening is concerned. Every one of my gardeners who is sound has joined the colours. One…has been killed – another permanently maimed – and several wounded…No less than sixty went from here…I have to carry on as best I can with such old men of non-military age or younger men unfit as we can secure from the ranks of the unemployed. It makes gardening very difficult and I fear – nay I know – that our collections are suffering sadly.[1]

At least two new species discovered by Forrest, *Roscoea humeana* and *Buddleja fallowiana*, were to be named after young RBGE gardeners who were killed in the war (Plate 91).

Opposite:
Plate 90. *Lilium ochraceum* var. *burmanicum*. Forrest collected bulbs and seeds of this lily. The flower shown was grown in Elwes' garden. It was illustrated by Lilian Snelling in Grove's supplement to Elwes' Monograph on the Genus *Lilium*

Left:
Plate 91. *Roscoea humeana*. Introduced by Forrest, this flower was first cultivated at the Royal Botanic Garden Edinburgh, where it was named to commemorate David Hume, a young gardener on the staff 'who fell in action during the retreat from Mons, on 26 August, 1914'.

The national mood in Britain near the start of hostilities is caught in a letter from Prain, Director of Kew, to Balfour:

> Our own anxiety is keen, but my wife bears up wonderfully… As for the boy himself…he is probably happier in the trenches than I am out of them… Where is your son? Is he also among the fortunate ones who are at the front?[2]

(He did indeed enlist with the 14th Battalion of the Royal Scots.)

By November 1914 a conflict that had confidently been expected to be over by Christmas seemed set to last longer. For their own sanity, those at home needed something else to think about, and J.C. Williams wrote:

> It is hard to get away from the one subject for long, but it is certainly better to try to…. My sister's son went down in the *Mauritius*… all our 4 boys are in it somewhere…[3]

Many, like Williams, sought solace in gardening.

Seeds of joy

As the war continued, Williams' distribution of Forrest's seeds and specimens in spring 1915 brought particular pleasure to the Botanic Gardens of Edinburgh, Dublin and Kew. At Edinburgh Balfour was so pleased with the seed germination that he foresaw a 'superabundance' of plants. They agreed that any surplus should be sent to a nurseryman, Wallace of Colchester. Balfour also thanked Williams for the gift of *Primula sinolisteri*:

> one of the coming garden plants. Already at Wisley they have had some beautiful results from crossing with it…If Forrest had done nothing else but introduce *P. malacoides*…and *P. sinolisteri* …his name would have been enrolled on the scroll of leading benefactors to Horticulture.[4]

Williams agreed that *P. malacoides* was 'an unceasing delight' and wrote that the success of the seeds was because Forrest 'is an old hand at the business … I have learnt to look at home for the fault if his stuff fails.[5]

F.W. Moore, Director of Glasnevin Botanic Garden, Dublin also thanked Williams 'for the wonderful collection of seeds from Forrest' and paid this remarkable tribute: 'Forrest has been a wonderful man, and has done much, and suffered much, in introducing some of these fine new plants. His name will certainly now live for ever in gardens.[6] Does the tone of this accolade reflect its wartime background? It sounds like an epitaph, but happily, at the time it was written, Forrest was alive (although weakened by 'flu) and was being welcomed back to the Edinburgh Garden. Everyone wished to hear about his latest adventure and what he had found. 'Forrest was here… yesterday being pumped. We are far from knowing all we want from him, but in time will get all we can', wrote Balfour to Prain.[7]

Balfour had the double delight of receiving dried plants as well as seeds. On 'Spring Holiday' 1915 in Edinburgh, he examined the new treasure, eagerly anticipating what it might yield. He sent a fine series of twenty-two *Meconopsis* specimens to Prain to study at Kew, and commented that they were all 'of the characteristic Forrestian standard'.[8] There was a wonderful lot of good things, 'heaps of seed' and a pleasant prospect of flowers. Forrest had got at least one plant that was new and, as Balfour observed, 'In no place more than in plant collecting does the appetite grow!'[9]

Propagation or patriotism?

In Edinburgh, the germination of Forrest's seeds depended largely on the skill of one man in particular, the Plant Propagator, Laurence Stewart. He had joined the Garden in 1901, so would have been familiar with these seeds since Forrest's first expedition. When Balfour gave a Masters Memorial Lecture to the Royal Horticultural Society in 1912, he described him as 'the enthusiastic plant propagator, whom I am so fortunate as to have on my staff'.[10] But at the end of May 1915 Stewart was thinking seriously of enlisting. This prompted a revealing exchange of views between Balfour and Henry J. Elwes, whom we met in the Prologue in 1880. A wealthy gentleman landowner, farmer and former big game hunter, a keen naturalist and gardener, Elwes would have been a larger than life figure in any age. Since 1880 he had been elected Fellow of the Royal Society and awarded the Royal Horticultural Society's prestigious Victoria Medal of Honour. In 1913 he completed a seven-volume work, *The trees of Great Britain and Ireland*, in collaboration with Augustine Henry (Plates 90 and 94).

Now aged sixty-nine and still a fine figure of a man, Elwes expressed forthright views to Balfour:

> I cannot conceive that Stewart is serving his country better by going to the Army now than he will be if he sticks to the work no-one else can do so well while there are plenty of men younger and stronger to fight, and if he were my servant I should tell him this pretty plainly…[11]

Plate 92. Forrest's room in one of his bases in Yunnan. Packets of seeds hang to dry, animal skins act as rugs; his belongings are neatly arranged, including his leggings above his bed.

129

Plate 93. *Primula chionantha* ssp. *sinopurpurea* growing on Big Snow Mountain, Da Xue Shan. It gave great pleasure to Bayley Balfour when it blossomed in the Royal Botanic Garden, in the spring after his son was killed at Gallipoli.

Plate 94. Standing is Augustine Henry, who collected plants in China and advised Bulley to send his own collector there. Seated is Henry John Elwes, FRS, who collected birds, butterflies and plants in many lands. He was a prime mover in forming the syndicate that funded Forrest's fourth expedition.

Balfour replied firmly:

> I am afraid I do not agree with you about Stewart, who is a crack rifle shot and a splendid cyclist and motor-cyclist. He has done a great deal of scouting already and has gone through two or three ambulance courses. He is therefore an extremely fit man for the Army work …of a cycle dispatch rider. He is unquestionably a great loss to us, [but] what does our gardening matter in a crisis like this? If we lost our whole collection it could be worked up again in time …The scientific and propagating work which Stewart superintends for me…cannot be carried on as it has been, and personally I shall suffer immediately very greatly because a lot of experiments that are in progress will probably come to an end. I do not complain. It is an incident in the law of sacrifice. I should feel criminal if I had put the smallest obstacle in the way of his going…[12]

Faced with this idealism, Elwes wrote humbly, in a note from the Athenaeum: 'You are perfectly right about Stewart as he is such a good man. I stand corrected.'[13]

Stewart went to war. Forrest could hardly believe the news: 'Is he really going? His leaving means so much to me.'[14] This reaction was natural, for Forrest reckoned that Stewart knew 'more about the treatment of choice plants than any man in Great Britain.'[15] Williams, alarmed at the prospect of the Edinburgh Garden losing Forrest's seeds, generously offered Balfour £100 (about £4,000 today) to replace Stewart. The offer was refused, for a young man, trained by Stewart and discharged from the army, had returned to the Garden.[16] Balfour did not expect to be able to get anyone better, but admitted to Elwes that 'Now…there is nobody except Mr. Harrow [the experienced Curator, too old for military service] who knows anything about our plants.'[17]

Soon Balfour suffered a more grievous loss. His own son, also named Isaac Bayley Balfour, was killed in action at Gallipoli on 28 June 1915.[18] Poignantly, Elwes' next letter (on 13 July) was addressed to Balfour's Deputy, W.W. Smith: 'I am writing to you as I do not like to bother poor Balfour in his distress'. Smith immediately forwarded it to Balfour, who replied: 'My dear Elwes, Thank you for your consideration. Work is not a conqueror at such times but it is an anodyne.'[19] The following spring Balfour found consolation in seeing *Primula sinopurpurea* 'sending up bravely its glorious trusses'[20] (Plate 93).

How did the war affect Forrest himself? Throughout most of it he was over the age of conscription but, in 1918, even fifty-year-olds were called up. Forrest was then forty-five and expressed himself 'perfectly willing to serve' although, having had blackwater fever, he regarded himself as unable to withstand any long service in a hot climate.[21] He learned from the British Consul at Tengyueh in June that his registration papers were on their way but, before arrangements were complete, the war ended. Unlike the younger men, Ward, Farrer and Cooper, who also undertook plant collecting for Bulley, Forrest was fortunate in not having his work interrupted by any form of war service. Some of his specimens were lost when the *City of Adelaide* was sunk off the coast of Sicily by enemy action on 11 August 1918, but he had wisely kept duplicates in reserve. It was nothing to compare with Clementina's brother, Charles, being gassed at Gallipoli, or the death of two of J.C. Williams' sons, and on Boxing Day 1918 Prain wrote to Balfour: 'Alas! For us, as for you, what remains of life will be marked by that unfilled blank which causes a constant heartache.'

Forming the Syndicate

The mountains of Yunnan continued to beckon Forrest. 'I hope to go out again as soon as this wretched war is…settled', he wrote to his fellow plant collector, E.H. Wilson, on 14 June 1915.[22] But he needed financial backing. A few weeks later Forrest addressed the Royal Horticultural Society (RHS) in London on the flora of North-Western Yunnan. He began by telling his audience that its flora is 'one of the richest in the world, and the most likely to supply us with gardening novelties for many years to come'. The close of his lecture was a clarion call: 'Much of the province is yet unexplored…a great harvest awaits the first in the field, a harvest…which…will astonish us.'[23]

His call struck a chord in Elwes, who knew the thrill of hunting for plants and animals in distant lands. Elwes had followed in Hooker's footsteps and collected birds, butterflies and ferns in Sikkim before Forrest was born. Now he took the initiative in rallying support for Forrest, meeting him to find out whether he was willing to collect for a syndicate of wealthy gardeners, and what it would cost.

By June 1916 Elwes was contacting his friends in an attempt to raise the money. J.C. Williams told Elwes that he was 'very glad indeed for Forrest's sake that there is a chance of work for him' and offered to contribute £350 a year for two years, on condition that he got all the rhododendron seeds and specimens and had no involvement whatsoever with any other aspect of the expedition. He also urged that Forrest should go where he could make use of his trained men, who 'double his value as a worker'.[24] Within a few weeks Elwes had promises of £100 a year from the Duke of Bedford, Sir John Llewellyn of Penllergaer, Swansea and Col. Stephenson Clarke of Borde Hill, Sussex. Gerald Loder (who became Baron Wakehurst, whose garden is now managed by Kew) promised £50 per year and Elwes himself gave £100 a year for two years 'which is as much as I ought to spend'. He was delighted that 'a new man called Cory' was willing to give £150 a year and he also hoped to secure backing from the RHS.

These seven gentlemen were part of the horticultural elite of the day. All were from the South of England or Wales (Plate 95). All but two were offered the coveted VMH at some stage of their careers. The oldest of the group, Llewellyn, now aged eighty, had chaired RHS Primula Conferences in both 1885 and 1913. Reginald Cory and Stephenson Clarke were to be amongst Forrest's most important sponsors.

Cory, a director of colliery, shipping and oil firms, was a cultured and generous man who had extended and remodelled the gardens at his family seat of Duffryn near Cardiff (Plate 96). Assisted by the editor of the *Gardeners' Chronicle*, he had recorded the Royal International Horticultural Exhibition of 1912, that had been housed in what was then the largest tent ever erected. Cory had impressed Elwes by 'buying plants at fabulous prices' at an RHS sale in aid of the Red Cross, 'where he must have spent near £1,000 [equivalent to £34,000 today]'.[25]

Stephenson Clarke had much in common with Elwes. Both men had been army officers with sons who fought in the Great War. Both had hunted big game. They were farmers, and both were fine all-round naturalists with specialist knowledge of trees and birds. In the 1920s Elwes became President and Clarke Vice-President of the British Ornithologists' Union.

Four of the seven sponsors were members of the recently formed Rhododendron Society. The popularity of the genus was increasing as new Chinese species were introduced by Wilson, Forrest, Ward and Farrer, and the new Society provided a forum for exchanging plants and seeds and disseminating ideas on propagation. The founding members of the Rhododendron Society were J.C. Williams (Chairman) and his cousin, P.D. Williams of Lanarth, Charles Eley of East Bergholt (Secretary) and J.G. Millais of Compton Brow, Horsham (son of the distinguished Pre-Raphaelite painter). Membership, by invitation only, was soon extended to Stephenson Clarke, Llewellyn and Loder.

Millais never sponsored Forrest, but was one of his many correspondents. He was keen on birds (and shooting) as well as rhododendrons. He was also adept at spotting gaps in the literature. As a boy, he had realised the need for books on ducks, and his volumes on British surface-feeding ducks (1902) and diving ducks (1913), illustrated by Thorburn and others, became classics. Now he saw that there was no book on the new rhododendrons, so he planned to write one and asked Forrest for his help.

At the end of June 1916, Elwes still needed to secure the RHS's contribution to the syndicate and he wanted Balfour 'to father the scheme' and name the dried specimens. He was concerned at Forrest's terms. 'If he sticks to £1,000 a year for salary and expenses + £250 for outfit and passage out, which is what he talked of when I saw him, I fear it will not come off at all'. Telling Balfour that 'Scotchmen [*sic*] are much better at driving hard bargains than we are', Elwes asked the Regius Keeper to 'see what [Forrest] really will go for'.[26] He wanted to know quickly at the Athenaeum.

Balfour replied that he would be very happy for the RBGE to name the plants, saying that 'We have the finest West China collection in the world and … Smith

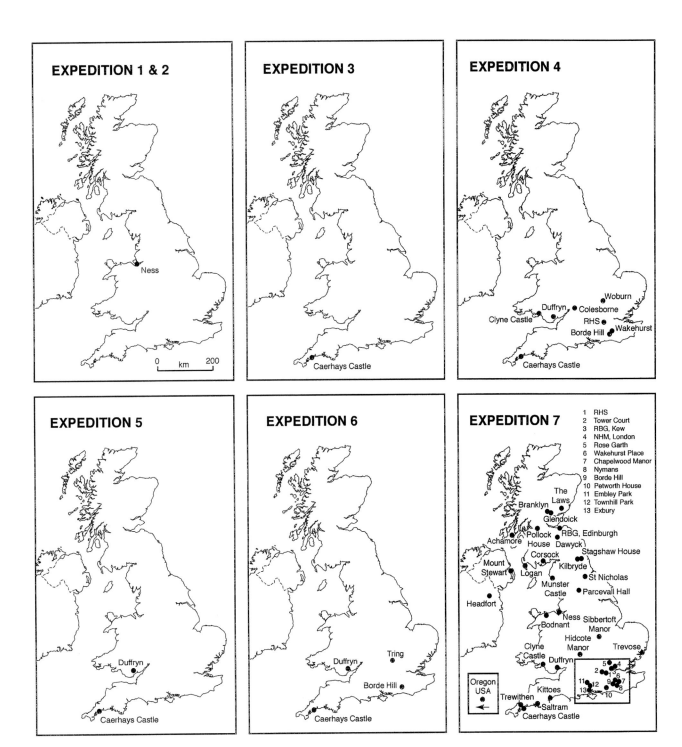

EXPEDITION 1 & 2

Ness

0 km 200

EXPEDITION 3

Caerhays Castle

EXPEDITION 4

Woburn
Duffryn ● Colesborne
Clyne Castle ● RHS ●
Borde Hill ● Wakehurst
Caerhays Castle

EXPEDITION 5

Duffryn
Caerhays Castle

EXPEDITION 6

Duffryn   Tring
Borde Hill
Caerhays Castle

EXPEDITION 7

1 RHS
2 Tower Court
3 RBG, Kew
4 NHM, London
5 Rose Garth
6 Wakehurst Place
7 Chapelwood Manor
8 Nymans
9 Borde Hill
10 Petworth House
11 Embley Park
12 Townhill Park
13 Exbury

The Laws
Branklyn
Glendoick
Pollock ● RBG, Edinburgh
Achamore House Dawyck
Corsock   Stagshaw House
Mount   Kilbryde
Stewart Logan   ● St Nicholas
Munster ● Parcevall Hall
Castle
Headfort
Ness Sibbertoft
Bodnant Manor
Hidcote Trevose
Clyne Manor
Castle Duffryn
Oregon Kittoes
USA Trewithen Saltram
Caerhays Castle

Plate 95. The distribution of sponsors of George Forrest for his different expeditions.

and Craib know more about these Chinese plants than anyone else in the country'. But he refused to be drawn into negotiating with Forrest. He observed that the syndicate gave Forrest no promise of future work, and advised Elwes that 'Forrest having given you his terms, you will find it difficult to get him to look at less. If you give him them, he will slave for you. If he be pinched, it soon becomes a grievance'.[27] Balfour also pointed out the importance of agreeing in advance the ownership of letters and photographs.

Elwes had the ear of Dr Keeble, Director of the RHS Gardens at Wisley, who was keen that the RHS should take part. On 1 August, Keeble secured the RHS Council's agreement to contribute £250 a year. The RHS was also to represent the syndicate in correspondence and distribute Forrest's seeds.[28] Sir Harry Veitch,

Plate 96. 'Duffryn', the home of Reginald Cory, who sponsored four of Forrest's expeditions. Forrest was invited to visit Cory in December 1920, but was unable to do so before leaving for his fifth expedition. This view of the house was painted by Edith Helena Adie in 1922/3.

Sir David Prain, Mr E.A. Bowles and Dr Keeble represented RHS interests on the syndicate. Later that day, members of the syndicate met Forrest and we can imagine them sitting round a table. If all were present, there would have been one duke, one baron to be, three knights, at least two other ex-army officers, and at least two company directors. Forrest was not deterred by this august gathering, and they agreed to pay him £500 a year salary (as on his previous expedition for Williams), £700 a year expenses and £500 down for outfit and passage to Bhamo. Elwes reported to Balfour that 'It is practically settled and the money found'. There was no time to settle all the details of an agreement, and it was left to Forrest to prepare a draft.

A month later Forrest's draft was circulated and Elwes objected to 'two conditions that I thought quite unreasonable'. One was that the money should be free of income tax, the other that a year's salary as well as the £500 for outfit and passage should be paid in advance. 'I told him that he had better withdraw these two conditions, but have had no reply', he wrote to Balfour.[29] Elwes was also anxious to

Plate 97. *Rhododendron impeditum*. Discovered by Forrest in alpine meadows in Yunnan in 1910, this compact shrub was in cultivation in Britain by 1916. It is widely available and has been used to produce well-known hybrids (see Appendix 7).

settle where Forrest would go and repeated an earlier request to Balfour to advise him on the matter, referring to 'an excellent map by Major Davies' (Plate 27).

Balfour advised Elwes to let Forrest choose where to go:

> He has been over more ground in the extreme west of China than anyone else…he is sufficiently jealous of his work and reputation to select a promising area and you will be well advised …to let him have his way. He has always been a free lance and you'll get little out of him if you try to prescribe particular areas to him.[30]

Behind the scenes, Balfour confided to Williams that 'knowing Forrest as I do, you will agree I am wise in declining to give any advice. Forrest needs a loose rein', to which Williams replied 'If they really want to get the best out of [him], they should ride him on a snaffle and not a curb'.[31]

On 10 September Elwes wrote to Balfour that he feared 'the Forrest arrangement' would break down. Forrest refused to divulge his plans until the agreement was signed.

> This means that we are to bind ourselves to find £2,500 for a journey of which the plans are to be arranged entirely by him. I am writing to tell him that I for one shall withdraw if he adheres to this … It is quite a new idea to me that a man should demand £1,500 <u>in advance</u> for a journey of [whose] plans… we are to remain ignorant. Does he really want to go or not? G. Loder seemed to think [Forrest's] wife was against it. What do you think?

Again Elwes was keen for a prompt reply and asked that it should be sent to him c/o Secretary, RHS, Vincent Square, where he would be meet 'Keeble and others' in two days' time. His anxiety to hear from Balfour prompted him to write a postcard from his home at Colesborne, Gloucestershire shortly before leaving for London. The PS informed Balfour that 'If you have not written about the F. affair, I shall be in town [London] Wednesday morning [13 September] at the club'.

Balfour's reply on 11 September is worth quoting in some detail, for it reveals his deep understanding of human nature and of the individuals concerned, as well as his desire for an amicable and fair agreement. He admired Forrest and had his future at heart. Speaking up for the collector and his wife, he wrote:

> Your doubt of Forrest's sincerity is hardly fair to him. Mrs. Forrest hates the life – but what is the alternative? – this is no factor in the situation. You seem to have drifted on the rock of which I warned you and, if you are not to shipwreck, you must get some pilot to steer you. You and Forrest are both too masterful for the negotiation …I take it Forrest's position is:- 'You (Elwes) asked me to go out. I did not ask you to send me. There have been difficulties over the finance already, and now you want me …to tell you all I know about areas of exploration in Yunnan – to give away to you all my experience – without guarantee that you will sign the contract. You won't trust me. How am I to trust you? You may insist on my going to some area that I think is no good, and I won't risk my reputation. Better end the business now…' That, or something like it, is no doubt passing through Forrest's brain. Absurd you will say. Well, you do not know Forrest. If Forrest has said what you tell me, he will stick to it, and if you stick to your statement there will be an end of your project. You may easily find a way out of the impasse by getting, say, Mr. Williams to deal with the matter. Forrest will never be moved by threats nor will he give his best if he harbours a suspicion of being bullied – but he is most amenable to gentle treatment. Like many other men he is most intractable behind his pen. …Tell him the sort of plants you want and he'll get them if they exist – trust him as he fully deserves to be trusted and he'll bring you a rich harvest. You've made an unfortunate start… Your only chance of [a] successful result is to let him go without the smallest suggestion in his mind of a grievance.[32]

Members of the syndicate met Forrest again on 10 October. Balfour's words must have been taken to heart, for Elwes reported that the meeting with Forrest went off 'much better than I expected. He withdrew both the conditions which we objected to, told us his plans, and made no difficulties of any sort'. Veitch had also been present at the meeting and Elwes told him later in the day that he was extremely pleased that Forrest was not 'difficult'. Recalling this conversation, Veitch remarked: 'It did not, I suppose, occur to him that his manner of treating Forrest when talking to him may have had something to do with making him "difficult"'.[33]

It remained for a lawyer to produce a printed legal form of the agreement. When completed, it ran to eight pages. Forrest was to collect 'bulbs, seeds and plants of horticultural value, and also botanical specimens of plants'. He was also to take photographs of 'plants, scenery and objects of interest'. For the first time in any Forrest contract that has been preserved, zoological collecting is mentioned, Forrest having to 'direct and supervise the work of any zoological collector or collectors who may accompany the expedition'. Elwes, Stephenson Clarke and Cory were probably the syndicate members who encouraged Forrest to widen his collecting to birds, butterflies and mammals (see Chapter 10). All the rhododendron material was to go to J.C. Williams. Everything else was to be divided between the other members in proportion to their financial contributions. The expedition was to be for the years 1917 and 1918 in the first instance, with Forrest agreeing to stay for 1919 on the same terms, if notified by 1 October 1918. The first page of the agreement bore four stamps of the Commissioners of Inland Revenue, and each of the signatures was witnessed (in Forrest's case by Balfour).

Forrest received his copy of the printed agreement in mid-December. His eagle eye spotted a clause apparently requiring him to present vouchers or receipts to the syndicate in support of his statement of accounts. He fired off a four-page letter to Dr Keeble protesting that this had not been his understanding of what had been agreed face-to-face on 10 October. 'Am I to be trusted or not?' he demanded. 'If the latter, then a thousand times rather I should keep out of it.' A small flurry of correspondence ensued, Keeble writing to Wilks (RHS Secretary) and both Keeble and Wilks writing placatory letters to Forrest. The lawyer who drew up the document had been wrong to retain the word 'vouchers'. It had been an oversight. The last minute hiccup was over.

Forrest and Balfour had done their own preparation for the expedition. Balfour made sure that Forrest was familiar with all the Edinburgh rhododendrons from Yunnan and the borderlands of Tibet, that he knew which ones were in cultivation, and how to distinguish difficult forms. He provided a list 'as complete as I can make it' of all Chinese rhododendrons and a package of about 130 dried plants collected by Forrest himself. Balfour gave Forrest the opportunity to learn about colour photography. The bond between the two men could not have been stronger, and Forrest knew how fortunate he was to have such close links with a botanic garden. 'Accept my warmest thanks for the reprints of your most interesting papers. I am grateful for your remembrance. I was pleased to learn of the improvement in your condition…', wrote Forrest to his mentor.[34] Balfour was pleased with his protégé, and told Williams that '[Forrest] will … start on his rhododendron work better equipped than any previous collector and will doubtless obtain correspondingly better results'.

Forrest sailed from Liverpool on 11 January 1917 aboard S.S. *Chindwin* bound for Rangoon. He had been home for nearly two years and enjoyed holidays with his family by the sea at Crail and in the Highlands at Balquhidder, near the foot of Ben More. They had moved back to the district of Lasswade, to Broomhill House, where their young sons could roam in two acres of garden. Here Forrest planted over 1,000 daffodil bulbs, due to flower for the first time in the spring. Perhaps neither parent knew that a third child was on the way.

CHAPTER EIGHT
Rhododendrons Galore

Perhaps we are not all quite sane on the subject of Rhododendrons
J.C. Williams at a meeting of the Rhododendron Society on 6 May 1925[1]

The fourth expedition was a bold plan, especially in wartime. Three weeks after leaving Liverpool, Forrest reported that S.S. *Chindwin* was about to dock at Dakar on the west coast of Africa and that it had been 'an anxious time for all'. Tongue in cheek, he told Keeble that French censorship forbade him to reveal his route, but there would be no further stop before Rangoon, so he would not be able to write from the Cape! On reaching Rangoon, he described his voyage as 'tedious and most uneventful', to which Balfour responded that it was preferable to '24 days in an open boat after the visit of a U-boat'.

The home of rhododendrons

The desire to find new species of rhododendrons was a strong motivation for Forrest from his third expedition onwards, just as the desire to grow them was an abiding passion for his sponsor, J.C. Williams. Ever since 1912 Forrest had a theory that the richest area for rhododendrons lay in 'those high alpine regions on the Chino-Tibetan frontier, which form the basins and watersheds of the Salween, Mekong and Yangtze.'[2] His search for this 'home of the genus' was akin to the quest for the Holy Grail. It was a search for perfection, but with no certainty of its existence.

At this point another motivating factor came into play: competition. It affected Balfour at home and spurred on Forrest in the field. Balfour had compared the numbers of Chinese rhododendrons introduced into cultivation by different collectors.[3] 'You will see', he wrote delightedly to Forrest in April 1917, 'that you top the list beating Wilson easily'. As for discoveries of new species of the genus, 'your record nearly doubles his' (Plate 99). Some collectors might have rested on their laurels at this news, but not Forrest. Balfour told him that the Paris Herbarium were sending all their unnamed rhododendrons to Edinburgh for him to work up,

Opposite:
Plate 98. *Rhododendron rex* ssp. *fictolacteum* towering above the deep pink flowers of *Rhododendron principis* in Ness Botanic Gardens.

Left:
Plate 99. George Forrest's photograph of *Rhododendron rex* ssp. *fictolacteum* in Yunnan. Several forms are in cultivation (See Plate 98).

'so please bustle up when you get on the Mekong-Salween where Soulié collected, as I would rather name the plants as yours'.[4]

At Bhamo Forrest met 'all the best' of his collectors: 'my head-man and fifteen others, the cream of the crowd'. They had been waiting for him for three weeks, not knowing that he had been forced to go round the Cape. He told Keeble that he expected to make 'a big haul' and vowed that 'I shall do my utmost to make it a record'. He travelled via Tengyueh and Tali, leaving a small party of men in each place. Those at based at Tengyueh were to collect on the Shweli-Salween divide, whilst those at Tali would work the western flank of the Tali Range before moving to a range of hills to the north-east where Delavay had collected. Forrest intended to establish his own base for the 1917 season at Tsedjrong, a few miles north of Tsekou, where he escaped from the lamas in 1905.

By 5 May he had reached Tali and found the central part of Yunnan in a very disturbed state. The route to Yunnanfu was virtually closed by robber bands and disbanded soldiery who plundered and murdered over a large area. To the north the remnants of White Wolf's gang were still dangerous, but Forrest assured Keeble that he would 'scrape through, if my usual luck holds!' Happily, it did, for by mid-June he had reached his destination and camped in the house of a Tibetan farmer, 'an old friend of mine of 1905'. The house stood on a flat area of land at Shiemalatsa in a big bend of the Mekong river where the valley was 'a mere gorge' 2,000ft. (600m) deep whose flanks were angled to 70° (Plates 42 and 101). He described the scene:

On every side we are enclosed by mountains, the divides rising to about 15,000 feet [4,500m], with isolated peaks, such as the sacred mountains, Doker-la and Ka-gwr-pu,…of 20,000 feet [6,000m] or even more, snow-capped and glacier-clad! … At our feet runs the Mekong, a raging cocoa-coloured torrent of 200 yards [180m] breadth, with a ten-knot current, rising and falling like a gigantic pulse, 16 feet [5m] or more, day by day.[5]

Forrest wrote regularly to the RHS and to Balfour. His letters to the RHS were circulated to members of the syndicate and published in the *Gardeners' Chronicle*. His correspondence with Balfour in this period reveals both the respect and deep regard that each man had for the other. There was an age gap of twenty years between them. Balfour had recently lost his only son. Much earlier, Forrest had lost his father. Is it too fanciful to suggest that their relationship corresponded in some degree to that between father and son? What is apparent is that Forrest's letters and specimens re-invigorated the sixty-four year old Balfour and gave him new zest for his work. By this time Forrest was a most experienced collector, as Balfour acknowledged:

I congratulate you…It is quite evident that you are at the top of your form and I am sure that you are going to reap a rich harvest that will repay you for all you are going through to get it. I confess that after reading your letter one of my first thoughts was – Why has Forrest not written a book upon his explorations? I hope, now that you are able to look at all your surroundings with a mature mind and with more knowledge than any other explorer in these regions has had, that you will put it all down as a story.

Balfour was thrilled at Forrest's descriptions. 'Every paragraph of your letter fills me with delight tinged … with sorrow that I cannot go out myself to see the plants in their native habitat. How I wish I were ten years younger!'[6] (Plate 100)

In 1917, letters took at least two months to go between Yunnan and Edinburgh, but Balfour and Forrest appear to be resuming a conversation dropped only minutes ago. Forrest refers to 'many species, old friends and new', including

Rhododendron wardii. Balfour responds that they have not got it growing at Edinburgh, so please would Forrest get seed and, if possible, compare it 'on the spot' with *Rh. croceum*. Also, could Forrest distinguish in the field between different forms of *Rh. saluenense?* The complexities of rhododendron identification became apparent as geographical variations within some species were discovered. Forrest wrote that:

> The wealth of rhododendrons is almost incredible, and the number of new species and forms more than confusing. I have really given up attempting to define the limits of species; each individual seems to have a form, or an affinity, on every range and divide differing essentially from the type.

He collected 'a very great number' of specimens to help Balfour sort them out.[7]

Forrest had a keen eye for colour. Some of his descriptions of colour variation in rhododendrons would not be amiss in a fashion writer's column. In *Rh. proteoides*, a species he had discovered in 1914, the type was 'pale canary-yellow, beautifully marbled deep crimson', whilst on some plants the flowers were 'white flushed rose', on others 'pure rose', 'yellow' or even 'white'. The flowers of *Rh. campylogynum* varied from 'almost light pink' to 'the deepest plum-purple'. But would any fashion writer have described one colour form of *Rh. sanguineum* as 'black-crimson – the colour of dried bullock's blood'?

He was prepared to go to great lengths at all seasons in search of new plants. In autumn 1917 near Shiemalatsa in the Upper Mekong, Forrest and his collectors did a most exhausting climb of 6-7,000 feet (2,000m), a steady grind from 6.30am till 4pm, with the last 2,000 feet (600m) 'up faces of rugged limestone and slate cliffs, hand and foot work all the time, in drenching rain and blinding mists'.[8] He had to dispense with boots, the going was so bad. Sometimes they had to push through thickets of 'most evil smelling' *Rhododendron hypolepidotum* (now *Rh. brachyanthum* ssp. *hypolepidotum*), where the odour was 'really sickening'. Later during this fourth expedition, J.C. Williams observed to Balfour that 'where Forrest serves us so well is in the iron way in which he battles to get the seed when most men would abandon the task as hopeless after the early snow has set in'.[9] Balfour's reply, that Forrest had 'more grit than any of the other collectors', echoed and confirmed what he had written to Bulley in 1904, that Forrest 'seems to me to be of the right grit for a collector'.

On 1 February 1918, Forrest wrote to Balfour's Assistant Keeper, William Wright Smith: 'Dear Mr. Smith, Don't you think we might drop the "Misters" between us now as we have known one another so long?' For the previous twenty-five days Forrest had been in Tengyueh 'pinned to a chair for 8-10 hours a day' writing up the dried specimens collected in 1917. With the job completed, he was in a relaxed and expansive frame of mind, enjoying reading the gossip from Edinburgh in Smith's letter written four months earlier. Smith, like Balfour, had suggested that Forrest could write a book. 'I have no doubt I could', replied Forrest, 'but, like the man who hadn't changed his shirt for 2 years, I have so much else to think of! I may some day, when I get a nice cosy job in the RBG or elsewhere.'

Forrest was glad to learn that Smith still had some time to examine plants from Yunnan. Had he received those sent from the Upper Mekong in the autumn? 'I have been <u>more</u> than successful this season – you and the others will have enough to rummage in for the next 3 or 4 years, never mind what I bag <u>this</u> season'. He had amassed 2,509 spp. in Herbaria and 300 or 400lbs (160kg) of seed, covering 6-800 of the best species, including seed and fruiting specimens of nearly all the rhododendrons he had missed on his previous expedition. 'It is a glorious haul and

Plate 101. *Rhododendron mekongense* flattened by winter snow near the Doker La, at about 12,000ft. (3,500m). Forrest sent seed to Britain in 1917 and 1922.

I've had to work some to get it. <u>But</u>! If those submarines bag it, you'll never see me again, for I'll take to drink or do something even worse!' Forrest was ecstatic. The rhododendrons were 'excellent, more than excellent!', with enough new species 'almost to <u>duplicate</u> Millais' monograph' of 1917.[10]

> Oh! If I only had the freedom, time, money and men to do the NW of this Province as I would like to, I'd cram my theory down the throats of all doubters that it is the richest rhododendron area in the whole world. I <u>know</u>, though I have only scratched it, I know! What I have seen, what I have done this last season is proof enough for me! But this damned war has spoiled everything, and I feel I'm getting old. Let us hope someone younger and more able for the work in every way may start out where I shall have to leave off!

Forrest had seen a little of the richness of the Salween-Mekong divide in 1905, when he had been forced to flee for his life from Tsekou. Political unrest prevented his return to the area until 1917, when he judged that 'the optimum of the genus' lay in Tsarong, the region of Tibet just beyond the north-west border of Yunnan. But he had no authority to go further and he kept his promise to the Consul and Chinese officials that he would not enter Tibet without a permit. He had glimpsed the Holy Grail, but could not grasp it. A further attempt by Balfour to secure a permit for him failed in 1918. Was his goal attainable?

As always, the resourceful Forrest had made friends with people on the spot, in particular with Père Valentin at the Roman Catholic Mission in Tsedjrong, just north of Tsekou (Plate 102). Valentin agreed to help by supervising some of

Plate 102. Père Valentin, a French missionary stationed at Tsedjrong, in the upper Mekong river valley, N.W. Yunnan, where he supervised some of Forrest's collectors. Forrest named a rhododendron, *R. valentinianum,* in his honour.

Plate 103. *Rhododendron griersonianum* was named by Forrest 'in compliment to R.C. Grierson Esq. of the Chinese Maritime Customs at Tengyueh, whose help I gratefully acknowledge'. Introduced in 1917, and valued for its geranium-scarlet flowers, it has produced many award-winning hybrids. (See Appendix 8).

Plate 104. George Forrest's fine close-up photograph of *Rhododendron edgeworthii* in Yunnan.

Forrest's collectors. They did not need permits to enter Tsarong. Balfour was so pleased at this news that he offered to pay for Valentin's help and left Forrest to make appropriate recompense. Their gratitude was also shown by the naming of *Rhododendron valentinianum*. In spite of border hostilities, the men managed to reach the sacred mountains of Doker-la and Ka-gwr-pu in 1918, securing specimens of nearly three hundred species, including fifty rhododendrons.

Forrest continued to collect for the syndicate in 1919 and Valentin continued to help him. (There were some changes in the syndicate at this time, Elwes withdrawing, and Bulley, who had already been getting seeds from Elwes, joining in. See Appendix 3.) Under Père Valentin's supervision, three of Forrest's collectors set out for Tsarong in late May 1919 with two mules, a map drawn by Valentin and 'some small presents' for the headmen they met on their way. Valentin told them 'to work their very hardest', concentrating on rhododendrons and primulas. Their wages would be augmented by 'a small reward for each new species found'. Valentin was aware that a Chino-Tibetan armistice might not hold and he told the men where to go if this happened.[11] Forrest was deeply grateful for Père Valentin's help and sent him a stock of drugs for his medical work.

Meanwhile, the discovery of new plants in Yunnan and Tsarong provided much excitement and a 'mountain' of work for staff at the RBGE. The thrill of unpacking Forrest's cases of collections was like opening a treasure chest. The senior botanists, Balfour, Smith and Craib, gathered round and had a 'field day'.[12]

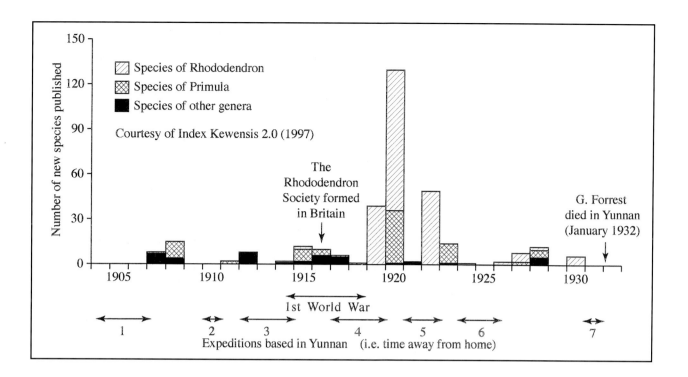

Laurence Stewart, back in harness after the war, not only raised seeds sent by Forrest, but 'got a fine armful of seeds' from Forrest's herbarium specimens. At the start of 1919 'shoals' of Forrest seedlings were coming up. Surveying the scene, Balfour proudly surmised in a letter to Forrest: 'Next to Mr Williams' collection of rhododendrons at Caerhays we have, thanks to your efforts, the finest collection of species in the world.'[13] Moreover, the collection was expanding. By the autumn three pits at the back of the RBGE were completely filled with Forrest's rhododendron seedlings.[14] Anticipation was high that plants from the mountains in and near Tsarong would be hardy and not difficult to grow.

As for the dried specimens, the naming and describing of so many new forms made it impossible to keep up with the number that were coming in. In October 1919 Balfour had worked on Forrest's specimens for two whole months and arranged all his rhododendron specimens ready for Williams to come and discuss. He wrote to Forrest, 'It has given me cause to marvel more than ever at what you have done... I shall not be surprised if your rhododendron collection furnishes us with at least 250 new species'.[15] He looked forward to filling many subsequent pages of the Garden's *Notes* with descriptions of Forrest's finds, which were adding to the prestige of the Edinburgh Garden, as well as to Forrest's reputation.

Such an immense collection had wider implications, too. Forrest's rhododendron specimens were aiding the evolving classification of the genus and, when his conifer specimens of the genus *Tsuga* were compared to those in the Paris Museum, they also challenged former ideas of classification.[16]

The increasing numbers of newly discovered plants gave Forrest an excellent opportunity to honour and show his gratitude to relatives, friends and acquaintances by naming plants after them. A new species, *Rhododendron traillianum,* honoured his father-in-law, G.W. Traill. He named others after Customs Officers (*Rhododendron griersonianum*) (Plate 103) and missionaries (*Rhododendron genestierianum*) and Williams' head gardener at Caerhays (*Rhododendron martinianum*) (Appendix 6). The increase in new rhododendrons and primulas which Forrest named is shown in the graph of Plate 105, and reflects the close relationship built up between Forrest and the taxonomists at Edinburgh who dealt with his new plants.

Plate 105. New plant species, discovered by Forrest, for which he was author or co-author. The graph shows the upsurge of new rhododendrons that he had a part in naming and/or describing after the First World War.

Illness

Plate 106. 'The Boozers' Club', Tengyueh, April 1919, where Forrest probably discussed Farrer's telegram with his pals. On 14 April Farrer wired Forrest to order his collectors to leave him alone in Burma. Consul Affleck (seated next to Forrest) advised him to give a brief civil reply.

Forrest witnessed a lot of suffering and endured a lot of illness himself on many expeditions, but especially in 1919. The original plan was for him to return home at the end of 1918, after two years in the field. Forrest's contract, however, stipulated that he would continue to work in Yunnan for a further year, if the syndicate informed him by 1 October 1918. The cable conveying this wish did not arrive until the second week of December. As this was well beyond the agreed date, Forrest had assumed that he was free to return home, so had already booked his passage and sold his tents. Greatly annoyed, but still loyal, Forrest cancelled all his arrangements and stayed for a third year. Apart from not seeing his family, this change of plan affected him in two ways. A worsening exchange rate forced him to lay off men at one point, and he missed some much-needed rest.

Forrest was ill in November 1918. His friend Hanna diagnosed possible appendicitis but, by early December, Forrest was recovering, convinced that it had been 'a bad attack of congestion of the liver'. From Lichiang he travelled south through Tali to Tengyueh. The journey became a nightmare, vividly recalled in a letter to the RHS and, months later, in one to Wright Smith.[17] The 1918-19 world-wide epidemic of influenza followed by pneumonia was ravaging some of the valleys of Yunnan, 'full 50% of the population gone – in many cases much more'. When Forrest passed through Tali in December, the trouble was at its height, 'people dying by scores daily'. He tried to keep his men off the market to isolate them from infection, but this did not succeed in its aim.

> [I] lost several of my men, 2 chairbearers and 3 muleteers, and arrived here [Tengyueh] with two of my collectors delirious, touch and go with them for several days. Two days out from here my cook, Yang, died of it after only a few hours illness and we brought his body in lashed to his pony. I had to be doctor, cook, and everything else and cannot yet imagine how I escaped infection. Poor Yang had served me for eight years. I'll never get another fellow to equal him and I miss him very much indeed.

Plate 107. *Cotoneaster forrestii* growing in the rock garden at Ness Botanic Gardens. This plant, with the field number F19875, comes from a 1921-22 collection which was originally grown at the RBGE.

In Tengyueh Forrest was diagnosed as having kidney trouble, probably brought on by drinking heavily limed water and 'aggravated by exposure and overwork'. The doctor strongly advised him to make Tengyueh his base for the 1919 season (Plate 106). Despite accepting this advice, Forrest got flu at the end of April, then, on recovery, he had a long and severe tussle with malaria. When he got about again an accumulation of work made him feel 'more sick than when down with the fever'. He had a second bad attack of malaria in the first half of August, writing on 16: 'I'm a bit shaky yet and my head feels as if filled with cotton-wool!' One of his men had blackwater fever, another was sickening for it. By 23 August Forrest was still not very fit. The monsoon had been abnormal, with little rain and great heat, and all Europeans in Tengyueh had been down with fever or dysentery. At the end of October he learned that Père Valentin had been seriously ill with typhoid for two months.[18]

It is a wonder that any collecting got done under these conditions. However, Forrest in Yunnan was not a one-man show, but a reliable network of friends and helpers. In 1919 groups of his collectors, including those supervised by Valentin, were sent out to collect plants on at least six mountain ranges reaching between latitudes 25° and 29°N, the furthest group being as far as 250 miles (400km) from Tengyueh. Forrest always did his best for the syndicate. Knowing members' interests, he was particularly pleased to get 'quite a number of fine epiphytic orchids' that were new to him, and he planned to collect pseudobulbs. On learning in September that J.C. Williams wanted more seed of certain rhododendrons, Forrest sent herbarium specimens north to Tsarong to show his collectors which ones to look for. 'It's a last chance!' he wrote to Balfour, 'They may fail with most, but are sure to succeed to get some'. Thanks to his collectors, he was able to report:

> I have done fairly well this season, not the bumper hauls of past seasons, but quite satisfactory in every way. Excluding the collection from Tsarong, I shall have fully 1,000 spp. in the herbaria here by the end of the season, most new to previous years.[19]

'My men worked admirably during my illness', wrote Forrest on 7 January 1920. He had been up for twelve days, but had to husband his strength to get through a day's work. About four days later he was on the road. On 15 he wrote from Bhamo that, although he had been very weak at the start of his journey from Tengyueh, he regained much of his strength on the way, doing two and a half or three hours steady marching at the finish when only three weeks out of bed! On 30 January he wrote from Rangoon: 'I am fairly fit though I haven't regained my full weight as yet, some 20lbs [9kg] short'.[20] Forrest pushed himself to the limit to achieve his goals.

The incorrigible collector

It is hard to say whether Balfour or Forrest was more excited by the thought of finding the 'home' of rhododendrons. The older man was convinced that Forrest had been collecting 'on the fringe of the chief centre of Rhododendrons in Asia' and egged him on by writing:

> It will be the creaming of the richest area in the world – and the last to be explored – when some one gets into those high hills that rise about where Tibet, Burma, Szechwan and Yunnan meet. I hope this will be your work.[21]

Forrest could not resist the challenge. At the close of the expedition in early January 1920, when still very underweight, he wrote to Williams about a further trip, but urged him 'to say nothing to Mrs.F.'[22]

In order to rest and recuperate, Forrest returned to Britain as the only passenger on a cargo steamer, S.S. *Sittang*. As he relaxed, he looked forward to seeing his family; his youngest son would be three in the summer, but they had not yet met. His eldest son had just started in secondary school. 'Kids are a great responsibility, even when distant a few thousands of miles!', he had written to Smith.[23] The dilemma of spending so many years away from home resurfaced. It was the price he had to pay for his collecting life, and it was certainly a hard life for Clementina.

After only ten months at home in 1920 Forrest made two more expeditions in quick succession. Overall, he was at home for less than two of the nine years from January 1917 to March 1926 (Plate 105). Clementina had no choice. She would have understood why the wife of an England cricketer wrote a book entitled *Another bloody tour…*,[24] even though she would never have used such language herself.

To do one thing supremely well, as Forrest did, other aspects of life often have to take second place. The inbuilt irony for Forrest was that, in searching for the 'home' of rhododendrons in 1917-26, he sacrificed being in his own home in Scotland.

When considering Forrest's decision to revisit Yunnan in this period, it is important to remember some relevant facts. His annual salary had stayed at £500 for each of his six years away between 1912 and 1919. Inflation saw this drop in value during the period from about £27,000 to £12,000 in present-day terms. Williams and Cory doubled his annual salary to £1,000 for the 1921-22 and 1924-25 expeditions, equivalent to an average of about £25,000 for each of the first two years and £29,000 for each of the last two as the value of the pound rose. In addition, he received £375 (equivalent to £11,000) per year from Lord Rothschild to collect birds in 1924 and 1925. The salary was attractive.

Plate 108. The Beima Shan, at 15,000ft. (4,500m), reminded Forrest of Scottish moors around the headwaters of highland streams, with patches of snow, the Scottish heather being replaced by mile upon mile of dwarf rhododendron. He wrote that 'the raw, damp wind strengthened the impression for me and, as I stood there, my heart warmed to it and I could almost imagine myself at home' ('Plant collecting in China', *Gardeners' Chronicle,* 27 October 1917, p.165).

Edinburgh staff realised the added burden that Forrest's collecting placed on his wife, and both Balfour and Smith felt a responsibility towards her. In July 1919 she consulted Balfour about the choice of secondary school for her eldest son. Balfour not only recommended that the boy should go to George Watson's College in Edinburgh, but wrote to the Headmaster on Mrs Forrest's behalf, referring to the boy's father as 'the distinguished scientific explorer of Western China'.[25] The boy was accepted. Smith and his wife kept in touch with Clementina by visiting her and, on one occasion, knowing her Orkney background, Smith sent her a ticket for a Botanical Society talk on Orkney plants.[26] It was typical of their thoughtfulness and support.

What then, of the home of rhododendrons? Between expeditions, in 1923, Forrest lectured to the Rhododendron Society:

> Our finds on the great ranges of the Tibetan marches during 1917-20, astonishing as they undoubtedly proved, were totally eclipsed by the multitude of beautiful species and forms discovered by us during 1921 and 1922 on the Salween-Kiu Chiang divide – a wealth of rhododendron beyond our wildest expectation. Plants new to us were seen and collected every other day, even to the last day of our search, giving promise of even greater riches farther north-west.[27]

The concept of a 'home' of rhododendrons had given Forrest a thrilling and very fruitful journey. And for him, as for so many explorers, there was always the possibility of finding more wonders just over the horizon.

CHAPTER NINE

Rivalry Resurfaces

In such country as this, one looks on a spot already visited by half a dozen
whitemen, as almost as populous and overtrodden as Piccadilly!

Reginald Farrer to Francis Younghusband, 13 September 1920[1]

Imagine three determined, ambitious plant collectors, all of them strong characters on individual missions, yet all searching for new discoveries in neighbouring mountain ranges. If they were to come rather close to each other, you might expect at least some wariness. So what happened when Forrest overlapped with Reginald Farrer or Kingdon Ward?

The scene is set on the borders of North West Yunnan and we shall focus on the post-war period when Forrest is well established and extending his collecting from his core area outwards. He is confident, experienced and well organised, with his bands of collectors doing forays in various directions. His main territory for collecting has evolved over many years, but its boundaries are fluid, and his plans are purposely secretive. No-one is ever quite sure where he or his men might turn up next.

Ward is a free spirit, even more unpredictable in his movements, and given to exploring further afield. He has a long-term goal of reaching the Brahmaputra River, and exploring more of the Himalayas, yet the botanical riches of Yunnan are still tempting. His impulsiveness can lead him into trouble, and since before the War he has not been allowed a passport into China. For the moment he is exploring Burma before, he hopes, going into Yunnan. But no-one is quite sure where he will go next.

Farrer enters on stage, nervous that he might upset Forrest or Ward by poaching their territory, but eager to stake a claim to collecting in this botanically rich area. His last expedition was in the north of China, and this is his first expedition to the mountainous region of Burma, west of Yunnan. He has a companion, E.H.M. Cox, and he has collected intensively in the European alps, but Farrer lacks the confidence and experience of the other two in tackling the remote, mountainous wilds. However, he had written to the wise Balfour for advice.

Seated in his office in Edinburgh, Balfour cannot understand why there should be any problem. Looking at the Foreign Office map of the Sino-Burmese border, there were unexplored areas waiting for such men. He advised Farrer to go to the very north of Upper Burma, with Putao as his base, far from Forrest's sphere of influence.

People in this country seem to imagine that these highlands between China, India, and Tibet, form an area which any one man could easily cover. Twenty men working for twenty years won't exhaust it.'[2]

Forrest – Farrer rivalry

In March 1919 Reginald Farrer stayed at the comfortable Minto Mansions Hotel, Rangoon, having seen the pyramids at Cairo en route. 'Just off, my dear, on the great adventure', he wrote to his mother, before setting off for the high alps of Upper Burma. The War was over, his two volumes of *The English Rock Garden* were published and he was looking forward to collecting seed of alpine flowers for British gardens. He was now relishing the thought of the floral riches of the Burmese mountains, although he was not heading as far north as Putao; he was going to an area near the Yunnan border. Ward had previously shown it was rich in new plants.

Farrer took the railway north to Myitkyina where he collected mules and began

the fortnight's trek up to Hpimaw Fort (Pianma). A day's journey never exceeded 15 miles (24km) and every night a wooden bungalow was provided for travellers, so if he started at six a.m. there was time in the afternoon to rest and read old papers and books that previous travellers had left behind. Farrer was in his element, for he liked his comforts and amenities as well as the mountains.

By mid-April he was settled in a bungalow at Hpimaw Fort, 'the last outpost of England'. There was a gurkha garrison to keep the Chinese out, and a breathtaking view of the nearby ridge of snow-capped mountains which formed the official Burmese boundary. All was peaceful, but Farrer admitted to his mother that 'the vastness of the country and the depths of the forest and its pathlessness, all combine to daunt one a little'. And inside him lurked the fear that Ward and Forrest had been to this area in the past and might already have taken the best of the plants. However, as the spring unfolded he went up to the pass and there, under the bamboo brakes and among the rhododendrons, he found a most beautiful primula – a harbinger, he hoped, of many more to come.

Unfortunately, he was not the only person looking for primulas. Farrer reported to his mother, 'Imagine my horror and disgust …when into Hpimaw came walking five Chinese, who turned out to be collectors of Forrest's, with commission to collect hereabouts and prospect!'[3] Farrer immediately sent Forrest a wire via the British Consulate: 'Am collecting round Hpimaw and northward myself this year, so could your collectors move elsewhere, please wire orders'. Forrest considered this message to be 'cool impertinence'. He wanted to snap back but, advised by Consul Affleck,(Plate 106), he replied laconically, 'Regret cannot recall men'.[4] He had men on the west and east flanks of the N'Mai Kha–Salween divide, so Farrer's deepest fears were coming true (Plate 109). In 1917 Balfour had advised him to go much further north to avoid the possibility of a series of raids by Forrest's men.[5] Elwes had warned him to keep out of Forrest's territory. But Farrer felt affronted at Forrest's men invading what he viewed as his territory and sent a long letter to

Plate 109. The Salween river valley (Nu Jiang) looking north, just north of Liuku. Forrest collected on the ranges either side of the valley. The watershed of the western range forms the Burmese border. In 1919 a group of Forrest's collectors surprised Reginald Farrer at Hpimaw, when they crossed over the range to collect in Burma.

Forrest repeating his request. It was a clash of wills, and Williams remarked to Balfour, 'No two less suited to each other can possibly be found'[6]

Ward arrived in Burma, too, and, although he disappeared over the ridge to collect on a neighbouring range, he made Farrer feel that the district was 'rather overpopulated with botanists'.

Two weeks later, Farrer was painting a rhododendron with an umbrella in one hand, while enveloped in a fog of midges and of stinging smoke designed to keep them off, when a pink-turbaned Lisu 'policeman' brought him a letter from his mother. He replied disparagingly about Forrest, showing the strain: 'It is indeed a nuisance to find Forrest's collectors perpetually coming up into this region, while the great man himself sits down at Tengyueh'.[7] (Forrest had been instructed by his doctor to stay in Tengyueh that year.) Farrer felt unnerved by the presence of Forrest's men, as if Forrest had octopus tentacles, and one kept reaching out to him.

By September Farrer was wishing he could have been at Ingleborough to see the illuminations celebrating peace. And in October, before he and Cox set off to camp for two weeks at 11,000ft. (3,350m) on the Upper Chimili, in search of new plants, he wrote to his mother requesting special luxuries like '12 tins of pressed American caviare, or Asparagus or of those delicious soups in tins, – hare and oyster and so on…'[8] as if this might provide some compensation for his disappointments.

Forrest haunted Farrer thereafter. Neither Farrer's seeds nor his dried specimens compared favourably with Forrest's. He found no new primulas or rhododendrons in 1919. When he heard the news from Balfour it was an awful blow. He wrote to his mother, 'I see Forrest's anticipated a <u>huge</u> majority of my finds'. Balfour wrote earnestly to him in early 1920, 'If you want to make history as a Botanical Explorer and as a benefactor to Horticulture you must go North [away from Forrest]'. To add insult to injury he continued, 'Forrest ought to be home in the course of a month or two with abundance of spoil'.[9]

With Forrest in Scotland, Farrer thought he would collect with no fear. Then he heard a rumour that Forrest was coming out again. Farrer wrote pleadingly to Wright Smith, '<u>Please</u> don't let him and his [collectors] come trespassing in my direction again!'[10] For Farrer, it was no fun competing with Forrest.

On the other hand, Forrest did not always feel very secure either. The plant collector's life is a big gamble in many ways and, when Ward unexpectedly turned up on Forrest's next expedition, it was Forrest's turn to be unnerved.

A storm over Kingdon Ward

On 16 November 1920 George Forrest gave a lecture to the Rhododendron Society in the august surroundings of the Linnean Society's Rooms in Burlington House, Piccadilly. He spoke enthusiastically of recent discoveries of rhododendrons in China and assured his audience that all this was 'but a tithe of what is yet to come, not only of Rhododendrons, but of many other genera – *Primula, Gentiana*, etc.' He had heard from missionaries that country to the west and north-west of Batang was clothed in Rhododendrons, great and small. 'Can we doubt the existence of many other beautiful and new species?' (Applause.)[11]

There was good reason for Forrest's heightened sense of expectancy. J.C. Williams was in the chair at this meeting and less than three weeks earlier he and Cory had signed an agreement with Forrest to engage him for a period of two years in N.W. Yunnan and S.E. Tibet.[12] He was to 'collect bulbs and seeds of plants of horticultural value and botanical specimens'. Forrest had already received his first year's salary – £1,000 – in advance, and £800 for equipment and his passage, and he would have an annual expenditure allowance of £1,400. This generously allowed for inflation. He now had six to eight weeks left for preparations before departure. He was confident of a successful expedition with only two major patrons to please in his botanical work, and extra funding due for any zoological collecting he could fit in (Chapter 10). Everything seemed in hand.

But in December Forrest was forced to bed with 'a bad influenza cold' and he was not in the best of spirits to receive Cory's next letter. First Cory suggested that a young man should accompany Forrest for meteorological work. Forrest squashed that idea immediately. He was going to a sensitive border area where there had been 'frontier trouble' in 1916-17, and he feared causing any further stir. However, when he read that Bulley and Cory were also sending Ward to Yunnan, Forrest's fears soared. Panic gripped him.

Ward had not been in Yunnan for six years, so this was a complete surprise to Forrest. The blue skies suddenly gathered clouds. A confusion of thoughts overtook him in a whirl of strong, disparaging, views as he wrote to Cory:

> Results have shown that Ward has no interest whatever in botanical or horticultural work…Ward's interest in the botanical aspect of this venture is merely a side-show, a greasing of the wheels of the other machinery…Mr Bulley talks very largely of controlling Ward's movements in Yunnan!…Once Ward gets into Yunnan, Bulley will have as little control of him as he has of the wind currents of the South Pacific![13]

There was no logic in this outpouring. If Ward had no interest in his botanical work, why was Forrest worried? The next minute he was saying, 'I don't care a row of pins where Ward goes, for there is little fear of competition from him.' Was this true? In view of his reactions, his words have an empty ring. Forrest's fear of competition was probably greater than he ever admitted. Ward had an instinct for a good garden plant and Forrest knew this. Moreover, the fact that Ward fitted in other successful activities keeping him in the public eye cannot have helped.

To make things worse, past grievances over Bulley were never forgotten, so the combination of Bulley and Ward was likely to produce a heated reaction from Forrest. He even became suspicious that they had heard of his plans and then sprung this surprise on him. He was like a cat arching its back and bristling with a combination of fear and aggression towards the invader of his territory. He had expected a 'clear run' at collecting, when in walked Ward, backed by Bulley and Cory.

Moreover, Ward had a history of unpredictability and a knack of causing trouble. Before the War he had used surveying equipment that made people suspect that he was a spy. In the winter of 1913-14 he tried to enter Tibet without a passport, his helpers deserted him and the Chinese authorities subsequently refused him a passport to re-enter China. Frontier trouble or social unrest of any kind was the last thing that Forrest wanted. Eight months before Forrest's planned departure, Balfour had applied to Viscount Harcourt for assistance in obtaining a special passport for Forrest to enter Eastern Tibet, principally the provinces of Tsarong and Chamdo.[14] Success in this had not been a foregone conclusion and Forrest didn't want these careful preparations wrecked by Ward. 'Trouble is sure to arise… and almost surely it will affect the results of my work.'

Fortunately, Forrest went to Balfour, who counselled that there should be room for them both. It was agreed to let the matter rest. Ward had proposed 'spheres of influence' for each of them. Forrest replied magnanimously, claiming no jurisdiction over his movements or any particular area of Yunnan. Each should have freedom to go where he pleased. The storm had passed.

Forrest apologised to Cory, too, retracting some of his wilder outburst:

Believe me, when I say that I had not the slightest intention – as I had no right to – criticise your action. I am not so foolish as to consider that because of your kindly participation in Mr Williams's expedition, you are bound in any manner to refuse a share in any other.[15]

He could not refrain from reminding Cory that 'I would like all of you to most thoroughly understand and appreciate that the last thing I anticipated any danger from was competition through Ward'.

Two days after seeing Balfour, Forrest was full of big plans once more. 'How many men Ward may have I cannot say but I expect to have fifty or more at work and I expect we shall cover most of the N.N.W. and N.E. of the province as well as S.W. Szechuan and S.E. Tsarong.' He hoped that it would be possible to have a few moments with Cory before he sailed for Rangoon, whereupon Cory invited him to stay at Duffryn. All seemed well.

However, sensitivities towards Ward were still high. When Forrest reached Bhamo, on his way to Yunnan, he wrote a P.S. in a letter to W.W. Smith: 'No sign of Ward yet. Commissioner here says he doubts if he shall be allowed to cross the frontier!'[16] Two months later, Balfour wrote nervously to Clementina: 'I hear that Ward is in Yunnan and making north for Atuntzu, which will be very bad of him.'[17] In September, Forrest wrote to Cory, showing clearly that his wariness of Ward was the same as ever:

Ward is in the province, and the chances are, should he hear of any success we have had this season, and learn where, or of our prospects for next, he might be tempted to anticipate. Personally I don't mind that a bit, for I'm not such a curmudgeon as to grudge any other a bit of success, but have only your and Mr. Williams' interests at heart, still, should Ward be drawn north he would in all probability end by stirring up the natives, as he has done on every occasion he has been here, and so make the country too hot for any of us…[18]

It is hard for leopards to change their spots.

Right:
Plate 110. George Forrest's photograph of *Rhododendron decorum* growing in the wild.

Opposite:
Plate 111. *Rhododendron decorum* growing in Benmore Botanic Garden, on the west coast of Scotland. It was a rare plant in cultivation until introduced by Forrest.

CHAPTER TEN

Birds, Beasts and Butterflies

I…was astonished at the magnificently fine birds to be found in the part of the world where you are going…

R. Cory to G. Forrest, 17 January 1921

It comes as a big surprise to the gardener or botanist to see drawers full of Forrest's pheasants from China. There seem to be hundreds of them lying hidden in the outpost of the Natural History Museum at Tring in Hertfordshire. On a smaller scale, there's a drawer in London packed with Forrest's butterflies (see Plate 125), whilst cupboards hold many different kinds of mammal that he found. And stored behind-scenes in the National Museums of Scotland in Edinburgh are delicate dragonflies that Forrest collected in Yunnan. Curiosity draws one to ask: 'How did they get there?'

They came because Forrest was a countryman imbued with a deep love of nature. In the mountains of north-west Yunnan, as at home, he was alert to all forms of wildlife. He was a collector to his fingertips; collecting came as naturally to him as walking. If he was gathering plants, why not butterflies or birds? That was the tradition of naturalists in the Victorian era into which he was born.

The breakthrough to Forrest making his largest zoological collections came on planning his fourth expedition, 1917-1920. His versatility and organisational strengths were becoming more widely known and two new sponsors asked him to collect zoological specimens as well as plants. Colonel Stephenson Clarke of Borde Hill requested birds and mammals and Reginald Cory of Duffryn asked for butterflies. Accordingly, Forrest's legal agreement for that expedition was that, without further salary, he should direct and supervise the work of any zoological collector or collectors who might accompany the expedition, provided the sponsors paid their wages and any other expenses connected with this.[1] Instructions for Forrest seem to have been minimal. 'Collect what you can' was the gist of the message.

Forrest was happy and willing to do this. He would organise the collection of animals alongside the plants, and at either side of the plant-growing season. We have to remember that he shot birds for food and loved the sport of shooting as relaxation; if the same birds' skins could be used for science, all the better. The possibility of a bird or mammal being named after him probably added to the excitement and allure of the expedition. At the time few people saw anything wrong in this: they were continuing the culture of collecting that had its hey-day in the nineteenth century with the foundation and expansion of those great museums that are part of our heritage. Animals seemed plentiful, ideas about conservation were only just emerging and there was no prohibition to the international transfer of skins for scientific purposes.

Bagging birds for the Colonel

Colonel Stephenson Clarke had a twinkle in his eye and he wrote from his highland estate at Fasnakyle of 'having good sport with Brown trout'.[2] At the age of sixty-eight he still took a boyish delight in measuring the height of trees in his garden at Borde Hill in Sussex, to determine which trees were 'Champions' of their species.[3] He said that in his youth he had a somewhat illicit acquaintance with French bird-catchers.[4] He was an energetic traveller and had collected birds in New Zealand and Africa. He was adept at taking opportunities and in 1916 he was

Opposite:
Plate 112. Temminck's Tragopan, *Tragopan temmincki*. After seeing this illustration in William Beebe's monograph, Reginald Cory asked Forrest to collect the ornamental skin for him (see also page 161).

Forrest's first sponsor for birds. There was no request for live or decorative birds – Stephenson Clarke wanted bird skins for science.

Stephenson Clarke was a well-known figure at meetings of the British Ornithologists' Club. Akin to the Rhododendron Society (to which he also belonged), this club was important socially: the gentry, clergy and services dined, chatted and exhibited their new birds. Colonel Stephenson Clarke and Walter, 2nd Baron Rothschild had also both been members of the British Ornithologists' Union for over twenty years and would often have socialised at Club meetings at Pagani's Restaurant, 42-48 Great Portland Street. Rothschild was chairman. Stephenson Clarke arranged that Rothschild should study Forrest's birds in his museum at Tring. The type specimens were to be presented to the Natural History Museum[5] and half the remainder to Rothschild, who may even have bought them.[6]

Forrest's letters to Stephenson Clarke reveal their shared enthusiasm as Forrest began to build up his bird collection in Yunnan. They show Forrest's keen eye for birds – a skill that probably went back to his early years in Scotland. He was able to identify many British birds and knew the terms for different feathers. On his first expedition to Yunnan Forrest travelled with an avid amateur bird collector, Lt.-Col. George Rippon,[7] and must have learned a lot from him. Over the years Rippon found new species of birds in N.W. Yunnan and adjoining areas and presented 3,000 bird skins to the Natural History Museum.[8] In 1916, ten years after meeting Rippon, when Forrest was asked to collect Yunnan birds, the challenge seems to have given him great pleasure. By then he was familiar with many of them. The mountains were alive with birds, from those pecking in the undergrowth, or gathered noisily in bamboo thickets, to the birds busy in the crowns of flowering trees and others flocking above the forested slopes.

In 1918, Forrest and his collectors hunted birds in the Lichiang Range (Yulong Shan). In July he wrote to Stephenson Clarke: 'I'm no ornithologist, but I can place a few in their groups'. He estimated that his burgeoning collection included eight or ten species of thrushes, eight species of tits, six of finches, five of woodpeckers, three of cuckoo and three species of wagtails. He went on to list the flycatchers, warblers, shrikes, nightjar, chough, pigeon, magpie, oriole, quail, partridge, jackdaws, larks, etc. that he and his men had bagged. He then gave a happy running commentary, as more birds were brought to him:

Just as I write, my boy has come in with two fine specimens – males – of Geoffrey's Blood Pheasant …or at least I take it to be that species: ground colour dull grey, under-tail coverts magenta, wing coverts and back feathers bright green, about twice the size of our home partridge. He has also three more Warblers, another flycatcher – male and female, and another bunting.[9]

Plate 113. Two birds from N.W. Yunnan named after George Forrest by Lord Rothschild. They are illustrated by Terence Lambert from Forrest's own specimens. The top one is a golden-breasted fulvetta, *Alcippe chrysotis forresti*. The bottom one is a slender-billed scimitar babbler, *Xiphirhynchus superciliaris forresti*. The type specimens came from the Shweli-Salween Divide.

Forrest's slight doubt about the identification of the blood pheasant was understandable, as there are several races differing in plumage details. Rothschild examined many more specimens before he settled on the name of this one from the Lichiang Range, where it forages in flocks among the rhododendrons. Rothschild first named it *Ithaginis clarkei*, in honour of Stephenson Clarke. Later he recognised it as a local, endemic race of a more widespread species and renamed it *Ithaginis cruentus clarkei*, as it is today.

Forrest had made a promising start and, at the end of 1918, he and his men had gathered 825 zoological specimens, mostly birds. They were packed into four cases for dispatch to the Colonel.

In 1919, Forrest made bird collections further west, around Tengyueh, in the Shweli valley, and on the Shweli-Salween dividing range. Forrest's letters continued to show his thrill and wonder at the beauty and variety of birds: 'Only two evenings ago whilst returning from the hills I saw a pair of Falcons new to me: beautiful steel-grey plumaged birds with ruddy beaks and claws. They were as large as our Gyrfalcon.'[10] He happily described a new goat-sucker (a bird that flies at night with a gaping mouth like a highly efficient flying insect trap). It had ears almost as distinct as the long-eared owl, a great spread of wings, and beautifully marked plumage, much richer in colouring than the common nightjar. He commented on some finely coloured finches, one resembling the hawfinch at home, and another that was almost completely black with 'just a wee touch of white' on the primaries when the wing was opened. The adjectives 'dazzling', 'magnificent', 'beautiful' and 'brilliant' were all part of his joyful list of birds.

Forrest also enjoyed his men's company and joked about their yarns of brilliantly coloured birds that they didn't capture – 'yarns … I neither believe nor disbelieve'. Above all, he recognised the debt he owed the men for their dedication, energy and enthusiasm in their work. In particular, he was full of praise for the way they collected on the Shweli-Salween divide, finding shrikes and bee-eaters that were new even to them, while Forrest himself was prostrate with enteric fever. He wrote, 'My men worked splendidly, even better I think because they knew I was helpless. They are a fine lot of fellows.'[11]

Somehow, Forrest had communicated his extraordinary enthusiasm and drive to his men in the collection of birds as well as plants. They were all essentially countrymen 'at home' in the mountains with nature and each other, and his men seem to have been pleased and proud to be part of the work.

As Forrest surveyed his bird collection in September 1919, he saw that the birds secured in this western area tended to be distinct from those of the Lichiang Range further east, although there were laughing-thrushes and other birds in common. The collection was smaller than in 1918, but satisfying, and in February 1920 two more cases containing 625 specimens were shipped by Bibby Line from Rangoon to London, on S.S. *Oxfordshire*. Forrest wrote to Stephenson Clarke 'You will I think find the collection I send you a very interesting one'.

Assembling the collection, however, involved time-consuming chores. Forrest's men recorded details of each bird in Chinese. Apart from supervising the preparation of skins, Forrest had then to write up labels in English. This was in addition to the plant work, and there was no slack in the system – no-one available to deputise for him. In both 1918 and 1919, when time pressed or he was ill, some labelling got left until later, even until he got back to Britain, and sometimes he did not complete the task. He frankly admitted this failing, but Stephenson Clarke was sympathetic. After all, there were hundreds of bird skins properly labelled and in good condition, and Forrest was exhausted.

Plate 114. Sclater's Impeyan pheasant, *Lophophorus sclateri*. This illustration in William Beebe's monograph prompted Reginald Cory to ask for its beautiful iridescent plumage. Forrest sent specimens from the Shweli-Salween divide.

As arranged, Stephenson Clarke sent the bird skins to Lord Rothschild to study in his private museum at Tring Park nestling in the Chiltern Hills. Ever since the age of seven, Walter Rothschild had had the ambition of having his own museum. Indeed, at the time he received Forrest's specimens he was on the way to assembling the biggest collection of natural history specimens ever made by one man. This was to include 300,000 bird skins. He was an amateur with an FRS, and his collections were so magnificent that on the Continent Tring was regarded as a highly successful rival of the Natural History Museum.[12] It was his life's work and he attended to his research with single-minded devotion and a passion for detail. To him each animal was an object of wonder. He had a phenomenal memory for them and a huge capacity for hard work. There was a great thrill whenever a new bird collection was unpacked, so we can imagine Forrest's birds being welcomed by this enormous man and immediately studied with characteristic, boyish enthusiasm.

Lord Rothschild pored over Forrest's collection and wrote of certain birds 'This is a most interesting discovery', or 'This appears to be the first certain record for China'. He found that Forrest had collected a remarkably large proportion of the known species and subspecies of Yunnan. From the mountains he had generally collected many birds characteristic of the Himalayas, whereas in valleys, especially nearer Burma, were birds of warmer climes. Forrest collected birds that were new to Yunnan and others that had never been recorded before. Many of these, like the new form of blood pheasant named after Stephenson Clarke, represented geographical subspecies or races discovered by relatively intensive collecting of selected areas, and several beautiful birds were named after Forrest (Plates 113 and 115 and Appendices 9 and 10). These newly found specimens became the basis for Rothschild's original descriptions, becoming 'type specimens' in the process and conferring an added importance to the whole collection. As in plants, each type specimen is the unique representative of that particular species or subspecies, and is forever of key value.

Fourteen new taxa were described based on material from Forrest's 1918-1919 collection,[13] and they are all now in the Natural History Museum.[14]

The quality and range of the bird specimens was so impressive that Stephenson Clarke continued his sponsorship for birds during Forrest's next expedition, 1921-1922.

Pheasants tempt Cory

Forrest was soon off to China again and, at the very last minute, in late January 1921, Reginald Cory was tempted to ask for pheasants. Being a collector of rare and sumptuously illustrated books, Cory had recently perused a monograph of pheasants by William Beebe, the Curator of Birds of the New York Zoological Park. Beebe had been to the Far East and subsequently assembled beautiful colour plates by leading American and English artists to illustrate the pheasants he had seen (Plates 112 and 114). Cory was astonished at the 'magnificently fine' birds to be found where Forrest was going[15] and asked him to obtain a sample of ornamental pheasant skins – not more than one of each. This was a request made on a whim, but Forrest was a servant of the wealthy, at the right price.

He was astute in his reply. Secretly Forrest regretted not collecting more pheasants before, and did not know whether all Cory's desired pheasants lived in the mountains of Yunnan. He agreed to do his best to get Cory skins of 'the finer birds' such as pheasants, hawks and falcons, and shrewdly suggested: 'I'll put on an extra man for your work – the cost won't be much – if you wish me to'.[16] He whetted Cory's appetite by listing pheasants he knew he could find on the Tibetan-Yunnan frontier, including the Kalege, the Tragopan, the Silver, and Lady Amherst's, and he enticed Cory to consider the White Eared pheasants on the Lichiang Range, 'huge birds, as large as the Capercaillie, with beautiful plumage'. Cory gladly agreed to pay the expenses of an extra man and, using Beebe's book, he listed the most beautiful pheasants he desired, rating them by the number of stars he put against each name. He sent the list to await Forrest in Rangoon and left Forrest to do the rest.[17] Cory had the pleasure of anticipation, Forrest gained a worker in the field, and this extra hunter also meant more pheasants for the drawers of the Natural History Museum.

One of the most highly starred pheasants listed by Cory was Sclater's Impeyan pheasant, an inhabitant of the eastern Himalayas, usually near the snow line (Plate 114). Beebe had made the first record of this pheasant in western Yunnan, in the mountains near the source of the Salween river in 1910. He was laboriously climbing up a small side ravine, when the male bird's brilliantly coloured, iridescent plumage caught his eye, and he watched what he claimed was 'the first wild Sclater's Impeyan ever seen by a white man'.[18] No wonder Cory wanted it; the combination of beauty and rarity was irresistible to him. Forrest knew the bird, having already killed and eaten one on an earlier expedition, before he collected birds for sponsors. But it was to be 1925 before Forrest sent back this magnificent pheasant from the rocky slopes of the Shweli-Salween divide, and Forrest's two female birds were the first to come to England.[19]

In contrast, another of Cory's starred pheasants, Temminck's Tragopan, was more easily obtained (Plate 112). The bird is a short-tailed, strikingly handsome and beautifully patterned pheasant. It roosts on low branches among the rhododendrons in the subalpine forests, and Forrest and his men collected it six times on this 1921-22 expedition. Something of Cory's delight can be imagined by Beebe's description of this bird as 'showing like a glowing coal' against the autumn foliage of Yunnan.

Plate 115. The white-bellied woodpecker, *Dryocopus javensis forresti*, illustrated by Terence Lambert from Forrest's type specimen at the Tring outpost of the Natural History Museum. It was found by Forrest in the upper Mekong valley in 1921 and Lord Rothschild described it as a 'wonderful discovery' *(Novitates Zoologicae*, XXX (1923), p.38).

Plate 116. Forrest's birds, dried, stuffed and labelled, ready to send to Lord Rothschild for identification.

Plate 117. Forrest's 1921 gun licence issued and stamped by the Taotai, head of the Tengyueh prefecture. It allows Forrest two hunting guns and 1,500 bullets in the tenth year of the Republic of China, and is to be shown at all check points.

Rothschild wants more

Rothschild also requested more pheasants, but not just one or two. As a scientist he wanted Forrest to collect large series of birds, so that he could study the variation of form and colour within each species. He had been disappointed that there were no long series from Forrest's 1918-1919 expedition. Only large numbers of birds would enable Rothschild to sort out the variation across the geographical range of a species. So the pressure on Forrest was now for quantity as well as quality, and a series meant collecting males and females, juveniles and even chicks and eggs where possible.

Forrest's employment of local men served well for this purpose. He combined the men's use of traditional weapons, skills and local knowledge with his provision of guns and organisation (Plate 117). In November 1921 Forrest engaged four men to hunt for birds on the north-west flank of the Lichiang Range, where the mountains dramatically drop from their highest altitude, at about 20,000ft. (6,000m), down to the water's edge of the Yangtze river. They camped at 10,000ft. (3,000m) and snowfalls had begun. The men knew the best places to search for particular birds and were used to tracking them. At the end of November Forrest reported that the birds were mostly snared, some were shot with the crossbow and blunt bolt, so that there were few damaged specimens. One amazing day his men brought in nearly one hundred birds and it took a sustained effort to gut and clean all the birds before they rotted. Each bird was laid on its back, and its skin removed as neatly as possible, leaving the skull to preserve the shape of the head. Arsenical soap was applied to the inside of the skin before stuffing and returning the body to its natural shape (Plate 116).

During the year Forrest would often give his collectors a gun for a day's shooting. He had taken two .40 guns with him on this expedition, but after seven months of frequent use the locks became too worn for safety. In readiness for the following season, he asked Stephenson Clarke to send out two more guns, 'a long barrelled .410 gun, single barrel…and an ordinary double-barrelled 12 bore muzzle-loader… as an emergency gun'. He saved his breech-loaders for his own use.[20]

At the end of 1921 the year's bag included beautiful birds new to Forrest, and he delighted in sending Stephenson Clarke detailed descriptions of some of them, including a fine grosbeak and a pretty finch that strongly resembled a brambling.

Plate 118. One of Forrest's collectors standing by a line of Lady Amherst's pheasants. Below them are stacks of drying papers and a crate labelled 'Johnnie Walker'.

Plate 119. White-eared pheasants from the Yulong Shan. Forrest compared their size to the capercaillie. Lord Rothschild probably exhibited this photograph at a meeting of the British Ornithologists' Club in London. Note the piles of dried plants being pressed by boulders in the doorway.

He was full of wonder as he held them in his hand, before packing them for the long journey to England and the attention of Lord Rothschild.

Rothschild was in a very privileged position. He had an excellent and experienced curator of birds and no distraction of other duties. He had a brilliant brain and concentrated with intense enthusiasm on naming, describing and classifying birds from all over the world. He was a prodigious worker for ten to twelve hours a day. Forrest's birds were compared in every detail with others in his huge collection, and lists of all Forrest's species and subspecies were written up in the Tring journal, *Novitates Zoologicae*, in remarkably quick time.

This is in notable contrast to the naming of Forrest's botanical collections by staff at the Royal Botanic Garden Edinburgh. They were inundated with greater numbers of Forrest's specimens, they had less time each day in which to work on them, and a far larger task as the basic classification of the huge genus of Rhododendron had to be worked out as they went along. The time lag between Forrest collecting a plant specimen and knowing its name was frustrating for everyone.

The relatively quick feedback given by Rothschild must have been very encouraging, spurring Forrest on to even greater endeavours. Rothschild reported that the making of the skins was generally excellent and he praised the series of pheasants. Indeed, long lists of names and numbers come pouring out in a flood from the pages of Rothschild's papers. Among these there was the 'exceedingly rare' species of koklass pheasant, a 'very rare' species of pheasant grouse, new to Yunnan, and a 'magnificent' series of the Lady Amherst pheasant, of which wild shot examples were very scarce in museums.

Rothschild was so delighted with Forrest's haul that he sent his curator to show a selection of Forrest's birds to fellow members of the British Ornithologists' Club. The naturalist from the Shackleton-Rowett Expedition to the Antarctic was a guest speaker when eleven of Forrest's new Yunnan birds were there for everyone to see. They included the first three-toed woodpecker to reach England and a new large white-bellied woodpecker that Rothschild named after Forrest, *Dryocopus forresti* (now *Dryocopus javensis forresti*)[21] (Plate 115). Forrest was becoming noticed among distinguished ornithologists.

Meanwhile, in the distant mountains of Yunnan, Forrest kept collectors on the Lichiang Range from February to November 1922. He took photographs of the birds they bagged, and one of these photographs (Plate 118) encapsulates the life they led. One of his men stood proudly by a line of Lady Amherst's pheasants hung from a bamboo cane across the doorway of a house. The birds' elegant, long striped tails dangled down and almost touched piles of plant specimens drying between papers. Crates hide their contents from us, but one had the give-away writing of 'Johnnie Walker', the whisky gratefully imbibed after a day's hard slog.

When Rothschild received a selection of Forrest's bird photographs, he was soon proudly exhibiting three of them at another meeting of the British Ornithologists' Club. They showed a 'bag' of white eared pheasant and Plate 119 is probably one of the photographs displayed.

Rothschild was so impressed by Forrest's ability to organise a successful zoological collection that he offered to sponsor him for another expedition. Rothschild sponsored many bird collectors, but had high standards for his museum. This was an honour: Forrest had 'arrived' in ornithological circles.

Forrest wrote out the contract in careful longhand for Rothschild to sign. The agreement was for Forrest to collect zoologically for two years (1924-1925) in accessible areas of West and North-west Yunnan, China and South-east Tibet. The

Plate 120. The identification labels of Forrest's rock squirrel, *Rupestes forresti (now Sciurotamias forresti).* Forrest's original label (white) with his collecting number, hand-writing and signature, and the type label (pink) added by the Museum. The squirrel was named in Forrest's honour, for his 'valuable Yunnan collections' and the 'great interest in his mammal work' (O. Thomas, *Annals and Magazine of Natural History,* II, 1923, pp.655-663).

whole results of the work were to be Rothschild's exclusive property. Annual remuneration for Forrest was to be at the rate of £375 sterling (about £11,000 today), half of it to be paid to his wife twice yearly in March and December.[22]

Brigands and general unrest placed severe restrictions on Forrest's travels, but he still managed to collect seven new taxa of birds. When added to those of previous expeditions, a total of thirty-six new taxa of birds had been collected between 1918 and 1925.[23] These results were written up in five main papers of *Novitates Zoologicae,*[24] and they demonstrate the value of Forrest's work, when ornithology in Yunnan was still at a pioneering stage. His bird collection was approaching the size of Rippon's, making a fine contribution to science. More was learned about changes in seasonal plumage, places of breeding and patterns of migration. More was known about birds' geographical distribution and variation. It emphasised the diversity of birds in this mountainous region.

A raccoon in the cupboard?

Let's have a peep at two samples of mammals that Forrest sent to the Natural History Museum in London. They are carefully stored among stacks of cupboards in an area where only researchers normally go.

When the door of one particular cupboard is opened, you see the skin of an animal with raccoon-like markings, a bushy tail and long hair, and a label with the unmistakable handwriting of George Forrest. It comes as quite a shock. Did Forrest shoot this? Surely raccoons don't live in China? 'Look at the skull', the expert says. 'The skull shows that the animal isn't a raccoon, but a raccoon-like dog. Both skull and skin are needed to properly identify this animal'. Forrest had provided both and this is a type specimen used for reference by taxonomists. It also marks the furthest west that the raccoon-dog has been found in China. Forrest and his men did well to collect it, for this animal is nocturnal, solitary and hard to find, though widespread in China to the east of Yunnan.

In another cupboard on the fourth floor is a type specimen of 'Forrest's rock squirrel'. Suddenly the past comes vividly to life. Attached to one foot is the

Plate 121. A giant flying squirrel, *Pteromys alborufus* (now *Petaurista alborufus*) collected by Père David near Moupin. Forrest discovered a new subspecies in N.W. Yunnan. After dusk it spreads its feet to extend its parachute membrane, and leaps from tree to tree, or from caves in the limestone cliffs of the Yulong Shan to feed in the tops of trees (M.H. Milne-Edwards & M. Alphonse Milne-Edwards, *Recherches pour servir à l'histoire naturelle des mammifères,* Planche 45, 1867).

original goatskin parchment label, provided for Forrest by the Natural History Museum over eighty years ago (Plate 120). The label was resistant to getting wet or torn, and Forrest wrote on it in indelible ink his collecting number for that specimen and the stark field note, 'Shot amongst rocks and scrub'. He also neatly recorded the date, 5/6/21, the location, altitude and latitude, before he signed his name. Attached to the squirrel's foot is also the distinctive red label used by the Museum for its type specimens. On arrival at the Museum, the squirrel was described and named by the taxonomist who specialised in mammals, Mr Oldfield Thomas. To him it was a 'special zoological prize', and he wrote on the red label the Latin name that he gave it, *Rupestes forresti* (now *Sciurotamias forresti*). Formerly all rock squirrels in Yunnan had been called 'Père David's rock squirrel', as that was well known further north in China. For the first time it was recognised that the rock squirrels that frisk around rocks and crevices of mountain cliffs of Yunnan are different. Yunnan has its own species of rock squirrel, named after Forrest.

When other cabinet doors are opened we see the variety of mammals that Forrest collected, from several genera of squirrels to bats, Chinese field mice and voles. We remind ourselves with difficulty that these were simply a sideline to Forrest's plant collecting. Kingdon Ward made two useful collections of small mammals when he first began plant hunting, and happily recorded when two men trapped some voles and skinned and fried them for supper.[25] Forrest's mammal collection is on another scale. In addition to other mammals, he collected about one hundred specimens of voles[26] in one of the most interesting collections that the Museum had received for many years.

How did this happen? Oldfield Thomas, the mammal specialist at the Natural History Museum, first wrote to Forrest in 1909 to ask if he would collect mammals on his next expedition. Forrest replied with keen interest, but as there was no money to pay him the idea seems to have fizzled out until Stephenson Clarke came along. He was the key man, being a new sponsor for Forrest and a benefactor to the Natural History Museum. He provided the vital link between collector and taxonomist.

The emphasis in the 1918-1919 expedition was on birds, but when Forrest sent back new type specimens of squirrels, Oldfield Thomas made a plea for more mammals next time, and Forrest rose to the challenge.[27] From then and onwards, on every expedition, significant numbers of mammals and birds were shot or trapped as Forrest and his men traversed Yunnan.

Forrest's fifth expedition, 1921-22, was particularly successful. Not only was he collecting whole series of pheasants, but a bumper crop of mammals. Month after month produced new taxa that were identified in the Natural History Museum, and three hundred specimens of mammals were collected on the Lichiang Range alone (Plate 121).

The early 1920s were vintage years for Forrest's collections of animals and we can be sure that he and his men enjoyed the variety and satisfaction of the chase. They had fun comparing the collections made in different parts of the province and he listened eagerly to the local gossip: 'The people here say there are three distinct species [of pole-cat or martin] …I may get them yet, if not this, then perhaps next year'.[28] Forrest's appetite could never be satiated.

Where have all the butterflies gone?

Forrest delighted in the colourful and varied butterflies of Yunnan. He collected them as a present for his fiancée on his first expedition, and years later he enclosed samples when he wrote letters to their sons. When we search for his insect collections in the museums of London and Edinburgh, we find awesomely rare and beautiful creatures, carefully kept in some of the smallest museum drawers. Unknown to many people, Forrest collected insects on at least five out of seven expeditions.

When he first set off for China he must have taken entomological nets and collecting material, probably including small jars with cyanide crystals and specially folded entomological papers into which to place the insects. No-one had asked him to do this; he took the initiative and, on his second expedition, he collected over 2,000 insects from the area around Lichiang. The variety suggests that some were swept into a net, while others were probably caught at night by shining light on to a white sheet. It probably took one person two weeks to collect and paper them all,[29] and Forrest presented this collection to what is now the National Museums of Scotland.

Forrest's first payment for insects came on his fourth expedition, which was the great leap forward in his zoological collecting. Alongside his collection of birds and mammals, he was catching butterflies for Reginald Cory and for a new sponsor, Mr M.J. Mansfield, whose collection is now in the Natural History Museum. Here

we find small drawers with rows of Forrest's butterflies and, in particular, a beautiful and very rare swallowtail butterfly (Plate 123) that was first collected by Forrest and has been the subject of much taxonomic curiosity.[30]

Two Edinburgh contacts then come into the picture. Mr W.E. Evans, the curator of the herbarium at the Botanic Garden, named many of Forrest's plants and also asked Forrest to collect some insects for him.[31] And, when Forrest returned from his sixth expedition, he presented a collection of dragonflies to a fellow Scot, K.J. Morton, a great enthusiast who had retired from the British Linen Bank in order to further his studies. He described and published two new species of dragonflies from Forrest's collection, with the splendid understatement, 'Little has been written on the dragonflies of Yunnan'.[32] (see Plate 126.)

The present collections of Forrest's insects may only be a small proportion of what he actually collected. Some were lost by accident, as when Forrest's first butterfly collections went up in smoke at Tsekou. Private collections, like Cory's, can easily 'disappear'. The following incident shows how one large loss occurred.

In 1920 Forrest asked Cory, '[Do] you wish the butterfly-collecting to be continued this journey? It seems a pity not to carry on the work now that I have the trained men and every probability of new species…'[33] Cory probably wanted no more butterflies, but Forrest continued to collect them. He assembled five or six boxes of butterflies. He took the risk that he could sell them.

There was a well-established Natural History Agency in London, Messrs Janson & Son, that had its base in Great Russell Street (Plate 122). Established in 1852, this family firm bought and sold natural history specimens from around the world and had corresponded with many distinguished naturalists, including H.W. Bates and A.R. Wallace, who collected in Amazonia. Forrest wrote to the agency:

> Dear Sirs, I have a collection of insects, mostly Lepidoptera, made during 1921-22 in the subalpine and alpine regions of N.W. Yunnan and S.E. Tibet, which I wish to dispose of. The specimens are still in paper and number 3-4,000.[34]

The firm expressed interest, provided that the specimens were in good order and contained some interesting species. They asked Forrest to send a box for them to examine. Forrest was pleased and optimistic, telling the firm that he was soon returning to the same region, and he could collect again.

Plate 122. The shop of Messrs Janson & Son in Great Russell Street, London, to which Forrest sent a collection of Lepidoptera specimens in 1923.

Plate 123. *Bhutanitis (Yunnanopapilio) mansfieldi,* a rare and beautiful swallowtail butterfly discovered by George Forrest. This is Forrest's type specimen in the Natural History Museum, London.

Plate 124. *Herochroma mansfieldi,* a moth discovered by George Forrest in the district of Tengyueh (Tengchong). This is Forrest's type specimen in the Natural History Museum, London. The label top left shows the place it was found in Yunnan and 'Type' denotes its value to taxonomists.

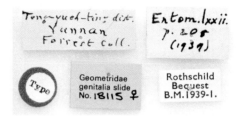

Then came the bombshell. Janson & Son went through the collection and found it 'very disappointing'. In their opinion there were very few species, mostly common ones, and – most damning of all – they concluded they were probably remainders. Unfortunately, they continued, the moths were also put flat in the papers, spoiling the upper surface of the wings.[35]

Forrest was not used to such a rebuff. He had been over-optimistic and had misread the market. When he first went out to China, French missionaries were selling butterflies in France, but in 1920s Britain, the Victorian heyday of natural history agents was well past. This was not a good time to be selling Lepidoptera. There was little demand and the agency probably had a large stock and could be fussy over what it bought. Perhaps, too, Forrest had over-reached himself and had not supervised the butterfly collecting properly. We have seen how difficult it was for Forrest to keep up with labelling.

A deflated and disappointed Forrest had to receive a returned box of specimens. He was just about to sail to Rangoon again. Presumably Clementina was left with the boxes. What did she do with the specimens?

Forrest had to be pragmatic. He could not let a setback weigh him down for long. He had to carry on to his next goal. Time was always pressing. Maybe, in his zeal he sometimes took on too much, yet without that zeal and determination he would not have accomplished what he did. On the expedition immediately after this setback, he maintained his self-belief and the belief that there were still new insects to be found. And what happened? He produced the two exquisite new dragonflies (Plate 126).

Looking back, we can see that Forrest was at an interesting stage in history. He was born into the heyday of Victorian naturalists and in many ways he was carrying on that tradition. He was collecting a diversity of wildlife, keeping taxonomists busy at the forefront of knowledge in the study of the plants, birds, mammals and insects of Yunnan.

However, by the mid-1920s many of the plants and butterflies of Yunnan were already known. In order to discover new plants and animals, Forrest had to concentrate on less studied animals, like the dragonflies, or more complex genera of plants, like rhododendrons. Fortunately for Forrest, old and new sponsors continued their interest in his work, and his museum collections remain for posterity.

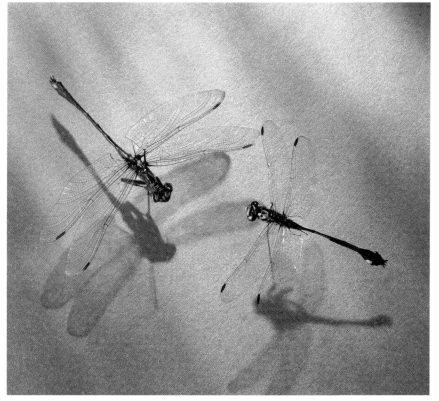

Plate 125. 'Drawer 7478' of Forrest's specimens of Lepidoptera in the M.J. Mansfield collection in the Natural History Museum, London. Typed labels indicate the collection of specimens in Yunnan in 1918.

Plate 126. Two dragonflies discovered by George Forrest in Yunnan, and named in 1928 as the type specimens of *Gomphus corniger* (the bigger one) and *Temnogomphus forresti* (the small one on the right).

172

CHAPTER ELEVEN

Recognition

…the well-known George Forrest,
who has a world reputation as a plant collector
W. Wright Smith to H.S. Harrington,
Dunloe Castle, Killarney, 13 December 1929

Even in the most active lives, there are times of recollection and taking stock of what has happened and what has been achieved. For Forrest such a period probably arrived in 1926, on his return to Scotland at the end of his sixth expedition. He was fifty-three, held in high esteem, and wanted to make the very best use of each year of his life. Ten years earlier he had written 'a year gone at my time of life is a year completely lost'.[1] Was he now too old go on another expedition?

Honours

When Forrest returned from his fourth expedition in March 1920, Balfour was looking older and not in good health (see Plate 100). The war, the loss of his only son and years of overwork had taken their toll. Before setting out on his fifth expedition, and no doubt aware that they might not meet again, Forrest asked Balfour for an autographed photograph of himself, telling him 'I shall prize it above most things'.[2] Happily, Balfour lived long enough to share Forrest's pleasure in the award of two special honours.

The first came from the RHS, who had co-sponsored his fourth expedition. On 30 November 1920 the Council of the RHS voted to give Forrest the Victoria Medal of Honour. The draper's son, who had been glad of a minor job in the Edinburgh Herbarium less than twenty years earlier, had always wanted to prove himself. The award of the coveted VMH marked Forrest as a member of the horticultural elite. It was an award held by the Directors of the Royal Botanic Gardens at Kew, Edinburgh and Dublin (Glasnevin). Of his sponsors, only Elwes, Sir John Llewellyn and Lord Rothschild held the VMH by 1920, although it had been offered to both Bulley and

Opposite:
Plate 127. Forrest reunited with his family in Scotland, 1920-21. It was the first time he had met his youngest son, Charles. Forrest stayed at home for only ten months before setting off on his fifth expedition.

Left:
Plate 128. Forrest relaxing with his dog in camp on a hot day, with a whisky and soda to refresh him, on his fourth expedition.

173

Plate 129. 'Flotilla House' in Bhamo, home of Captain Medd, the agent of the Irrawaddy Flotilla Company, after whom Forrest named *Rhododendron meddianum.* Forrest was staying here in January 1923 when he heard the sad news of Professor Bayley Balfour's death.

J.C. Williams. Comparing himself to other plant collectors, Forrest must have been particularly pleased to hold the same award as E.H. Wilson and Augustine Henry. Farrer died (aged forty) in 1920 without a VMH. Kingdon Ward did not get his until after Forrest's death. Forrest was so pleased with his VMH that he even put the initials after his entry in the telephone directory.

Another honour that Balfour would have known about was the award to Forrest of the George Robert White Medal of the Massachusetts Horticultural Society. White, a great benefactor of the city of Boston, endowed a gold medal for the 'man or woman, commercial firm or institution in the United States or other countries that has done the most in recent years to advance interest in horticulture in its broadest sense' or, as put later, 'for eminent service to horticulture'. In the Society's 1924 Yearbook, the medal was described as America's highest horticultural award. E.H. Wilson had received the medal in 1915. It was awarded to Forrest in 1920, so in that year he held the premier awards of both Britain and the USA.

On a smaller scale, he was elected an Honorary Member of the select Rhododendron Society in the same year. The secretary, Charles Eley, conveyed the news to Forrest and the two men became friends, Forrest staying at Eley's home in East Bergholt, Suffolk around the time of both his 1920 and 1923 lectures to the Society in London. Balfour had been one of the first to be elected to Honorary membership of the Rhododendron Society and had travelled to London 'to support Forrest' at his 1920 lecture before giving a vote of thanks.[3] Balfour retired in 1922 and went to live in Haslemere, where he died on 30 November 1922, four days after Elwes. It was the end of an era.

The news of Balfour's death reached Forrest at the end of his fifth expedition, in January 1923, when he was staying in Captain Medd's house in Bhamo (Plate 129). He wrote from there:

My dear Smith, I got in here on the 10th and found your letter of 5th Dec awaiting me! Though for the past 3 months I have dreaded receiving such news as it contained, yet it came as a very great shock to me. It has killed life for me for the time being, even much of the interest in my home-coming is lost for I had so hoped to see him again. I'd gladly give a year or two of my life could he have been spared to us for a while longer, not from any selfish reason, but just because of what he was to all of us. As you say, it is a grievous loss to science and I doubt if we of this generation shall see his like. I for one have lost a friend whose place shall never be filled.

And Forrest, full of news at the end of his expedition and well used to sending letters of up to twenty pages and sometimes many more, only managed four, admitting poignantly 'I have no heart to write'.

Forrest knew how much he owed to Balfour, who had made Forrest's career possible and had supported, advised and befriended him for nearly twenty years. Balfour understood Forrest, his ambition, his enthusiasm and his every mood better than almost anyone else. Happily, Forrest's friend, Wright Smith, was appointed Professor and Regius Keeper in succession to Balfour, and the plant collector's strong link with the Royal Botanic Garden Edinburgh continued.

Further honours followed. In June 1923 the Committee of *Curtis's Botanical Magazine* dedicated Volume 148 (1922) to George Forrest

> as a token of our admiration of the energy, courage and sagacity with which he has in repeated expeditions since 1904 explored the flora of the borderlands of Yunnan and Tibet, and … as a special tribute of our gratitude for the introduction of the many new and beautiful plants which horticulture owes to him and of which not a few adorn the pages of this volume.

Forrest must also have treasured the special copy of Volume 88 of *The Garden* (1924), bound in dark green leather and 'dedicated, by permission, to George Forrest, VMH'. The eulogy, presumably written by the Editor, E.H.M. Cox, referred to the fact that, by 1924, Forrest had collected over 25,000 plant specimens and discovered over 1,000 plants new to science. 'This is a significant total and proves Mr. Forrest's zeal and keenness for his work.'

In 1924 he was also elected Fellow of the Linnean Society, with the backing of the Directors of two Botanic gardens (Edinburgh and Kew) and three other Fellows. And in 1927 he was to be elected Hon. Life Member of the new Rhododendron Association, and awarded his third gold medal, the RHS Veitch Memorial Medal (Plate 131).

In a singularly happy touch, not only was Forrest elected an Associate of the Botanical Society of Edinburgh, but his wife and their two elder sons were elected Ordinary Fellow and Ordinary Members respectively during 1927-28. They surely deserved this gesture.

Above left:
Plate 130. *Magnolia campbellii* var. *mollicomata* at Ness Botanic Gardens; a deciduous tree first discovered in Yunnan by Forrest in 1914 and now recognised as an eastern form of *Magnolia campbellii*.

Above right:
Plate 131. Forrest's three gold medals: the Victoria Medal of Honour, the George Robert White Medal of the Massachusetts Horticultural Society, and the RHS Veitch Memorial Medal; a photograph taken by his great grand-daughter, Katherine Cameron.

What next?

Honours brought new demands for Forrest's acknowledged skills. Gardeners sought his advice, hoping for a visit from him. Wright Smith wanted his assistance in the taxonomy of primulas and rhododendrons, and fresh ideas circulated about another Forrest expedition.

Forrest returned home in 1926 to find the 'prevailing headlong Rhododendron rush' magnificently displayed at the Rhododendron Show in London in April 1926. Never before had so many species, varieties and hybrids of rhododendrons been exhibited under one roof. Forrest's plants were among those gaining awards. It was perhaps not surprising that a year later, in September 1927, a rhododendron enthusiast, Mr J.B. Stevenson of Tower Court, Ascot, asked Forrest whether he would consider a further expedition for one year.[4] Forrest was to send him a sketch of his plans, some maps and an estimate of finances, and it was to be called the 'George Forrest Expedition 1928-29'.[5] Wright Smith offered support and Forrest would depart at the end of 1928. But this idea, as we shall see, did not come to fruition.

In 1927 Forrest committed himself to helping Smith in a major work on a new classification of the large genus Primula. The proofs had to be ready for the end of December, in preparation for an international Primula Conference in 1928, and Smith admitted that he kept Forrest 'very closely tied down'.[6] Their paper was published to acclaim,[7] Stephenson Clarke maintaining it was 'the most valuable result of the Conference',[8] and in April Forrest went with his family for two weeks of fishing and hill climbing in upper Tweedsdale.[9]

However, when Forrest went shooting rabbits with his sons and missed some of his targets, the boys knew something was wrong. Forrest was having trouble with one of his eyes and an operation seemed inevitable. He postponed going to Ireland, had to forgo the Primula Conference and was admitted in July 1928 to a private nursing home in Edinburgh for an operation to his left eye.[10] Fortunately it was successful and in early August he went with his family to convalesce on the Isle of Arran.

Meanwhile another exciting proposal had emerged, which enabled Forrest to enjoy longer with his family and yet serve the insatiable demands of keen gardeners for more seed from Yunnan. It was to be a vicarious expedition.

Brainwave from Bodnant

When eager men meet, ideas flow, and on 7 June 1928, two weeks after the Primula Conference, George Forrest was visited by two of the most knowledgeable and accomplished amateur gardeners, the Hon. Henry D. McLaren (later Lord Aberconway) and Major Frederick Stern. It was a pivotal point at this stage of Forrest's career.

Neither visitor had sponsored Forrest's previous expeditions, but they had raised his seeds and had a high regard for his reputation. Stern, a soldier and merchant banker, travelled up from Highdown on the South Downs, where he grew *Primula forrestii* on his chalky soil with great success. McLaren, a land owner and barrister with business interests from china clay to ship building, came from Bodnant, near Conwy, North Wales. There he was experimenting with asiatic primulas in 'leaf soil' and raising rhododendrons from seed of Forrest's last two expeditions (Plate 133).

These two men were influential establishment figures at the forefront of gardening. They had ample funds at their disposal and both of them had previously subscribed to expeditions of Wilson and Kingdon Ward. Now they were seeking guidance from Forrest on how to acquire fresh seed of alpine plants in Yunnan. They came with a mission to the expert on that area.

The initiative for this meeting came from McLaren, who was a close friend of

Plate 132. George and Clementina Forrest enjoying each other's company on holiday in Scotland.

Reginald Cory and J.C. Williams, so familiar with Forrest's work. McLaren was a man of extraordinary drive, and he was flush with recent success at Chelsea (Plate 134). He and Lady Aberconway had received an award for an exhibition of Primulas that they and their head gardener, Mr F.C. Puddle, had grown at Bodnant. Furthermore, McLaren had just given a paper at the Primula Conference, on 'Asiatic Primulas for the Garden'. In this paper he highlighted the problem of how many primulas, since 1913, had 'passed out of cultivation in this country'.[11] McLaren understood the need for more seed stock, and where to go for it in China. At the same conference, he had heard Handel-Mazzetti stress that the real home of the genus *Primula* is in the highland and the high mountains of Yunnan and West Szechuan, where more than a third of all of the primula species are indigenous.[12] Handel-Mazzetti had met Forrest in Yunnan (see pages 123-4) and knew the value of this area. He ended his paper by wishing the audience success in 'transplanting' many plants to 'enjoy them without the evil accompaniment of sandflies, leeches, and Chinese soldiers…'. That was McLaren and Stern's inherent purpose in visiting George Forrest, the plant hunter.

In the course of discussion about China and Chinese alpine plants, Forrest mentioned that his collectors in Yunnan could be recalled to collect more seed, possibly as soon as that autumn, even without him being there. Why not use his collectors? He had tried this successfully in 1923, when a number of his men had continued collecting while Forrest was in Britain between two expeditions.[13] The idea had immense appeal to his visitors. It seemed a brilliant ruse. No previous plant hunter in that area could possibly have suggested this, as they had never built up such a pool of well-trained, reliable and loyal local collectors.

They discussed finances, Forrest agreed to contact his men, and McLaren was to ask two more gardening friends if they would like to join in this new project.

The next day McLaren confirmed the plan in writing, sent Forrest £50 for preliminary expenses and wrote to Lionel de Rothschild of Exbury and the Hon. Robert James of Richmond, Yorkshire.

Dear de Rothschild,
Stern and I … arranged that he [Forrest] should communicate with his collectors with a view to collecting seeds of certain selected plants, especially of alpines, in the Lichiang and Tali Ranges, the Lichiang Range especially appealing to Stern as providing the lime-loving plants. We thought that we should give him [Forrest], in addition to the £150, £50 for himself, in recognition of his arranging the matter, making £200 in all…I need hardly say that Stern and I would be delighted if you came in as a 3rd partner.[14]

Plate 134. Henry D. McLaren (the 2nd Lord Aberconway).

Rothschild immediately joined in and so did the Hon. Robert James, who thought it an excellent plan. They formed a cosy and select syndicate. Forrest was keen to keep the number of subscribers small, so that the seed could be easily divided, the RBGE having a selection if desired. Forrest emphasised that the project was a gamble, but to these enterprising and wealthy gardeners it was a gamble well worth taking. The scheme had the support of Wright Smith, who confirmed that those ranges in Yunnan had 'the most distinctive alpine flora in Asia'.

Within days Forrest assured McLaren that he was willing to assist them to the best of his ability, and he had already taken steps to get in touch with his men through missionaries and Chinese friends in Tengyueh and Lichiang. Ever obliging for his patrons, he was soon sending McLaren a list of names of the species to be found on the Tali and Lichiang Ranges, seeds of which 'we may manage to collect for you'.

Forrest had his eye operation the following month, happy that he had started on a new project. Characteristically, he even cabled to Upper Burma while he was in the nursing home; wherever he was, his cabling and letter writing never ceased. However, while he was convalescing with his family on the Isle of Arran he had bad news. He reported to McLaren, 'complete failure of telegraphic communication with Yunnan'. He had tried every route without getting through and found that all communications were affected by political disturbances in the province. With great regret he had to admit that it was getting too late in the season 'to get the machinery in motion with any prospect of a paying harvest'. All he could do was to offer to try again the following year, 1929, which would give more time to make the necessary arrangements. Determined and tenacious as ever, Forrest was keen to have another go, and he cannily challenged McLaren when writing to him: 'Even should you withdraw from the venture my intention is to carry it out alone'. McLaren rose to the bait magnificently, giving the go-ahead for the following year, sure that his three friends would be of the same opinion; if not, he would either take another share or replace one of them. He did not want to let the idea go. He wanted more seed. The arrangement stood firm.

In the spring of 1929 Forrest began to make plans for the proposed autumn harvest of seed in Yunnan, while McLaren wrote down a list of desirable plants from which he wanted seed. Forrest explained that whilst most of these would be within reach of his collectors on their best known beats, others would be more difficult. 'As most of the plants grow on screes and ledges of cliffs you will understand how difficult it is to get anything approaching a satisfactory quantity.'[15] Some plants would be too rare, or notoriously poor seeders or difficult to describe without showing his men the details. For example, he explained, '"a primrose by the river's brim" – may be said [by] many of my men as well as our own people here'. McLaren understood and was not put off.

A missionary now in Lichiang, Revd James H. Andrews, agreed to contact and help supervise Forrest's collectors, concentrating on the two ranges and districts of Tali and Lichiang, but with the possibility of exploring further afield in the Muli and Chungtien areas. They commenced collecting on 1 July, early enough in the season for all that was asked of them. Forrest was optimistic of their harvest, because the men employed had all served him for eight to twelve years.

Even on holiday with his family in Tweedsmuir, from the end of August to early September, Forrest was still at the helm, writing letters to Wright Smith, McLaren and to his men in Yunnan, to keep everything on schedule without a hitch. He could not resist the happy thought that there was a chance that his men might find something new, but, as always, he tempered hope with realism, and wisely wrote a warning, 'I've pushed the lever but once going I can only partially control the mechanism'.[16]

Forrest was in a strange but privileged position. He was advising and dictating what should be done in Yunnan, but that was the limit of his involvement and he was free to have a family holiday in the hills. The whole family was enjoying this, and Forrest was glad to be away 'from the beastly city', reporting that 'the fishing has been poor, but we have lots of fun amongst the bunnies. The country is very bare and with a .22 rifle the sport is almost as exciting as deer stalking'.[17] He was happy and well and could see with both eyes. Contact with his men was restored and dreams of returning to Yunnan in the future were being mulled over in his mind.

Meanwhile, administration by others continued efficiently, with Forrest's guidance. Forrest learned that the currency in Yunnan was debased, and the cost of living had risen almost 200 per cent since he was last there, but he used his bank account in Rangoon to send rupees into the country, and McLaren sent £100 to Andrew's account in the Hongkong and Shanghai Bank. It was then imperative to make sure that the collections were brought out of Yunnan with the greatest possible speed and without the cases being opened and re-packed, injuring the contents. Forrest approached this with as much care as others would give to the export of the most delicate and beautiful porcelain from China.

Forrest was used to pulling strings and making personal visits to key people with influence. The Chinese Maritime Customs were still administered from Britain, so he advocated a personal call at the Head Office in London where, 'a friend of mine', Mr Stephenson, was probably the Commissioner in charge. If not, 'another of my friends – Mr Shone – may be, … I am sure either of them will gladly assist you'. During his last three expeditions Forrest had also had to gain consent of the Inspector-General of the Chinese Customs at Peking. So Forrest advised,

> your best approach to him would be through the influence of the Foreign Office and our minister at Peking. … Sir Frances Aglen, late Inspector-General of the Chinese Customs could probably give you much information.[18]

Forrest knew how to make things happen.

It seems that Wright Smith and McLaren divided the jobs between them, Smith using his official influence as Regius Keeper of the RBGE. He was to be the official receiver of the crates in Britain, and, following Forrest's instructions, he wrote to key people in Yunnan and Upper Burma to request their help. He wrote to the Commissioner of Customs and H.M. Consul at Tengyueh to facilitate the dispatch of cases to Bhamo, in Upper Burma. He also wrote to the Commissioner at Bhamo to ask him to see that material was not held up there, and to Messrs Cook at Rangoon, to ask them to send the material by the first boat possible. McLaren agreed to pay the cost of freight into and out of Yunnan and homewards. Arrangements were well under way. Among themselves, the whole enterprise was referred to as the 'Forrest' expedition, even though Forrest himself did not go to Yunnan.

In late September a report was sent to Forrest that everything was running smoothly. The men were working well. They had made a collection of dried plants of over 400 species and the seeds of a good few plants were 'already in hand'. Then Forrest had the most 'heartening news' possible: his most reliable of men, his long-term headman, Chao, had somehow heard that Forrest had written and he had resigned a job in distant Tachien-lu in order to join Forrest's men at Lichiang. Forrest was thrilled and relieved to tell McLaren that Chao was now running the business,

> as I have every faith in him knowing he will do his utmost to make it a success … and when I think of the 250 miles, [of] rough and dangerous country, between Tachien-lu and Lichiang I am amazed, and not a little proud, of his fidelity. I hope we may meet again so that I can thank him.[19]

By the end of December 1929, the whole collection had been dispatched, comprising one case of seeds and two cases of dried plants for identification in the RBGE herbarium. Some of Forrest's men had taken the cases to the Commissioner of Chinese Customs in Tengyueh, with a covering letter requesting that they should be forwarded to Rangoon.

While the seeds were sailing to Britain, the news spread. The Marquis of Headfort wrote from his home in Ireland, on his personal blue notepaper, complete with Latin motto, to McLaren:

> I believe you are financing Forrest's collectors this winter in China and I was wondering whether it would be possible for you to let me have a small share in this expedition.

He and another gardener hoped to have a half share each: 'I should be very grateful if you would let me in with him'.[20]

As it happened, McLaren had been concerned that the money so far given would not cover all expenses, so he took another share in the 'expedition' for £50, and presumably this was divided unofficially between the Marquis of Headfort and his friend.[21]

In early April the cases arrived safely in Glasgow by S.S. *Burma,* and they were welcomed in RBGE by Wright Smith and Forrest, who immediately spent the weekend sorting through them. There had been some confusion in Yunnan in the numbering of species, Chinese characters being mixed with the numerals universal in the West, but there was plenty of seed. Forrest wrote jubilantly to McLaren:

> an ample supply of seed of some 220 species has been sent, many very fine things being represented …I feel sure you will be satisfied with the results.[22]

He listed some examples: species of Clematis, Gentian, Lilium, Magnolia, Meconopsis, Nomocharis, Primula and Saxifrage, and now that the collection had arrived, the last payment of £50 was sent to Mr Andrews in Lichiangfu. On 16 April 1930 Wright Smith sent the first consignment of seed to McLaren and the other shareholders. As there was a balance of £40.10.0 in the account, McLaren gladly paid this to Forrest.

There were smiles and congratulations all round. Stern wrote to McLaren:

> My dear Harry, Many congratulations on the success of the Yunnan idea. A wonderful lot of seed has arrived. It was your brain wave and a fine one.[23]

On the same day, Forrest also wrote to McLaren:

> Thanks for …the very kind way you write with regard to the little I have done. I also have had great satisfaction in the results of last year's work, if only in knowing that my men are still faithful, and eager to serve me…I was not expecting any gratuity to come my way, though it is very kind of you to think of it.[24]

Forrest reiterated his thanks to all the sponsors in his next letter to McLaren, and his genuine gratitude and appreciation for the money was partly linked to his recent move from Edinburgh. He was writing from a splendid, newly acquired, detached mansion called 'Bellfield', at Eskbank, Midlothian, where he and Clementina planned to enjoy the garden and countryside in his retirement. Knowing McLaren's pleasure at Forrest's help, he could not resist a personal *Post Script*:

> We have removed to the country, about 6 miles South of Edinburgh, and I should be greatly indebted if you could give me one or two shrubs for my place here![25]

McLaren's initial desires had been met, Forrest's reputation had increased and his spirits and confidence were high. Looking back to the early days of his plant-hunting

Plate 135. *Arisaema candidissimum,* discovered by Forrest in the Fengkou valley, N.W. Yunnan in 1914. It is hardy and widely available in Britain. From *Curtis's Botanical Magazine,* t.9549.

career, how far he had come! Originally he had been the servant of commerce, exploring and picking the plants with relatively little help. Now that he had trained a faithful band of experienced local collectors, and had the experience, friends and influence to 'pull the levers', he could stay in Britain, have an operation and buy a larger house in the country, while 'his men' still worked for him.

Looked at another way, he had acquired the cachet and experience to satisfy and serve the appetites and competitive urges of the capitalists, by producing the primary products, the seeds of plants for their gardens, without leaving home.

But essentially Forrest was still an explorer at heart, longing to return to his loyal men, the hills and people, the wilderness and dangers of Yunnan. His main aim, now, was to return one last time to Yunnan, and plans were already taking shape. In his mind he was there already, and it would take an awful lot to stop him.

Seeking sponsors

In November 1929 Wright Smith dined at a small elite club, the Garden Society, whose members all belonged to the RHS. He discussed with Lionel de Rothschild and other keen gardeners the possibility of Forrest going one last time to Yunnan for seed. After consulting Forrest, a clever plan emerged. Subscribers could be offered seed from two seasons for the cost of one expedition, if Forrest's men collected in autumn 1930 before Forrest arrived. He would stay in Yunnan until January 1932.

Plate 136. George Forrest happily chatting and gesticulating to a group of Ireland's most distinguished horticulturists in May 1930. To his left, Lord Headfort's gardener, Mr J.A. Boyle, takes notes. The trio in front of him are, from left to right, Hugh Armytage Moore of Rowallane, Co. Down (whose garden Forrest described as a 'bit of Yunnan'); Lady Moore, wife of Sir Frederick Moore, retired Keeper of the National Botanic Gardens at Glasnevin, Dublin; and Lord Headfort, who had grown Forrest's seeds since 1915 and was a subscriber to his final expedition.

Forrest estimated that £4,000 (£125,000 today) would be needed for the enterprise. The RBGE would be the administrative centre and Smith set about raising the money by writing eagerly to potential subscribers. 'Another Forrest expedition is on the way' proclaimed one letter.[26] The letters were not identical, but all stressed the richness of the Yunnan flora, Forrest's great experience ('a man who has never disappointed his subscribers'), and the fact that this would be his last expedition. Many letters contained a list of the genera of plants whose seed would be sought and indicated the collecting areas. Smith hoped to find eight people willing to pay for a £500 share, but realised that some shares might need to be divided. By 25 November 1929, £2,000 had been raised, a fact that Smith exploited in later letters, making it clear that readers should act quickly to take advantage of an offer that could not be repeated.

News spread, enquiries came in, and Smith liaised closely with Forrest. Bulley heard of the expedition from McLaren, and wrote immediately to Smith, asking for a quarter share of £125. Smith conveyed Forrest's assurance that he would be delighted to collect for Bulley. In October 1930 the RHS accepted Smith's invitation to take part and sent a cheque for £500 to Forrest. All previous sponsors of Forrest who were still alive supported his final expedition, with the sole exception of the Duke of Bedford, then deeply involved with establishing Whipsnade zoo.

Mrs. A.C.U. Berry wrote to Smith from Portland, Oregon: 'I cannot tell you how eager I am to become a subscriber to the expedition of Mr. Forrest'. She wanted primula seed, 'It's the only way we have any chance of seeing the lovely things, and I do enjoy the game for its own sake'. She paid £100, Smith telling her on 27 August 1930:

> You will be the only one in the USA who has a share in the expedition and, if all goes well, will be in possession of stores of things quite new to American gardens.[27]

The thirty-nine sponsors of Forrest's final expedition are listed in Appendix 3.

Many are well-known names. Some endowed horticultural cups (Cory, Crosfield, Loder, Lionel de Rothschild). Lord Walter Rothschild paid £500 to get birds for the Natural History Museum. Over half were keen growers of rhododendrons, many being members of the Rhododendron Society, with Lionel de Rothschild of Exbury and Admiral Heneage-Vivian of Clyne Castle, near Swansea, being respectively the first President and Vice-President of the Rhododendron Association. Among these experts was J.B. Stevenson of Tower Court, Ascot, whom Forrest had helped in the preparation of the long-awaited and classic handbook, *The species of Rhododendron*, which was published in 1930. Earlier, J.C. Williams had treasured Balfour's rhododendron publications, looking forward to reading them 'with greedy eyes', keeping them on his desk or by his bedside, and thumbing them 'into a disgraceful state'.[28] Now Lionel de Rothschild, who had been glad of Williams' advice when creating his garden at Exbury, read through the whole of *The species of Rhododendron* on holiday. 'I am leaving London today for a yachting cruise in the Baltic and shall not be back for six weeks' he wrote to Tagg, the rhododendron taxonomist at the RBGE on 17 July 1930. Another rhododendron lover was Col. (later Sir James) Horlick, whose business address was 'Horlick's malted milk Co., Ltd., Slough (Bucks)'.

Forrest's final expedition attracted eight Scottish and two Irish sponsors (Plate 95). The Scottish contingent included McDouall of Logan and FRS Balfour of Dawyck, giving their gardens an early historic link with the RBGE before being partially or wholly incorporated. Another Scottish sponsor was E.H.M. Cox, who accompanied Farrer on part of his last journey. Across the sea, Lord Headfort, President of the Royal Horticultural Society of Ireland, had received some seed from earlier Forrest expeditions, even though he had not been a sponsor. He invited Forrest to see his garden, and contributed £100 to the final expedition (about £3,000 today) (Plates 136 and 137). Headfort's sister, Lady Beatrix Stanley, was one of Forrest's more colourful sponsors. Married to the Governor of Madras, she was to be awarded the Imperial Order of the Crown of India, a bejewelled breast badge with Queen Victoria's monogram surmounted by an imperial crown. She was a talented botanical artist (some of her drawings of Indian plants are at the RHS), and she created a lovely garden in the hills of Ootacamund, but asked that Forrest's seeds be sent to her head gardener at Sibbertoft Manor, Market Harborough.

The Marchioness of Londonderry, Lady Edith Helen, of Mount Stewart, Co. Down, had visited McLaren at Bodnant for a gardening weekend in May 1930 and invited Forrest to visit her. But time was now pressing on Forrest and he had to defer this and other visits until his return in 1932. His very courteous reply to the Marchioness was appreciated so much that it was pasted in her diary.[29]

A total of £5,975 was raised, but only five full shares of £500 were taken and twenty-four subscribers paid £100 or less (see Appendix 3). The syndicate of thirty-nine who supported Forrest's final expedition was probably the largest that had then been assembled for a collector, with sponsors from all over Britain (Plate 95) and from gardens big and small.

In October 1930, only five weeks before departure, Forrest admitted 'time is all too short for what I have to accomplish'.[30] His friend, George Taylor, a future Director of Kew, would have loved to go with him, but was then working in the depths of the Natural History Museum. Forrest could not resist ending a letter to him: 'I trust … that you keep fit though working in that awful place. Think of me on the sun-lit ranges of Yunnan!'

Plate 137. George Forrest, photographed at Headfort, near Kells, north of Dublin, on 25 May 1930 by C.P. Raffill, who wrote on the back, 'With compliments and best wishes from your friend, C.P. Raffill'.

184

CHAPTER TWELVE

The Final Expedition

Death closes all: but something ere the end,
Some work of noble note, may yet be done

Lord Tennyson[1]

Beneath the bustle of activity Forrest had a steely resolution in preparing for this final expedition. He had a firm belief in his own continuing strength and ability. He knew his fitness from daily walking and family holidays in the hills; he might be fifty-seven years old, but he could walk thirty miles in a day. His zest and enthusiasm were undiminished and he relished the challenge of a new expedition. He was confident in the complete backing of Wright Smith, and that his wife understood his desire for one more, last, expedition. He expected to be away no longer than eighteen months and he would write to her regularly. He left home on the morning of 7 November 1930, keen to savour again the richest temperate flora of the world.

Fraught times with Major Johnston

Major Lawrence Waterbury Johnston, founder of the famous garden of Hidcote Manor, Gloucestershire, was a generous subscriber to this expedition. However, Forrest's decision to let Johnston join him in China soon proved to be mistaken.

Forrest had been rather mysteriously warned. 'Cherry' Ingram, Reginald Cory and George Taylor had recently been with Johnston on a plant-hunting expedition to South Africa,[2] and advised against him as a travelling companion. However, it seems that Forrest did not fully understand their reasons.

Lawrence Johnston was keenly interested in the plants that Forrest had introduced and longed for some seed for his own garden. In 1929 he wrote to H.D. McLaren, offering him £50 towards the syndicate that he was organising to fund Forrest's collectors.[3] He contemplated going to Yunnan alone, but then rejected this in favour of joining Forrest a year later.[4] Forrest wavered, but eventually consented. It is intriguing, for Forrest had never taken anyone with him from Britain before. He had invited the young George Taylor, who would have been an excellent, keen and fit assistant, but Taylor's new appointment at the Natural History Museum prevented him from taking up the offer.[5] We don't know what influenced Forrest to then accept Johnston as companion: perhaps it was Johnston's persistence – he had been helpful in enrolling subscribers – perhaps the £500 he invested in Forrest's expedition was a lever.

The two men approached the expedition very differently. This was partly because of their contrasting backgrounds, partly their personalities. They were roughly the same age, and Johnston was a keen and creative gardener who shared Forrest's enthusiasm for new garden plants, but their lifestyles were very different. Johnston was a wealthy American bachelor who had settled with his mother in England. He had spent twenty years in the Army, enjoyed 'Society' friends, house parties and antiques, and his social credibility was important to him.[6] He had two properties, Hidcote and La Serre de la Madone, near Mentone in the south of France. Just before he joined Forrest's expedition, Hidcote featured in the August 1930 edition of *Country Life*. In this garden Johnston employed a permanent staff of five gardeners, with local part-time help when needed.[7] In neither of his properties, in

Opposite:
Plate 138. *Iris wattii,* introduced by Major Johnston. The plant illustrated was shown by Lord Aberconway (formerly the Hon. H.D. McLaren) and given an Award of Merit in 1938.

England or France, did he ever need to get his hands dirty. He was not used to 'roughing it' in any way, since he enjoyed an ample income, a cultured milieu, his own valet, butler, housekeeper and a large domestic staff – a lifestyle epitomised perhaps by his habit of driving a Lancia himself, while his chauffeur drove the Bentley. Indeed, his chauffeur and valet accompanied him on the South African expedition. Forrest never owned a car.

With this in mind, it is perhaps understandable that problems arose. For Johnston, it was probably a 'holiday with a purpose', an opportunity to see and collect some new garden plants. For Forrest, his work was the whole purpose of the journey. This was to be the climax of his life's work before he retired. He had been commissioned and felt a strong sense of duty to use the expedition time well. Everything was familiar and he felt no wish to dally. He felt the pressure of his subscribers' expectancy as well as his own. He desperately wanted to push on, especially as there were many questions at the back of his mind: would his team of collectors be at Tengyueh to meet him? Had they found the seed his subscribers wanted? Would this expedition be a success? Tensions built up between the two men, especially when Forrest felt that Johnston was not helping.

Johnston, who has been described as a 'birdlike, ineffectual' man,[8] was drawn to socialising with the British community. Forrest, on the other hand, expected Johnston to share in the practical preparations as part of the expedition. It was not a situation likely to be friction free. Forrest described Johnston's aloofness in Rangoon:

> Everything devolved on me, securing passports and permits, calling on the various officials, booking berths and securing tickets, etc. etc. I had all the purchase of equipment to attend to and getting stores of food stuffs, drugs, tents etc.

Money problems made the situation worse:

> I ordered a sufficient supply of stores for a year, on the understanding that he would pay his share. He coolly informed me that making up lists of stores and purchasing them bored him to extinction almost, and besides it was much too hot to attend to such matters!! Then he left me to pay for the transport of the purchases to Bhamo and also to here [Tengyueh]. I am now out of pocket with that and other expenses for our journey to the amount of Rps. [rupees] 500/-!

Upon arriving in Bhamo, Johnston socialised with the hospitable British Deputy Commissioner and his wife instead of helping Forrest to prepare for the overland journey into China. Forrest was left to engage the chairs and chairbearers, coolies and mule transport. He graphically wrote of his frustration:

> I had only an Indian boy as help, and as my Chinese was a bit rusty I had a hard row to hoe and was well put to it at times. There was much he could have done to lighten my labours but he was busy gadding around every day…riding in the morning, tea and tennis in the afternoon and bridge at the club in the evening.

Forrest described how his resentment and anger built up:

> Knowing me as you do you may not believe it, but I was more than patient under all of it, but at last I did give way after I hadn't seen him for three days. I sent for him and asked him what he meant by all of it, and if he thought I was a Cook's courier arranging a tour for him and if he thought I was paid to attend to him.

However, Forrest realised he could not change anything and Johnston never apologised. So when Johnston then fell seriously ill, Forrest, who never suffered fools gladly, could not resist a cutting gibe: 'Apparently he had contracted a severe chill through exhausting himself in playing tennis and then sitting cooling off

Plates 139, 140 and 141. George Forrest gave a series of popular public lectures under the auspices of the Botanical Society of Edinburgh in the late 1920s. On 24 October 1929, he spoke on the 'Peoples and Customs of Yunnan'. These three photographs show the variety of illustrations he had available, including two examples of the many minority groups in Yunnan together with the captions he gave them.

Right:
Plate 139. An elaborate Chinese grave.

Below left:
Plate 140. A 'Heh-Mossoo lady'.

Below right:
Plate 141. A 'Black Lissoo' couple.

instead of changing'. Johnston's condition worsened:

> The Bhamo Divisional surgeon was called in to attend to him…he informed me that Johnston was in a very bad state internally, chronic congestion of the liver, lungs exceedingly weak, and heart and kidneys bad, and that it would be extremely dangerous for him to attempt such a journey into Yunnan as we had contemplated.

Johnston was forced to stay behind in Bhamo to recuperate. Forrest hectically cancelled the arrangements for Johnston's onward journey and left him behind, setting off, at last, for the Chinese border town of Tengyueh. On arrival, he poured out his troubles in a letter to Wright Smith. 'I have had a most harassing time', he wrote in February 1931.[9]

> Had I raked G.B. with a small tooth comb I couldn't have found a worse companion than Johnston, and I cannot say how often during the past three months I have cursed myself for being so foolish in consenting to him accompanying me! I have indeed paid for my folly!

However, a heart-warming welcome awaited him. The Commissioner of Customs gave him accommodation and Forrest's headman, Chao, and eighteen of his trained collectors were in town to greet him. The immediately recognisable and familiar figure of Forrest was present amongst them again, after a gap of four years. They proudly showed him their haul of the previous year, 'a collection of herbaria numbering nearly 1,000 spp. [species] with seed of some 3-400 of them'. Forrest was thrilled.

Forrest's rejoicing was interrupted by a determined Johnston who, against all advice, had undertaken a nine-day trek in sub-tropical conditions from Bhamo to Tengyueh. He had been carried in a sedan chair, but the track was uneven and progress slow as the old trade route wound through the mountains and the gorge of the Taping river. For a sick man used to the comfort of a luxurious limousine on English country lanes, the journey was a great strain. He became even more seriously ill. Indeed, Forrest feared 'poor Johnston would have gone under for keeps' if medical aid had not been quickly provided by the British Consul and the Commissioner of Customs. Johnston was warned by the doctor that he had a life-threatening condition and he decided he had better give up and return to his second home in the south of France. Forrest feared that Johnston would not abide by this decision. He wrote that as Johnston 'changes his mind more frequently than his socks' he would give no guarantee what the Major would do: 'Since the first demand made by him he has changed his mind repeatedly'. Forrest's fear was well founded. When Johnston was cautioned against attempting a strenuous trek north with Forrest, he still ventured outside Tengyueh, became seriously ill for a third time and had to S.O.S. for medical help.

One final impasse illustrates the difficulties and misunderstandings between these two men. As he prepared to leave, Johnston wanted to take his share of the stores, but Forrest pointed out that the cases had already been sealed for the next overland journey to Lichiang. Johnston wanted to break open the cases. However, the more experienced Forrest realised this would leave them prey to thieves, and the thought of re-packing and re-sealing them was more than he could countenance. Forrest felt that his plans and his leadership were being threatened by Johnston. He was not used to this on an expedition and he said that Johnston had 'fallen out of line'. Forrest offered to pay for his companion's share of the stores, but Johnston refused. Both men were intransigent. The tension was compounded by Forrest's own reaction: 'I can only construe his refusal as an attempt to give me further trouble'.

Plate 142. Under the heading 'New plants from China', *Androsace spinulifera* was introduced through Bees' Ltd, who called it 'a choice rock plant'.

Forrest exploded in outrage to Wright Smith:

> I have been so incensed over the whole affair that could I have communicated speedily with you I would have suggested returning him his share [subscription], turning him out of the syndicate and getting someone else to take his place.

His outburst flowed on, culminating in language that he would never otherwise use.

> He has irritated me so much and so constantly hampering me in every way, so that I am much behind in my work, correspondence, as well as all else. I can now realise perfectly what was behind all those warnings I received from Cory, Taylor, G. Loder and others. My God! if only they had been more open with me what a difference it would have made for me. Johnston is <u>not</u> a man, not even a bachelor, but a right good old <u>Spinster</u> spoilt by being born male. A person more utterly selfish I have yet to meet, and I'm not the only one here who thinks so.[10]

Forrest had two elder sisters who were spinsters and he loved and respected them dearly. The sentiments and language of his temper reflected the frustration and depth of his desire to get on with the expedition unimpeded. Forrest's desire for success was as deep-seated as the slow-burning passion which over nearly thirty years had shaped him into an outstanding collector. Never before had he been challenged to collect for so many subscribers, and he did not want to be deflected from this task.

Wright Smith knew Forrest very well and ignored his outburst. He knew the storm would blow over. He was also reassured that Johnston was on his way home and recovering his health, as Johnston had written to him 'in very good spirits and with a very commendable spirit of resignation'.[11]

Forrest and Johnston had arrived in China as spring was coming. Both men rejoiced in the camellias in flower and Forrest declared, 'I have never seen

Two contrasting bridges in Yunnan.

Above:
Plate 143. A chain suspension bridge over the mighty Mekong river on the main trade route between Tengyueh (Tengchong) and Talifu (Dali), taken in February 1906.

Opposite:
Plate 144. A precarious but beautifully-crafted liana bridge across the Yang-pi (Yangbi) river, a tributary of the Mekong river in N.W. Yunnan, in March 1906.

Camellia speciosa[12] as fine…and when Johnston saw it he nearly went dotty'. Despite his appalling health problems Johnston had tasted the thrill of plant hunting in China. On his way to sulphur springs near Tengyueh, he found a beautiful iris, *Iris wattii* (Plate 138) growing near an irrigation canal; he dug up rhizomes and subsequently planted them successfully in his garden near Mentone, France.[13] (This garden is now twinned with Hidcote Manor, Gloucestershire.) He also introduced to Hidcote the fragrant climber *Jasminum polyanthum* and two handsome shrubs, *Mahonia lomariifolia* and *M. siamensis*.[14]

As for Forrest, he was relieved to be rid of Johnston: 'beyond all things I'm thankful he accompanies me no further, that I'm quit of him from now on'.[15] With cheerful confidence, Forrest savoured the freedom and the joy of returning to be with the people and wildlife of the remote mountain areas of north-west Yunnan.

The bonus collection

Forrest's most urgent task upon meeting his welcoming party at Tengyueh was to sort the men's haul and dispatch it to Britain. This collection was the bonus he had promised to his subscribers. Delay would lead to deterioration of seeds, specimens, and public relations. Forrest prized all three. He settled down with the usual discipline aligned with his passion to accomplish any task he set himself.

It soon became clear to Forrest that his men had done a good job, and so had his friends who had overseen the work for him. The seeds had been collected mainly from the snow-topped ranges of the Muli and Yungning districts and the Chungtien plateau. Being a perfectionist, it was not easy for Forrest to accept that there had been some mistakes: his collectors had not always been sent in the

direction he had planned and they had underestimated the number of *Nomocharis* seeds to collect. But now that Forrest was back in Yunnan, he could put that right in the coming year. Meanwhile there was plenty of sorting to do.

The dried plants and majority of the seeds were listed and packed with their field labels in wooden cases. The large seeds were waxed for extra protection and groups of twenty to thirty seeds were wrapped in oiled paper alongside the dried plants. The five cases were loaded on mules and escorted by his men to Bhamo, whence Messrs Cook sent them on to Rangoon, by S.S. *Bhamo* to Glasgow docks and by train to Edinburgh – the total journey taking three months. Some seeds are best sown fresh, but this was the cheapest way to send the bulk of them to Britain since postal rates had risen far more than anticipated.

Packets of selected seeds were given priority and sent at intervals to Edinburgh in registered postal packets. Some seeds were selected to 'clear up the muddle'[16] of plants' identification and classification. This included the yellow-flowered tree peonies[17] and some very variable primulas and rhododendrons. Others, 'the much desired seeds of the better things',[18] were selected for horticultural purposes. Some of these were wanted for new trials as they had failed to grow before or survived only fleetingly. For example, the beautiful lily, *Lilium taliense,* first found by Père Delavay in 1883, had never been in cultivation. It grows wild in Yunnan and Szechuan (Sichuan) and seeds collected by Forrest's men were the first to flower in Britain (Plate 157).

As the registered packages of seeds began to arrive at the RBGE, there was a buzz of expectant activity. The contents of the first packets were sorted and sent to subscribers within two days, together with an estimate of the future number and

Plate 145. *Omphalogramma vincaeflora,* photographed by Forrest.

Plate 146. *Camellia saluenensis.* Forrest introduced this plant on his fourth expedition. In 1930 the RHS gave the species an Award of Merit. J.C. Williams crossed it with *C. japonica* to make the first of the *williamsii* hybrids.

timing of seeds expected from Yunnan. Anticipation mounted among gardeners round the country. Colonel Stephenson Clarke of Borde Hill replied that he was off to put up another range of frames and Mr Johnstone of Cornwall reckoned he would be kept busy for some years. As for camellias, Wright Smith assured Forrest:

> You will certainly please Mr Williams [of Caerhays] very much with the *Camellia* seed for he reckons that it is in his opinion the best shrub which has come from China. He says with him it is hardy and vigorous, varies much in colour, foliage and habit, but all the variations are good. He states, moreover, that he gets charming flesh-pink hybrids by crossing with *Camellia japonica* and these are even more vigorous than the mother plant.[19]

No collector could hope for better news to boost his morale. Forrest had first introduced *Camellia saluenensis* in 1917 (Plate 146) and these hybridisation experiments of his sponsor, J.C. Williams, were epoch-making in producing the first series of beautiful plants hardier than *C. saluenensis* itself. This includes hybrids like 'J.C. Williams', of great garden worth.

A few weeks later, when eighty-nine packets arrived from Forrest all at once, and all in excellent condition, there were enough to send some of them to all thirty-nine subscribers for seeds. The staff at the RBGE sorted seed and sent out 3,000 separate packets within five days. Forrest was also sent the news that three more of his plants were illustrated in a recent issue of *Curtis's Botanical Magazine.*

Some subscribers were in such a hurry to grow the flowers that they sowed seeds like camellias without removing the added wax coating. More careful gardeners had good germination results. At Branklyn garden in Perth, Scotland, Dorothy Renton had previously obtained some rhododendrons with Forrest numbers, but this was the first time she had subscribed to a Forrest expedition. She and her husband, John, were eager for more plants for their new rock garden. When they received Forrest's seed they methodically 'set to' with a will. She had a canvas-backed pocket note-book headed 'Forrest Expedition 1931' in which she carefully listed columns of the plant names, their Forrest number, date sown and date of germination, and the month in which the seeds were pricked out.[20] The germination rate was pleasingly high, including primulas, meconopses and gentians. A few years later she had the pleasure of being awarded three 'George Forrest' medals by the Scottish Rock Garden Club. Her interest in the Sino-Himalayan flora was established in this beautiful, intimate two-acre garden, overlooking the River Tay and distant hills. It became renowned for its choice collection of plants and is now in the care of the National Trust for Scotland.

Forrest's collectors and the panda

Forrest had brought with him a book to read that he knew would have a special resonance. It recounted an American expedition to hunt for the giant panda in the region north of Yunnan in 1928-29 when Forrest was still in Edinburgh. The authors were two brothers, Kermit and Theodore Roosevelt, Jr., sons of President Theodore Roosevelt. A giant panda was shot and the dead animal sent triumphantly to the States, being among the first panda specimens ever exhibited there. It created a sensation, as many zoologists had thought that the giant panda was extinct. This was before any giant pandas were captured and taken live to zoos, thrilling millions of visitors.

Forrest looked forward to reading about this hunt and one day the opportunity came to relax with his collectors. He opened the book, *Trailing the Giant Panda*.[21] Forrest's headman, Chao, looked over to see the pictures and recognised some of the people, because he had been partly involved. Chao had been hired to assist Herbert Stevens, an English naturalist on this expedition. Stevens was the man left in the lurch when Chao returned to lead Forrest's men for a season's collecting before Forrest arrived (Plate 147). As several of Forrest's men had also been part of the panda expedition, they were eager to know the Roosevelts' version of events, and they all got caught up in the story.

According to the book, a Lolo hunter had first seen the panda emerging from the hollow of a spruce tree and the Roosevelt brothers were signalled to come and see the animal. Just in time, before it was lost from sight in the bamboos, the Roosevelt brothers 'fired simultaneously at the outline of the disappearing panda. Both shots took effect'. The panda was 'floundering through the drifted snow', so the brothers fired again. The panda fell, but recovered and made off through the densely growing

Plate 147. Forrest called his headman Lao Chao, seen here on the left, 'my best card in this business'. Forrest had great faith in him, knowing he would do his utmost to make the collecting a success.

bamboos … then, to quote the book, 'the chase ended in seventy-five yards. He was a splendid old male'.

Forrest's men laughed when they heard this. They were sure that the Roosevelts were lying and that they never actually killed the giant panda. In a chatty letter to McLaren of Bodnant, Forrest recounted the tale as told by his men:

> 'The Giant Panda' the Roosevelts secured had been tracked by a local Lolo hunter, shot by him, and sold to the party for 200 Syechuan!!! … Now the truth is out … everyone is chortling. Lying like that is beyond my conception. If there was one such a[s] G. Washington in America then the Good Lord must have broken the mould as soon as it cooled.[22]

So, who killed the panda? There is agreement that the Roosevelts shot and wounded the panda. The book implies that the animal died as a result. From the evidence of Forrest's collectors, the Roosevelts were economical with the truth and a Lolo made the final shot that actually killed it. Forrest was certainly influenced by his chortling collectors. Whatever the truth about the panda, the story shows how well he got on with his collectors. There was a rapport based on years of working together, a *camaraderie* that strengthened bonds. He enjoyed sharing the story with them, the laughter relaxing them and motivating the team spirit, which was essential when there was much still to do.

Spring, the sweet spring

Forrest was keen to plan the year ahead with his collectors. They must collect more *Nomocharis* to meet the demand and go to new localities where the men had previously found much-wanted plants (Plates 148 and 149). These included the breath-taking, brilliant red flowers of *Meconopsis punicea* and a yellow-flowered form of *Primula dryadifolia* that had been recently found by Joseph Rock. Forrest, the ever-competitive hunter, was instinctively keen to find the same primula that Rock had found. Chao thought he knew where Rock had collected it, because he saw them when with Mr Stevens. Forrest listened carefully and strategically dispersed groups of them on different errands. His own appetite for exploring grew again. This was the life he loved.

As Forrest found time to explore, his sense of awe and wonder was as sharp as on his very first expedition to Yunnan. When he trekked into the virgin forest north of Tengyueh, he was still 'astounded' by the size and majesty of the highest trees. When he rediscovered a small, dainty primula, he was still overcome by its beauty. There was never a feeling of *déjà vu*. Pages of his long letters were brim full of enthusiasm for the beauty and diversity of the flora, irrespective of whether the plant might be suitable for gardens in Britain. However, if he thought that a plant might be hardy, his descriptions would whet the appetite of any subscriber awaiting seeds.

When he wrote to H.D. McLaren of Bodnant, who was partial to magnolias, he described some cousins of the magnolias that he saw in the early spring. He wrote:

> In one large gully, at well over 9000 ft. [2,700m], the whole of one flank was forested with immense specimens of *Manglietia Forrestii* bare silvery grey pillars of 90 or more feet [27.5m], topped by widely spread masses of…glistening foliage…the ground was thickly littered with last year's leaves and cones.

He assured McLaren that he had taken a photograph and then he speculated: 'Seeds of the species from that high altitude might, I think, give us a breed hardy enough for Ireland and England, and possibly the South of Scotland'.

He continued, 'One of the finest [large trees] was *Michelia manipurensis* 60–80 ft.

(18-24m) in height, yellow with butter coloured blooms, scenting the air for hundreds of yards around'. Forrest even shared his wish that the climate of Britain might be a bit milder, so that he could introduce even more of the wondrous plants he saw. He reported:

> *Rhododendron mackenzianum* [now *R. moulmainense*] was everywhere magnificent, up to 40-60 ft. [14-20m] laden with masses of bloom, ranging in specimens from white to the deepest crimson-magenta, with bare smooth mahogany red pillared stems. If we could grow that species at home as I saw it this time the enthusiast would kneel in worship to it.

The sheer scale and majesty impressed him so much that his writings could have featured in a tourist brochure for fellow-lovers of such plants. But those times had not yet come. Instead, Forrest felt it his role to describe to his gardener-subscribers back home where the seeds had come from and what the plants looked like in their native habitat, as if he were writing a private nursery catalogue. For *Camellia forrestii*, he described how it grew in the upper Shweli valley:

> It is the dominant shrub for 30-40 miles [50-65km] …Mile upon mile of the valley hillsides were absolutely covered with it ranging from clumpy bushes of 2-3ft. [1m] to shrubs of 10-20ft. [3-6m]. All in full and most abundant flower, in colour running from the palest shell pink, and nearly white to the deepest shade of rose, almost a crimson in bud…and if all goes well I hope to harvest a large quantity of seed this autumn.

The hunt for giants

Forrest and his collectors showed amazing perseverance in hunting for plants. A key example on this expedition was their search for the largest specimen of *Rhododendron giganteum* [now *R. protistum* var. *giganteum*]. When Forrest first discovered and named this species in 1921 some people did not believe its enormous size. Characteristically, he wanted to prove his point.

It was not easy, because ten years earlier he had found only three trees, but Forrest was sure that others grew in the area. He sent scouts to the headwaters of the Shweli river and they reported many 'immense trees' greater in girth and height than the original three giganteums. However, Forrest wanted to be sure that these trees were exactly the same as the species he had previously named and described. He asked his men to go ahead to make a further search, and to bring back a cross section of the largest bole they could find. It was intended for the Garden Museum at the RBGE.[23] He planned to come on later and photograph the best specimens. He wrote excitedly to both his wife and Wright Smith, even asking Clementina to pass on the news to the professor, in case his post went astray. Clementina was the ever-dependable personal link between the home team at Edinburgh and the overseas team led by Forrest in Yunnan. Her sense of humour saw the lighter side of Forrest's earnest endeavour as she wrote to the professor that Forrest and his men had gone 'to cut down one of the Giants!'[24]

A month later Forrest reported his trek to the giants:

> Our last camp was 6 days north of here [Tengyueh]: where the breadth of the Shweli is less than that of the Esk at Lasswade, at an altitude of about 8000 feet [2,500m]. Then the day following we struck still further up the valley until the stream was so small it could be stepped across.
>
> There, to the east the watershed, the Shweli-Salwin divide towered abruptly above us to an altitude of 11-13000 ft. [3,500m], fairly well snow capped, the forest in the gullies and on the spurs flanking it being the home of *Rhododendron giganteum*…

They were in virgin country, 'the very devil to get about in, not a track of any

Plate 148. *Nomocharis pardanthina.* First introduced by Forrest from his second expedition for Bees Ltd, it was awarded a First Class Certificate in June 1916 and its seed was increasingly in demand.

Plate 149. *Nomocharis aperta,* photographed by Forrest.

kind', and Forrest was astounded at the great size of the specimens. He wrote:

> It is indeed rightly named! …great towering boles of 80 to 120ft. [24 to 36m] … We found it at its best, in almost full flower…thousands of trusses of huge blooms of varying shades of rose-pink to almost magenta-crimson, crimson blotched at base. The ground under each tree littered inches deep with the huge fallen corollas.

With great difficulty they found a space amongst the forest trees where a felled tree would fall clear, across the bottom of one of the gullies. A photograph of a standing tree was impossible but Forrest was keen to record the event:

> I exposed a hundred ft. [30m] of ciné film in the felling of our specimen and the cutting of the section from it, the cut being taken a good 12-14 ft. [4m] from the base. The section is fully 6 ft., nearly 7 ft. [2m], in circumference and I shall be much interested to know if [Mr] Tagg can fix approximately the age of the tree from it.
>   It was a hefty day's work for all us and when I got back to camp at 6.30 I was more weary than I have been for many years having been going hard for fully 12 hours.[25]

Forrest only thought to mention 'a most appalling earthquake' much later in his letter. It happened the previous night, and was the worst he had experienced in Yunnan. The strongest tremor came at midnight when he was almost thrown out of his bed, and several of his men fled into the open, screaming in terror. Forrest had great difficulty in pacifying them. Vibrations continued till 2 am, accompanied by terrifying rumblings like a distant rock avalanche. He admitted to being 'more than a bit windy' himself, as they were camped on a very small meadow – the only

Plate 150. *Michelia doltsopa* in flower at Caerhays. It was introduced by George Forrest in 1918. The clustered flowers are fragrant and the genus is a cousin of Magnolia.

level bit of ground they could get – by the side of a stream with cliffs soaring more than 2,000ft. [600m] above them. He spent a 'most uneasy night' fearing that at any moment some of the cliffs might fall on top of them.

Next morning, their tents were sheeted with ice and the margins of the stream frozen. They made a dash for their goal, *Rhododendron giganteum*, and were overjoyed at the size and splendour of the trees.

After cutting one down, they made cross-sections through the trunk and began the seven-day trek back to Tengyueh with their large load. There, the cross-section was carefully stencilled:

Rhod. giganteum.
Specimen of fully 90 ft.
Section cut 12 ft. from base
Cut 15.3.31.
G.F.

Triumphantly, their trophy was placed in a wooden case and sent by sea to Professor W.W. Smith at RBG Edinburgh. There the cross-section was given a place of honour and Forrest was so proud of it that he told McLaren to see it when next he was in Edinburgh.[26] He secretly estimated to Lord Headfort that the tree might be about two hundred years old and he hoped it would be 'an object of interest to those rhododendron people who may visit the R.B.G. during the season' (1931).[27]

However, proof of the enormous size of these giant trees was not the only challenge to be met. By 1930 it was thought that there were intermediate forms between *Rhododendron giganteum* and another species, *R. protistum*.[28] Forrest wanted to sort this out. When he examined the leaves of the felled tree, he found three strikingly different forms on the single large tree. The hairiness of the underside of the leaf seemed to vary with leaf maturity. As this had been the main diagnostic feature separating the two species, he wrote:

> I finally proved one thing, that *Rhodos. giganteum* and *protistum* are one and the same species…So you'll have to cut out one name…I should like *giganteum* to stand, for…the name is most fitting! Don't you agree?[29]

The professor must have smiled, for they both knew that this was impossible as the code of nomenclature gives priority to the first name given to a plant or animal. However, in a more recent reassessment, Forrest would have been pleased to know that the name *giganteum* has been retained for a variety of *Rhododendron protistum*.[30]

Forrest's persistent questioning and turning to the facts mark him out as a scientific explorer. He had not been in 'that corner of the woods for fully 10 years'. He searched afresh for evidence, examined it carefully and, to the best of his ability and knowledge, drew his conclusions. He could not resist mentioning his personal preference, but he deferred to the experts in Edinburgh.

Hailed as a great acquisition, this handsome rhododendron can only be grown out of doors in a few favourable gardens on the west coast of Scotland and in Cornwall. In 1953 a First Class Certificate was awarded to Her Grace the Duchess of Montrose, Brodick, Isle of Arran, Scotland, for one that bore the Forrest number F. 19335. The wheel had turned full circle. The Scottish isle that probably inspired Forrest in his youth, and provided happy holidays for his family, now harboured a rhododendron whose giant size had gripped his memory and imagination.

An abundant harvest

News of other plant collectors in the region was sent to Forrest and in early April 1931 Wright Smith reported, 'I hear of Ward being at Fort Hertz [Upper Burma]'. Ward had not been in Yunnan since 1922 and he had become far more interested in the mountain ranges further west, in Burma, north India, the eastern Himalaya and southern Tibet. In contrast, a prime aim of Forrest now was to revisit the Lichiang Range of Yunnan to collect plenty of seeds for introduction or re-introduction to Britain.

Before Forrest had even set off for Lichiang, another collector, Joseph Rock, was also heading there. A talented and ambitious Austrian, who had been Professor of Botany and Chinese at the University of Hawaii, Rock had first entered Yunnan in 1922, by which time Forrest had a head start, being on his fifth expedition. Rock followed Forrest's example, staying in Snow Mountain Village and employing Nakhi collectors, and it is not surprising that Rock's biographer recounts that Forrest, Kingdon Ward and Rock were 'wary of one another' when they first met in 1922.[31] Rock's presence in Yunnan and even in the same village probably irked Forrest,[32] who found him a 'most unreliable person'.[33]

Between 1922 and 1931 Rock travelled widely in China, and in Yunnan he began his keen observations of the people and collected herbarium specimens, seeds, birds and mammals, making valuable collections of rhododendrons, of which thousands of seeds germinated. But, as the mountainous areas of Yunnan had already been worked by Forrest and Kingdon Ward, Rock discovered few new plants and he never caught up with Forrest's collections of birds, either in total number of specimens or number of species.

During 1928-9 Rock had spent the winter in Snow Mountain Village while Forrest was in Britain, and Forrest's return in 1931 prompted memories of their first meeting in 1922. Rock wrote in his diary on 18 February, 1931: 'Forrest and I sat

together then among the graves and lunched, this was ten years ago. Today I sat alone in peace and quiet…' He did not seem to want to meet Forrest again. When he heard that Forrest was coming, he wrote in his diary:

> Hochi told me that Forrest is coming and that a house has been rented for him in the upper part of the village. I really do not relish this intrusion and I shall move northwards to Yongning and Muli.[34]

Dodging an encounter with Forrest, Rock hurriedly departed.[35] We do not know Forrest's reaction to Rock's sudden exit, but they continued their expeditions apart.

Forrest mainly sent his men to collect seed while he concentrated on sorting and dispatching packages to Edinburgh. In turn, knowing Forrest's particular interest in primulas, Wright Smith sent him happy reports of their propagation: 'Your Primula seed has done particularly well and we have a fine braird of plants'. [Braird is a Scottish term for the first shoots to appear above ground.] He continued: 'I do not think that I have ever seen so many Primula plants as there are now at the back – not even in our best years".[36]

Wright Smith also hinted of demand for other plants like *Nomocharis* (Plate 149). An article in the *Journal of the RHS* was extolling their beauty and Stephenson Clarke and others wanted seed. So Wright Smith wrote tactfully to Forrest, 'I belicve seed of various species of that genus will please your subscribers more than anything else. Everyone seems keen to try it'.[37] And Forrest and his men did their best to oblige.

As encouragement, Wright Smith sent Forrest good news of his subscribers. In June he reported that Lord Headfort, in Ireland, had sent an extra £100 for Forrest's expedition, and the newly knighted Sir William Milner, of Parcevall Hall, Yorkshire, had secured a new gardener who was likely 'to do your plants well and he is looking forward to excellent results'.[38] By November, a delighted Milner confirmed his pleasure at 'the good germination' of practically everything he had received.[39]

The seeds kept coming from Yunnan and a ripple of pleasure spread through his sponsors. By mid-December Stephenson Clarke of Borde Hill reported, 'I have this afternoon received Forrest's 18th consignment of seeds, they are an interesting lot, I hope that I may have luck with them'.[40] On the last day of the year Clarke received six packets of seed in the twentieth sending of Forrest's packages. There was no doubting the hard work that was going on in Yunnan and the gardeners who sponsored him were kept very busy too.

The value of Forrest's seed was displayed in style in November at an Exhibition of Conifers held by the RHS in London. Lord Headfort won the gold medal for the finest exhibit in the show, the samples from his garden including the silver fir

Plates 151 and 152. A panorama of the eastern flank of the Lichiang Range (Yulong Shan), taken by Forrest on his fourth expedition, by pasting together two photographs. The huge scree on the right-hand peak can be seen from the Snow Mountain Village (see Plate 155).

Plate 153. *Osbeckia yunnanense*. Forrest introduced this flower to cultivation through seed sent in 1931. This specimen, raised from Forrest's seed, was sent for illustration in *Curtis's Botanical Magazine* (t.9588) by Lord Headfort.

Plate 154. The silver fir, *Abies forrestii*.

Plate 155. View of the Lichiang Range (Yulong Shan) from the gateway of Joseph Rock's former house in Snow Mountain Village. The same striking shape of a huge scree can also be picked out on Forrest's panorama of this range.

Abies forrestii F.6774 (Plate 154) and the spruce, *Picea likiangensis* F.6746, both grown from seed collected by Forrest twenty years earlier. The exhibition fortuitously aroused fresh interest in the new Chinese conifers just as Forrest and his men were providing more conifer seed. The momentum of expectancy was kept going and the range of Forrest's seeds was emphasised.

Meanwhile, letters of mutual reassurance and news went to and from Yunnan and Scotland. Forrest assured Clementina that everything was going well in spite of heavy rains and occasional earthquakes. Wright Smith told Forrest not to waste time writing to him, as he would rely on news coming via Clementina, and he gathered snippets from Forrest's middle son, Eric, who was a student in his botany class at the

University. Smith also sent news of auspicious visitors to the Garden, the King and Queen and Sir David Prain, the former Director of Kew. He kept Forrest up to date with peoples' promotions and deaths and sent him newspapers covering the elections. Above all, Smith confirmed to Forrest that he was in one of the best places in the world for collecting, as the Chinese-Tibetan region still seemed to be richer than the Rockies and he had not yet heard of a Chinese collector in Yunnan. Forrest seemed to be in the best place from every point of view.

The only possible regret expressed from Edinburgh was the long wait for the seeds to arrive by ship. Wright Smith had just had a visit from an acquaintance who was going by aeroplane to the Equator to explore Mt. Ruwenzori.

> On the last occasion he brought a few plants back in his aeroplane…This is a new way of doing things, but I guess it will be some time before Yunnan is treated similarly.

Forrest was one of the last British plant collectors in China before the era of air travel.

As the collections were brought in, Forrest became totally focused on sorting and packing them. It was an unremitting battle against time. He settled in Tengyueh for this huge task, which included animals as well as plants. The collection of birds and mammals for the Natural History Museum had been a sideline gently carried on through the year. As early as March 1931 he had reported that 'the bird business is going on all right. Already I have well on towards 200 skins and also a few mammals!'[41] There were still more birds and mammals to collect through the winter months, but Forrest dispatched his men to hunt while he carried on with the labelling and packing. Pressure always piled up at this stage of an expedition, but Forrest seemed to have everything in hand until the Commissioner of Customs warned him in early December that the regulations for the export of bird skins had been tightened up in recent years. Forrest would have to seek special permission to send the bird skins to Britain; the Consul in Tengyueh had been transferred to another post, so there was no one to write on Forrest's behalf.

However, Forrest was not a man to be defeated at the last hurdle. He wrote a courteous and informative request to His Excellency Sir M.W. Lampson, K.C.M.G., C.B., Envoy Extraordinary and Minister Plenipotentiary, British Legation, Peking. Forrest explained that he was accredited by the Foreign Office:

> …The object of this letter is to solicit Your Excellency's valued assistance in facilitating the export of the zoological collection I have made and hope to add to during the next three (winter) months. Would you kindly help me by arranging with the present Chinese authorities? All interested in the venture would be under the deepest obligation.
>
> My zoological collection consists of skins of small birds, with included, a small percentage of the smaller mammals.
>
> As I say, it has been made solely for the British Museum [Natural History] which's financing that part of my work and is of course purely scientific.
>
> The number of cases containing it will, I expect, be some 5 or 6, the number of skins from 1,500 to 2,000. The insured value, approximately £350 [£12,000 today]…[42]

Then Forrest left the wheels of officialdom to turn, while he sorted and packed more seeds. On Boxing Day, 1931, he wrote 'Chao and his men have done well this season, beyond my expectations'.[43] Seed packing would take him at least a week and he would have over 1,000 sheets of plants to write up and the birds and mammals. It was hard work but, when he realised that this was the largest haul that he and his men had ever made, an overwhelming sense of victory seized him. He wrote a triumphant letter to Edinburgh:

Of seed such an abundance, that I scarce know where to commence, nearly everything I wished for and that means a lot. Primulas in profusion, seed of some of them as much as 3-5 lb. [1.75kg], same with Meconopsis, Nomocharis, Lilium, as well as bulbs of the latter. When all are dealt with and packed I expect to have nearly if not more than two mule-loads of good clean seed, representing some 400-500 species, and a mule-load means 130-150 lb [60-70kg]. That is something like 300 lb.[136kg] of seed. If all goes well I shall have made a rather glorious and satisfactory finish to all my past years of labour.[44]

Forrest had fulfilled the task entrusted to him. He was in the final stage before returning home and looked forward to retirement with Clem in their lovely new home. He visited the new Consul and his wife when they arrived before Christmas, cheerfully discussed his plans, and they expressed the hope that Forrest might just have time to help them lay out their garden in the New Year.

The New Year began happily and on 4 January 1932 the Regius Keeper of the RBGE, Wright Smith, wrote an appreciative letter, having just received the latest package from Forrest that morning. He told Forrest that the *Meconopsis* expert at the British Museum, Mr George Taylor, happened to be at the RBGE and would immediately be examining Forrest's recent dried specimens of the poppy. The seeds of *Nomocharis* were giving subscribers particular pleasure, and seeds of the lilies *Lilium taliense* and *L. ochracea* were 'attracting much attention' (Plate 157). The letter ended with the message, 'All good luck for 1932. Kindest regards from everyone'.[45] But Forrest never received it. Within two days of it being posted, he was dead.

Plate 156. One of Forrest's family wrote on the back of this photograph: 'Charles likes this one of his Daddy with the pet monkey best. It is very like him: but makes him older-like, and not too good'.

Lilium taliense

S.R-C.

CHAPTER THIRTEEN

Death and Aftermath

The little foreign cemetery here is in a good position, out on the hillside
overlooking the Tengyueh plain and with a view of distant snow mountains.

Mrs A. Prideaux Brune (the Consul's wife) to Mrs George Forrest, 15 January 1932

The telegram to Professor Smith, RBGE, was brief and bleak:

Deeply regret Foreign Office
received Tengyueh telegram
stating Forrest died suddenly
heart failure fifth January.[1]

It was the second telegram saying that Forrest was dead. His death was reported in 1905, but that proved to be untrue; unfortunately, this time it was true. He actually died on the morning of 6 January 1932, while out shooting in the country about four miles (6km) from Tengyueh (Tengchong). He was buried next day.

The British Consul and his wife both wrote to Mrs Forrest, giving details of what had happened. The Consul assured her that Forrest's death was very quick:

Three of his Chinese employees were with him at the time …he suddenly felt faint and called to his men to assist him. Two of them, who were close by, supported him on the ground, but he did not speak again and he only lived for a minute or two after the moment when he called them.

We buried him…in the little foreign cemetery on the hillside just outside the city. His grave is next to that of Mr Litton, his old friend…A Swedish missionary clergyman – one of Mr Forrest's friends here – read our English burial service, and it was attended by the European community and Mr Forrest's Chinese friends and servants …The Chief of Police came to represent the Chinese officials. We put a Union Jack on the coffin, and besides the wreaths from us Europeans there was a small one of white roses from his Chinese house-servant which we put in a place of honour.

This servant was deeply distressed, and I can see that he is a nice man who was greatly attached to Mr Forrest…You will know that Mr Forrest's last time out here was spent among kind and friendly people.

We are placing a wooden cross on the grave, temporarily, and we have sent out to the hills for red rhododendrons (now at their best) to make a cross which we'll put on the grave tomorrow, from you…

Mr Forrest was liked and respected by everyone who knew him, Europeans and Chinese. His loss is felt acutely by our little community, and we send you our heartfelt sympathy. The value of his work is, of course, widely known, both here and at home; one feels that it was a work of most uncommon value, and that he was singularly happy and successful in his lifelong devotion to it.[2]

Opposite:
Plate 157. *Lilium taliense:* Forrest found this lily on several expeditions, including his last, whence seeds were raised in Colonel L.C.R. Messel's garden at Nymans, Sussex. This illustration is from a drawing by Miss S. Ross-Craig of Colonel Messel's rare flowers. (Groves' Supplement to Elwes' Monograph of Lilies, Plate 24 (1939)).

George Forrest's eldest son was a tea planter in India at the time. He described his experience of his father's death: his letters just stopped coming.[3] Clementina and her younger sons had been looking forward to Forrest's return. She quietly summed up her loss: 'We meant so much to each other'.

Among people giving her sympathy and support was the lily expert, Arthur Grove, who wrote, 'To me, there is something singularly appropriate in the fact that the great explorer should have gone to his end on the mountains he knew so well…'[4] In the following years, Grove's Supplement to Elwes' Monograph on lilies included illustrations of Forrest's gatherings (Plate 157).

Meanwhile, gloom hung over the RBGE. Forrest had worked with staff there for twenty-eight years. Before his final expedition, when living at 17 Inverleith Place, he would walk through the back gate of the Garden and ask propagators brightly at 9 am: 'What's germinated this morning?'[5] By 9.30 he would visit the wooden huts where rhododendrons were studied, discuss taxonomic problems and tell stories of his adventures in China.[6] Cheerful and inspiring, freelance yet one of them. It was hard to realise that he would not be coming back.

A wide range of obituaries paid tribute to Forrest, one in *Nature* stating, 'His dried material forms one of the great collections, worthy of comparison with that of any previous explorer in any country.'[7]

But what happened to Forrest's collections that were still in Tengyueh after his death?

The bird specimens were the largest problem. There were five wooden cases of dried bird skins awaiting shipment to the Natural History Museum, London, but permission for their export was refused by the Chinese Government on 8 January.[8] (This was part of the world-wide movement to reduce trade in 'feathered skins'.) The Museum then enlisted the help of the Under Secretary of State at the Foreign Office to arrange for the specimens to be exported.[9] Pleas were made that Forrest had been commissioned and paid by the Trustees of the Godman Exploration Fund to make this collection for the Museum, it was necessary to complete the scientific knowledge of the Museum, and, if kept in China during the rainy season, the specimens would be ruined. There was a request for an exception to the rules in the interest of science: if their export were not allowed, a great scientific loss and useless slaughter would have taken place.[10] On 23 March 1932 Chinese officials relented, 'to assist the English scientific world', and a member of the Chinese Customs Service escorted Forrest's cases to Bhamo, to the forwarding agent for Britain.

Ironically, in the same month, on Friday 11 March 1932, there was a shock heading in *The Times:* 'Loss to British Ornithology. Rothschild Collection Sold'. The newspaper reported: 'Ornithologists have learned with dismay that the wonderful collection of birds in the museum at Tring has been sold and is going to the United States'. It was hoped that Lord Rothschild's private collection of birds at Tring, including Forrest's birds, would eventually go the Natural History Museum, London, but 'economic conditions have interposed'.

Lord Rothschild had been blackmailed by a peeress and forced to sell most of his bird collection to the American Museum of Natural History. Forrest never knew, but many of the birds he had earlier collected for Lord Rothschild were packed in cotton wool and newspaper and shipped in crates to New York.[11]

Forrest's botanical collections of his final expedition had a more straightforward course. After Forrest's death, his Chinese assistants helped the Consul to complete the packing of twelve cases of specimens and seeds ready for despatch to the RBGE. On arrival, the seeds were to be divided and distributed among Forrest's subscribers. When the first tea chest was opened at the RBGE, hundreds of large white ants swarmed out, but otherwise the specimens were in beautiful condition.[12] The subscribers received their rightful share of seeds, and a few plants even flowered in Britain for the first time (Plate 157). Two things Forrest had prized highly, trust and good organisation, enabled his final expedition to be brought to a successful conclusion.

When Forrest died, he had been on the point of concluding an arrangement for his collectors to carry on working for the Hon. H.D. McLaren of Bodnant during 1932. McLaren's confirmation of their plans reached Tengyueh a few days too late, but the Consul wrote offering to give assistance, and happily this collecting continued as Forrest had arranged.

Plate 159. The grave of George Forrest. Behind is the grave of Consul Litton.

Plate 160. *Camellia reticulata* was first grown by J.C. Williams at Caerhays from seed collected by Forrest near Tengyueh (Tengchong), in 1924. In March 1932, after Forrest's death, he sent this flower, F.25352, for illustration in *Curtis's Botanical Magazine* (t.9397) where J.R. Sealy wrote, 'After more than a hundred years, the wild form of the species has at last been discovered and introduced into cultivation'.

Plate 161. *Camellia* x *williamsii* 'Donation', the best-selling camellia in Britain. This delicate pink flower was produced by Colonel Stephenson Clarke, at Borde Hill, Sussex, when he crossed a form of Forrest's *Camellia saluenensis* with *C. japonica*.

CHAPTER FOURTEEN

George Forrest – A Perspective

Perhaps Forrest has spoiled us as a Prince of Collectors
Prof. Bayley Balfour to J.C. Williams, 22 February, 1920

Although the title of this book is *George Forrest: Plant hunter*, it should be clear by now that Forrest was much more than this. He was a man of the open air, a keen observer who appreciated the wilds and had a curiosity about everything there. Forrest had a background of hobbies in the countryside, fishing in Scottish streams when no taller than his grandfather's walking stick. He knew the birds of Scotland and their habitats, from the largest falcon to the smallest finch. His sound Scottish education had given him a broad understanding of the natural sciences, and he grew up to be an all-rounder with an interest in geology, plants, snakes, mammals, butterflies, and birds. A job in the Herbarium of the Royal Botanic Garden Edinburgh led him to collect dried plant specimens and seeds in N.W. Yunnan, China, as his primary focus of work. But zoological collecting became part of his later expeditions, whilst observing the customs of the varied minority groups added to the interest and enjoyment of his travels.

Forrest inherited a strong and sturdy physique and as a young man he proved his toughness and endurance, as well as his love of adventure, by gold-digging and exploring in Australia. Difficulties were a challenge, risks added spice to life. So when a Liverpool cotton broker, A.K. Bulley, was seeking a young man to collect eastern seed of alpine and hardy plants for his new plant nursery, Bees Ltd, Forrest immediately took the opportunity. Bulley sent him by the shortest route to the high mountains of Yunnan, in S.W. China, where a French missionary, Père Delavay, had made rich pickings of new plants, but relatively few seeds.

Forrest's first expedition was a huge success, even though it nearly cost him his life. He discovered new species valuable to science and gardens, he introduced many others and longed to return for more. The beautiful mountains of Yunnan were to become like a second home. They often reminded him of Scottish moorland and he spent slightly more of his married life on expeditions there than he did in Scotland.

Forrest's career evolved step by step, through a series of short-term contracts. One sponsor gradually led to another, each with new interests and demands. Bulley had wanted seeds of alpine and hardy plants; Williams wanted more shrubby, woody plants, particularly rhododendrons and magnolias; Elwes' syndicate organised for Forrest's fourth expedition included Stephenson Clarke, who was interested in mammals and birds; Lord Rothschild particularly asked for birds from Forrest's sixth and seventh expeditions. Each time Forrest obliged his sponsors, stimulated and encouraged by their fresh enthusiasm. He was driven by his own ambition and scientific curiosity, and by his sponsors' acquisitiveness. Forrest was satisfying the general desire of the time for new species, plants and animals.

He was always willing to explore another set of ranges that he had not been to before, optimistic that he would find new species. One driving force was his theory of a 'centre of rhododendrons' where their greatest diversity would be found. This idea drove him further and further north-west into Tibet and northern Burma. It was an enormously exciting period for all those involved.

As Forrest's reputation among gardeners grew, so did Balfour's praise for his scientific achievements. In 1912, when Farrer and Kingdon Ward were relatively inexperienced as collectors, Balfour wrote, 'Forrest is unquestionably the finest collector of modern times'.[1] In 1914, when Forrest was collecting prolifically for J.C.Williams, Balfour was comparing Forrest favourably with previous well-known and revered collectors in China:

> Forrest should now recognise that his position as an explorer of the vegetation of Western China is established for all time on the plane of Henry, Fortune, Delavay, Wilson, to name the giants.

High praise indeed. Balfour had already substantiated his view, based on herbarium material:

> Forrest's collection is, like all his previous ones, magnificent. He is undoubtedly the prince of collectors. No one approaches him, alike for the excellence of the specimens, proper selection of forms, and notes upon habitat…[2]

In an obituary of Forrest in 1932, E.H.M. Cox wrote that 'Forrest was certainly the greatest plant collector of his generation'.[3]

So what enabled Forrest to achieve so markedly?

For one thing, Forrest had incredible determination. As Williams wrote to Balfour in 1919: 'Where Forrest serves us so well is in the iron way in which he battles to get the seed when most men would abandon the task as hopeless after the early snow has set in'.[4] Balfour agreed that Forrest had 'more grit than any of the other collectors''[5] – an assessment that bears out Balfour's initial recommendation of Forrest to Bulley in 1904. This opinion would later be confirmed by the fact that Forrest collected in China for almost twice as long as Wilson.

Forrest was no saint. He would not suffer fools gladly and could become unduly suspicious of others. His temper blew up when he felt affronted, let down or not trusted, and Elwes described him as 'difficult'. But, in 1919, J.C.Williams picked out Forrest's particular assets: 'Forrest has his faults like the rest of us, but as far as the work he undertakes to do, his capacity, his energy and his knowledge are what we shall hardly see again in any one'.[6] In support of his genuine admiration of Forrest's qualities as a collector, Williams invested in five of Forrest's expeditions, to a total of £354,000, in present day value. (See Appendix 3.) And in 1922 the dedication of *Curtis's Botanical Magazine* to Forrest mentioned the combination of 'energy, courage and sagacity' with which he explored the flora.[7]

The Protestant work ethic was a feature of Forrest's upbringing, and this meant that, whoever his sponsor was, Forrest always felt it his duty to do his best for those who hired his services. As a man he was highly principled and keen to be trusted to undertake the work that he had said he would do. He was entirely focused on his job and could at times be disparaging of other collectors who, in his eyes, did not measure up to his level of dedication. Kingdon Ward, for example, first went to Yunnan as a plant collector for Bulley, but he had a wide range of other interests, from mapping and journalism to scientific theories. Forrest could hardly believe that Kingdon Ward should spend so much time 'playing around with a theodolite' when Bulley had paid him to collect plants. Similarly, unlike Johnston, on their ill-fated pairing at the outset of Forrest's final expedition, it never entered Forrest's head to spend time socialising when there was work to be done.

Along with this single-mindedness, Forrest had very high standards and wanted all of his work to be as good as possible. This meant that he could be a hard task-master, both of himself and of his collectors, and his organisational skills enabled his prodigious productivity of high quality specimens, as shown in a 1918 letter from Balfour:

> When one looks at the collection as a whole one cannot but wonder at the industry of the man and at the meticulous care with which everything is arranged. Certainly there never was a collector who sent home finer dried specimens. Wilson's and Ward's are very poor in comparison. The very few which Farrer has sent home are undoubtedly beautifully dried but then he has dealt with tens – Forrest has dealt with thousands…[8]

Balfour mused: 'Forrest has really spoilt us for the gatherings of every other collector…'[9]

Forrest's superb organisation was reflected in his planning. Before an expedition he drew up detailed lists of purchases needed in Britain and Burma (see Appendix 4) and when in Yunnan he arranged the shipment of his collections and their passage through customs. In the field he maintained overall responsibility for the life of his group: from camping to the medical care and feeding of animals and men, and the recording, drying and packing of specimens and seeds. Nothing was left to chance, yet if social unrest interrupted his plans, he adapted quickly and made new arrangements.

Forrest did not, however, attempt to do everything by himself. He had a natural ability to form bonds with people. He was open and companionable, and made friends with a wide range of people, the staff of the RBGE, gentlemen landowners, ships' captains, consuls, customs officials, missionaries and his own collectors. Wherever he went he built up a network of contacts which helped him to maintain some continuity between expeditions.

He appreciated the value of properly trained collectors. He learned the language sufficiently to train them until they were able to go with a trusted headman on mini-expeditions without him. Groups would go ahead into different mountain ranges, exploring new areas and collecting specimens of plants and animals. Each of his expeditions therefore covered a much larger territory than one man alone could possibly have done. The consequent size of harvest could lead to pressure of time to label all the specimens, leaving some to be completed on his return to Britain.

Forrest enjoyed a great rapport with his men and appreciated their comradeship. In fact, he got on so well with his Nakhi collectors that on his third expedition he lived in their village. He learnt from them about their customs, the mountain ranges, and the local wildlife, building up a good two-way relationship.

Loyalty was a big feature of Forrest's life. There was his personal loyalty to his wife, even though he was away from home for such long periods, and the trust and loyalty of his wife for him. There was his loyalty to the RBGE, to which he always wanted his plant specimens and some of his seeds to go; and the tremendous loyalty that he inspired in the local people that he employed in Yunnan. A core of Forrest's collectors worked with him on every expedition. They would sometimes travel hundreds of miles to welcome him back when he returned on his next expedition.

The bond between Forrest and his well-trained men was exemplified by the fact that between his fifth and sixth expeditions they continued collecting without Forrest even being in the country. With this experience, Forrest later organised a seed collection in Yunnan for a McLaren syndicate in Britain, whilst he underwent an eye operation in Scotland – an amazing and unprecedented situation.

If the case can be made that Forrest was 'a Prince of Collectors', it is perhaps puzzling that he is not as well known as Farrer and Kingdon Ward. One explanation is that part of the reputation of these two men springs from their writings. They were both gifted with words and conveyed the excitement and the romance of plant hunting to a wide home audience at a time when there was no competition to books from radio or television. Both Farrer and Kingdon Ward were self-publicists: Farrer wrote books that became garden classics, whilst Kingdon Ward captured the imagination of readers with the titles of his books – *The romance of plant hunting*, *The riddle of the Tsangpo gorges*, *Plant hunting on the edge of the world*. Wilson also wrote a book on his travels. Forrest, of course, did not write a book; he concentrated on his fieldwork and on writing up his collections. Forrest did write thousands of letters, which caused some to hope that he would turn his hand to a more substantial piece of writing. Balfour, for instance, wrote to Williams:

> I hope when Forrest comes home you will be able to persuade him to write an account of his journeyings. He began, but did not complete the story of his first trip. He has an easy pen – more graphic than that of Wilson – not ultra exuberant as in that of Farrer, and his great knowledge and experience would give his book qualities that are wanting in Ward's daring immature effort.[10] Taken when he is hot from the field, and before details of his collections accumulate to overweight him, he could produce a really good book.[11]

Even in retirement it is doubtful that Forrest would have written up his travels. He did not take easily to writing, except for letters, and if asked he would probably have continued to maintain, 'Like the man who hadn't changed his shirt for 2 years, I have so much else to think of!'[12] He liked to be busy, sociable, always on the move. His field observations were valuable to taxonomists. He took enormous pleasure from visiting keen gardeners to see his garden introductions and to advise on the conditions in which the plants might best thrive. He was a popular lecturer. And, just before his last expedition, he and Clem had bought an elegant detached mansion with a large garden awaiting attention.

Forrest is renowned for introducing some outstanding garden plants, from tall conifers *(Abies forrestii)* and small flowering trees *(Sorbus forrestii)* to the springtime delight of bushes *of Pieris formosa forrestii* and the bright blue flowers of the autumn gentian, *Gentiana sino-ornata*. His camellias, candelabra primulas and range of rhododendrons have been long accepted as part of our garden heritage and hybridisers have used his species to produce beautiful and useful new cultivars. What is less well known is the scientific importance today of his dried plant and animal collections that are used internationally for taxonomic studies, whilst his living, botanical, collections in botanic gardens provide more information for research, education and conservation. Some of Forrest's rhododendrons in the RBGE are being propagated and repatriated to Yunnan for use in the conservation of plant diversity on the Yulong Shan, the magnificent mountain range whose grandeur he admired, and whose wealth of plants and animals amazed him. Its slopes, near Lijiang, now support a field station, a new botanic garden and a nature reserve, easily reached by plane.[13]

The fascination of Forrest's life today is partly that it reflects a completely different era. From China he depended for communication on the telegraph and postal links of the British Empire, when the quickest way to travel to and from Britain was by a combination of steamship, paddle steamer, rail and mules. Only those with a pioneering spirit or a sense of mission undertook such journeys.

Whilst writing this book I have been struck by the number of people who have said that George Forrest is one of their heroes. Plant enthusiasts who visit Yunnan today speak with pleasure of walking in his footsteps. It is not only Forrest's achievements that evoke admiration. His capacity to excite and thrill us by his zest and determination, his spirit of adventure and sheer guts, is a personal legacy that we can all share.

George Forrest in His Own Words

The beauty of the country

In the morning – the sun as it touches the tops of the Mekong divide, sends shafts of turquoise light down the side gullies to the river which seems to be transformed to silver.

From Forrest's address to the Royal
Geographical Society, 1908

Next morning we were off very early, in moonlight…, and reached the summit [of the dividing range of the Yangtze and Mekong basins] after a tremendous climb of about 3 hours … the view from the top is entirely beyond my powers of description. The morning was wonderfully clear and we could see for hundreds of miles on all sides. Nothing but range after range of tremendous mountains, many of the peaks covered with eternal snow, and all glistening in the early morning sunlight like gems, lay before our eyes. Add to this billows of vapour rolling about in ceaseless movement in all the valleys and, above all, the intense stillness there was at this elevation, not even the rustle of a leaf, or blade of grass and you can perhaps have a faint idea of what the scene was like. I cannot tell you what my feelings were as I sat and gazed at it all. One feels in a place such as that that one is nearer something, call it by any name you like. I could have sat and dreamed all day, but time and tide wait for no man, and neither did Litton on me.

Undated 1st expedition letter from
Forrest to Clementina

Autumn on the Yulong Shan

Even in the green summer coating those [Sorbus] trees are a delight to the eyes, but after the arrival of the first frosts simply magnificent. The foliage then becomes the deepest richest crimson scarlet, and each individual tree stands out like a glowing torch on the hillsides, visible for miles…

Some of the patches of mixed forest I saw were marvels of beautiful colouring and I long for the power to photograph or otherwise record them; the pure golds of the birches, the silvery yellows of the poplars, the ruddy browns of oaks, and the yellows and reds of acers, backed and mixed with the black green of Abies and the lighter shades of Picea and larch make a picture beyond the power of any to describe. And behind and above all the bare limestone crags powdered with glistening snow and outlined against the deepest sapphire blue. It was grand! I got a few fairly decent photos of the scenery, but they express little of the grandeur as seen with the naked eye.

Forrest to J.C. Williams 9 November 1913

Cold

Eventually we gained the summit… after fully 8 hours' stiff climbing. This was… covered with snow from 12 inches to 4-5ft [30.5cm to 1.22-1.5m] in depth. A bitterly cold wind blowing from the N.W. didn't make it any pleasanter… I have experienced 40° [of frost], 8° below zero [Fahrenheit] in my time and that was nothing to it…The animals and we ourselves were so done up that I found it absolutely [essential] to camp…I got my tent pitched on about 14 inches [35.5cm] of snow … I never spent a more miserable night in all my life. I went to bed, of course, with all on bar my boots and in spite of this and a big heavy pugi or quilt,… I was half dead before daybreak. The whole interior of the tent was white, also everything in it, my hair, pugi, blankets, etc., all covered with frozen moisture from my breath and I rose in the morning for all the world like a Father Christmas. I had a bottle of water and my sparklet bottle … and these were both split … Felt much better after I had swallowed a pint of hot chocolate. Had breakfast then got dressed for the weather and started to do a little collecting. It was indeed a <u>little</u>, as everything was buried in snow…

Undated 1st expedition letter from
Forrest to Clementina

Wind

This bitter wind from the N.W. blowing over the snow-clad Tibetan mountains was a curse to us all the time we were on the plateau. It made every one of us as crabbed as the very deuce, and before a couple of days had passed I fear very much if you would have recognized me. My hands, face and lips were so severely chapped that every movement was torture to me and as for laughing, that was out of the question, even supposing there had been anything to laugh at.

Undated 1st expedition letter from
Forrest to Clementina

Danger

I spent two of the hardest and most dangerous months of my life there, a time I shall never forget. Roads of no kind; deep jungle-choked and panther-haunted gorges, bounded by break-neck precipices and dense forests at the lower altitudes, crane-brakes [?] and boulder-strewn, marshy moorlands with snow drifts and eternal mists at the higher, above all a chaos of screes, ragged peaks and glaciers with, however, flowers dominant everywhere! A place to visit once and have as a memory always.

Forrest to R. Cory 7 Sept 1921

Insects

Animal and bird life along the Upper Salwin is conspicuous by its absence – an important matter for the traveller, who cannot count on replenishing his larder with game. On the other hand, the river-banks at a low altitude, and where wholly sheltered from the north winds, have an almost tropical climate, and vegetable and insect life is both vigorous and troublesome. Creatures with inconveniently long legs plunge suddenly into one's soup; great caterpillars in splendid but poisonous uniforms of long and gaily coloured hairs arrive in one's blankets with the business-like air of a guest who means to stay. Ladybirds and other specimens of Coleoptera drop off the jungle down one's neck, whilst other undesirables insert themselves under one's nether garments. The light in the tent attracts a perfect army of creatures which creep, buzz, fly, crawl and sting.

pp.245-246 of G. Forrest, 'Journey on Upper Salwin',
October – December 1905, The Geographical Journal, *32 (1908) 239-266.*

His first wolf

Just about dusk I shot my first wolf. It was coming down the moraine quite boldly, probably after the horses, but when it saw it was detected slunk off in a cross-direction. I bolted after it but even the appearance of my chasing it did not make it hurry. Got my first shot in about 250 yds [230m], a clear miss, as likewise was the second, as the animal was going hard then. However, after running to a good distance, perhaps 7 to 800 yds [685m], something in front seemed to startle it, and it stood broadside on for a few seconds. This was my opportunity and I got in my third shot. It was a mere chance as my Winchester rifle is only sighted up to 300 yds [275m], but I did as I used to do in Australia when kangaroo shooting, cast up above the object to what I reckoned was the elevation, and I found I had not entirely lost my skill as I got it clean through the back part of the skull. It dropped stone dead of course.

Undated 1st expedition letter from Forrest to Clementina

Separation

Hoping to hear from you next week with all the love I am capable of and heaps of hugs and kisses from your own loving boy,

George.

My own sweet Clem. When will I have you in my arms again dear?

Undated 1st expedition letter from
Forrest to Clementina

Chinese and Burmese Place Names

The spelling of Chinese place names has often varied, but since the time of Forrest the official system for transcription has completely changed. In the text of this book the names are those used at the time. The following lists show the names currently accepted.

Names used at the time of Forrest   **Names used today**   **Names used at the time of Forrest**   **Names used today**

PROVINCES AND REGIONS

Szechuan . . . . .Sichuan
Tibet . . . . .Xizang
Tsarong . . . . .Tsarong
Yunnan . . . . .Yunnan

TOWNS AND HAMLETS

Atuntse, Atuntsi, ...Dechen, Deqen,
Atuntze, Atuntzu . . . . .Deqin, Dequn
Bhamo . . . . .Bhamo
Chengtu . . . . .Chengdu
Chung-tien . . . . .Zhongdian
Fengkou . . . . .Fengke
Hpimaw . . . . .Pianma
Lhasa . . . . .Lhasa
Lichiang, Likiang . . . . .Lijiang
Litiping . . . . .Litiping
Mengtze, Mengsi . . . . .Mengzi
Muli . . . . .Muli
Myitkyina . . . . .Myitkyina
Ningpo . . . . .Ningbo
Putao . . . . .Putao
Szemao . . . . .Simao
Tachien-lu, Tatsien-lu . . . . .Kangding
Tali, Talifu . . . . .Dali
Tengyueh . . . . .Tengchong
Tsekou . . . . .Chigu
Weihsi . . . . .Weixi
Yungning . . . . .Yongning
Yunnan-fu .Kunming

RIVERS AND LAKES

Lake Tali . . . . .Er Hai
Litang . . . . .Litang Qu
Mekong . . . . .Lancang Jiang
N'Mai Kha .N'Mai Kha
Salween, Salwin . . . . .Nu Jiang
Shweli . . . . .Longchuan Jiang
Taping .Daying Jiang
Yang-pi .Yangbi Jiang
Yangtze (upper) . . . . .Jinsha Jiang
Yangtze (lower) . . . . .Chang Jiang

MOUNTAINS AND PASSES

Beima Shan . . . . .Beima Shan
Chimili (Chimili Alps) . . . . . .(just north of Pianma)
Chungtien plateau . . . . .Zhongdian
Doker La . . . . .Doker La
Kari pass . . . .(near Fugong)
Lichiang Range . . . . .Yulong Shan
Litiping . . . . .Litiping (plateau east of Weixi)
Mount Omei . . . . .Emei Shan
Sung Kwei pass . . . . .Songgui
Tali Range .Cang Shan

George Forrest (1873-1932) – A Chronology

1873 13 Mar. Birth of George Forrest at Falkirk, Scotland

1885 Moves with his parents and sisters to join his elder brother, James, in Kilmarnock.
Attends Kilmarnock Academy until 1891.

1889 14 Sept. George Forrest's father dies.

1891 Starts work at Rankin & Borland's pharmaceutical shop in Kilmarnock.

1898 Inherits legacy and goes to Australia.

1903 21 June. Hon. John Abercromby writes to Prof. I. Bayley Balfour, Regius Keeper, RBGE, on behalf of Forrest.
7 Sept. Forrest starts work in the Herbarium of the RBGE.

1904 Apr. Arthur K. Bulley of Ness engages Forrest to collect seeds of alpine and hardy plants in N.W. Yunnan for Bees' nursery.
May. Sets sail aboard S.S. *Australia* on his 1st expedition to Yunnan.
Sept. Reaches China Inland Mission (CIM) at Tali (Dali), N.W. Yunnan.
Sept. to Nov. A 'preliminary canter' with Consul Litton to the Mekong valley.

1905 21 Jul. Lamas sack French Catholic Mission at Tsekou in the Mekong valley. Forrest flees with missionaries, who are later murdered.
17 Aug. Foreign Office telegram reports Forrest murdered on 21 July.
19 Aug. A further telegram reports that Forrest is alive and safe.
Oct.-Dec. Exploration of the Upper Salween with Consul Litton.

1906 10 Jan. (approx.). Death of Consul Litton.

1907 Apr. Forrest returns to Scotland and works in the Herbarium of the RBGE.
15 Jul. Marriage of George Forrest and Clementina Traill at Rosslyn Chapel.

1908 14 Aug. Resigns from the RBGE.
5 Sept. Meets Charles Sargent, Director of the Arnold Arboretum, USA at Veitch's Nursery, Chelsea to discuss collecting plants in N. China.
Nov. Forrest declines Sargent's offer.

1909 26 Mar. Birth of George Forrest's eldest son, George (jnr).

1910 2 Jan. George Forrest's mother dies.
Jan. Funded by Bees' nursery, Forrest sails aboard S.S. *Irrawaddy* on his 2nd expedition to Yunnan, his last expedition for a nurseryman.

1911 21/23 Jan. Departs from Rangoon on S.S. *Amarapoora*.

1912 7 Jan. Birth of George Forrest's second son, John Eric.
Feb. (or late Jan.). Funded by

J.C. Williams of Caerhays Castle, Cornwall, Forrest boards S.S. *Martaban* for his 3rd expedition to Yunnan.

1913 Clementina and sons move from Glenkevock House, Lasswade to Loaningdale, Peebles while Forrest in Yunnan.

1915 Jan./Feb. Departs from Rangoon on S.S. *Tenasserim*.
20 Jul. Lectures to the RHS.

1915 Nov. Family moves from Loaningdale, Peebles to Broomhill House, Lasswade.

1917 11 Jan. Funded by a syndicate of seven gentlemen and the RHS, Forrest departs aboard S.S. *Chindwin* on his 4th expedition to Yunnan. His contract includes making zoological collections.
8 Jul. Birth of GF's third son, Charles, at Broomhill House.

1918 11 Aug. Plants lost when the *City of Adelaide,* bound for Liverpool from Rangoon, is sunk by enemy submarine in the Mediterranean.

1920 6 Feb. Forrest boards S.S. *Sittang* bound for home
June. Elected Hon. Member of the Rhododendron Society.
16th Nov. Lectures to the Rhododendron Society.
30 Nov. Council of the RHS votes to award Forrest the Victoria Medal of Honour (VMH).
13 Dec. Notified that the Massachusetts Horticultural Society awards him the George Robert White Medal of Honour for eminent service to Horticulture.

1921 20/21 Jan. Funded by J.C. Williams and R. Cory, Forrest sets off on S.S. *Bhamo* on his 5th expedition to Yunnan.

1922 Volume 148 of *Curtis's Botanical Magazine* is dedicated to Forrest.
30 Nov. Death of Professor I. Bayley Balfour.

1923 Mar. Returns to Britain.
Nov. Lectures to the Rhododendron Society.
20 Dec. Lectures to the Botanical Society of Edinburgh.

1924 Jan. Funded by J.C. Williams, R. Cory and Lord Rothschild, Forrest sails from Britain on his 6th expedition to Yunnan.
Clementina and sons move from Broomhill House, Lasswade to 17, Inverleith Place, Edinburgh.
19 June. Forrest elected Fellow of the Linnean Society.
Volume 88 of *The Garden* is dedicated to Forrest.

1925 21 Nov. Death of George Forrest's elder brother, James.

1926 Mar. Returns to Britain.

1927 July. Council elects Forrest as Hon. Life Member of the new Rhododendron Association.
20 Oct. Elected an Associate of the Botanical Society, Edinburgh.
RHS awards Forrest the Veitch Memorial Medal.

1928 13 Jan. Lectures under the auspices of the Botanical Society of Edinburgh.
16 Feb. Mrs George Forrest elected 'Ordinary Fellow' and their two elder sons, George jnr. and John Eric, elected as 'Ordinary Members' of the Botanical Society of Edinburgh.
3 Mar. Lectures to the Kirkcaldy Naturalists' Society.
13 Mar. Lectures under the auspices of the Botanical Society of Edinburgh.
7 June. Discusses with Hon. H.D. McLaren and Maj. F.C. Stern the use of his collectors to send seed from Yunnan, whilst Forrest stays in Britain.
June. Has eye operation.
23 Aug. Death of George Forrest's sister, Isabella.
15 Nov. Lectures under the auspices of the Botanical Society of Edinburgh.

1929 Autumn. Forrest's collectors gather seed in Yunnan for Hon. H.D. McLaren.
October, RHS awards Forrest the Loder Rhododendron Cup for his introduction of new and rare species of Rhododendrons.
24 Oct. Lectures under auspices of the Botanical Society of Edinburgh.

1929-30 Prof. W.W. Smith organises subscriptions for Forrest's 7th and final expedition.

1930 31 Jan. Lectures under auspices of the Botanical Society of Edinburgh.
1 Feb. Purchase of Bellfield, Eskbank, Midlothian. Forrest family move from 17, Inverleith Place, Edinburgh.
25 May. Forrest visits Ireland.
19-21 Aug. Forrest visits Bodnant.
Nov. Funded by a syndicate of thirty-nine sponsors, Forrest sails with Maj. Lawrence Johnston of Hidcote Manor, Gloucestershire, to Rangoon.

1931 Mar. Major Johnston returns early.

1932 6 Jan. Dies suddenly near Tengyueh (Tengchong), Yunnan.

APPENDIX 3

The known sponsors of George Forrest

Contemporary documentary evidence shows that the following people and institutions sponsored Forrest on expeditions to Yunnan. For expeditions three to six written contracts exist and for the seventh expedition we have what appears to be a complete list of subscribers in Forrest's own hand.[1] Many who subscribed for Forrest's seeds shared some with their friends and later shared cuttings of the plants, so having a plant with a Forrest number is no proof of having been a subscriber. Where a sponsor had more than one garden, only one is listed below. Forrest's annual salary and the total cost of each expedition are given, if known.

Forrest's 1st Expedition (1904–07)

A.K. Bulley's nursery, Bees Ltd   Ness, Neston, Cheshire

Forrest's 2nd Expedition (1910–11)

A.K. Bulley's nursery, Bees Ltd   Ness, Neston, Cheshire
Bulley was the original sponsor on behalf of Bees Ltd, but J.C. Williams paid Bees for rhododendron and conifer seed. Forrest's annual salary was £200 and Bees' total expenditure was £933.9s.4d.[2]

Forrest's 3rd Expedition (1912–15)

J.C. Williams   Caerhays Castle, Cornwall
Forrest's salary was £500 per annum. He was also given a travelling allowance of £400 per annum, passage monies of £50 each way, and itemised initial expenses of £166.9s.6d. (in Britain) and £142.4s.0d. (in Rangoon). The total cost of the three-year expedition was £3,108.13s.6d.

Forrest's 4th Expedition (1917–20)

Sponsors listed on the original contract[3] are as follows. They are listed in order of the amounts they contributed.

7 parts	J.C. Williams	Caerhays Castle, Cornwall
5	The Royal Horticultural Society	Wisley, Surrey
3	R. Cory	Duffryn, Cardiff
2	Duke of Bedford	Woburn Abbey, Bedfordshire
2	Sir J.T.D.-Llewellyn	Penllergaer, Swansea
2	Col. Stephenson R. Clarke	Borde Hill, Haywards Heath, Sussex
2	H.J. Elwes	Colesborne, Gloucestershire
1	G.W.E. Loder	Wakehurst Place, Ardingly, Sussex

One part comprised £20.16s.8d. for initial expenses and an annual payment of £50. Four additional sponsors appear on a later list.[4] They joined later, when the expedition was continued into 1919. Their individual contributions are not given.

Lord Barrymore	Fota, Carrigtwohill, Co. Cork, Ireland
A.K. Bulley	Ness, Neston, Cheshire
C.C. Eley	East Bergholt Place, East Bergholt, Suffolk
M.Yorke[5]	

Forrest was paid an initial expenditure allowance of £500, a salary of £500 per annum and travelling expenses overseas of £700 per annum. The total cost of the three-year expedition was £4,100.

Forrest's 5th Expedition (1921–23)

Sponsors listed on a contract[6] are:

R. Cory   Duffryn, Cardiff
J.C. Williams   Caerhays Castle, Cornwall

They contributed equal amounts, paying Forrest an initial expenditure allowance of £800, a salary of £1,000 per annum and an expenditure allowance of £1,400 per annum. This two-year expedition cost them a total of £5,600.

Col. Stephenson R. Clarke seems to have sponsored Forrest to collect birds, for Forrest wrote to him in 1921 asking him to send him some new guns.[7]

Forrest's 6th Expedition (1924–26)

Two contracts for this expedition have survived.[8] The first lists two sponsors:

R. Cory   Duffryn, Cardiff
J.C. Williams   Caerhays Castle, Cornwall

As for the 5th expedition, they paid Forrest an initial expenditure allowance of £800, a salary of £1,000 per annum and an expenditure allowance of £1,400 per annum. In addition there was an allowance for an assistant of £500 per annum. This two-year expedition cost them a total of £6,600.

In the second contract, Lord W. Rothschild of Tring, Hertfordshire agreed to pay Forrest a salary of £375 per annum 'to collect zoologically for a period of two years'.

The total cost to Rothschild was £750.

The McLaren syndicate helped by George Forrest (1929)

The sponsors were:[9]

2 shares	=	£100	Hon. H.D. McLaren	Bodnant, Tal-y-Cafn, N. Wales
1 share	=	50	Hon. R. James	St. Nicholas, Richmond, Yorkshire
1 "	=	50	L. de Rothschild	Exbury House, Exbury, Hampshire
1 "	=	50	Sir F.C. Stern	Highdown, Goring-on-Sea, Sussex
Total		£250		

The RBGE received one share of seed gratis. Forrest was paid £50 for his services and a gratuity of £40.10s.0d., the amount left over after all expenses had been paid.

Forrest's 7th Expedition (1930–32)

Sponsors for seeds are listed in the order of their contributions:

£500:
The Royal Horticultural Society   Wisley, Surrey
Crosfield, J.J.   Embley Park, Romsey, Hampshire
Johnston, Major L.W.   Hidcote Manor, Campden, Gloucestershire
Rothschild, L. de   Exbury House, Exbury, Hampshire
£250:
Cory, R.   (for RBGE)   Duffryn, Cardiff
£200:
Williams, J.C.   Caerhays Castle, Cornwall
£125
Rothschild, L. de (for RBG Kew)   Exbury House, Exbury, Hampshire
Bulley, A.K.   Ness, Neston, Cheshire
Clarke, Col. Stephenson R.   Borde Hill, Haywards Heath, Sussex
McDouall, K.   Logan, Port Logan, Wigtownshire, Scotland
McLaren, Hon. H.D.   Bodnant, Tal-y-Cafn, N. Wales
Messel, Leonard C.R.   Nymans, Handcross, Haywards Heath, Sussex
Milner, Sir William   Parcevall Hall, Skipton, Yorkshire
Stevenson, J.B.   Tower Court, Ascot, Berkshire
Swaythling, Lord S.A.S.M.   Townhill Park, West End, Southampton, Hampshire
£100:
Bentley, W.   48, Rickmansworth Road, Watford, Hertfordshire
Berry, Mrs. A.C.U.   Portland, Oregon, U.S.A.
Cooke, R.B.   Kilbryde, Corbridge, Northumberland

Headfort, Marquess of	Headfort, Kells, Co. Meath, Ireland
Heneage-Vivian, Admiral A.W.	Clyne Castle, Blackspill, Swansea, Wales
Horlick, Lt.-Col. J.N.	Achamore, Isle of Gigha, Scotland
Johnstone, G.H.	Trewithen, Probus, Cornwall
Kent, Sir S.H.	Chapelwood Manor, Nutley, Sussex
Leconfield, Lady	Petworth House, Petworth, Sussex
Loder, Gerald, W.E.	Wakehurst Place, Ardingly, Sussex
MacEwen, Brig.-Gen. D.L.	Corsock, Dalbeattie, Kirkcudbrightshire, Scotland
Ramsden, Sir J.F.	Muncaster Castle, Ravenglass, Cumbria
Sandeman, F.D.S.	The Laws, Kingennie, Angus, Scotland
Straker, Mrs.	Stagshaw House, Corbridge, Northumberland
Younger, H.G	Kittoes, Bishopsteignton, Teignmouth, Devon

£62 10s:
| James, Hon. R. | St. Nicholas, Richmond, Yorkshire |
| Morley, Earl of | Saltram, Plympton, Devon |

£50:
Cox E.H.M.	Glendoick, Perthshire, Scotland
Renton, J.F.	Branklyn, Perth, Scotland
Guiseppe, Dr J.P.L.	Trevose, Felixstowe, Suffolk
Londonderry, Marchioness of	Mount Stewart, Newtownards, Co.Down, N.Ireland

£25:
Balfour, FRS	Dawyck, Stobo, Peeblesshire, Scotland
Stirling-Maxwell, Sir J.	Pollok House, Pollockshaws, Glasgow, Scotland
Stanley, Lady Beatrix	Sibbertoft Manor, Market Harborough, Leicestershire

In addition, Lord Walter Rothschild of Tring, Hertfordshire, subscribed £500 for birds and mammals to be collected for the British Museum (now the Natural History Museum), London. Counting Lionel de Rothschild once (he paid for himself and for Kew), Forrest had thirty-nine sponsors for this expedition.

Summary

During his career Forrest had forty-six different sponsors, of whom thirty-six only sponsored a single expedition. The total present-day (November 2003) value of sponsorship was £1,020,000, of which 85% was provided by his seven largest sponsors, with nearly three-quarters of the total being provided by just three men – J.C. Williams (36%), Arthur Bulley (19%) and Reginald Cory (18%).

The top seven sponsors of George Forrest by number of expeditions supported and total present-day value of sponsorship

J.C. Williams	5 expeditions	£364,000
Arthur K. Bulley	4	190,000
Reginald Cory	4	186,000
Royal Horticultural Society	2	40,000
Lord Walter Rothschild	2	39,000
Lionel de Rothschild	2	23,000
Col. Stephenson R. Clarke	3	18,000
Total:		£860,000

Notes:

1. Wherever possible, calculations are based on known written contracts and on data supplied by the Bank of England on the value of £1 sterling from year to year. Bulley's contributions to the first expedition and to the last part of the fourth have been estimated, as has Stephenson Clarke's contribution to the fifth.

2. Qualification: Sponsored two or more expeditions with a total contribution having a present-day value of at least £10,000.

3. The money given by Lord Rothschild was purely for zoological collecting.

4. Lionel de Rothschild sponsored Forrest on his final expedition and for the collection for the McLaren syndicate of 1929.

With thanks to Robin McLean

APPENDIX 4

Supplies for the Third Expedition (1912–15)

(as written in longhand by George Forrest)

List of necessary items for expedition which had best be procured here [Britain]: also other expenses

	£	s	d
Passage to Rangoon from Liverpool, train fare to Liverpool, insurance of luggage, porterage, etc:	50	0	0
Medicine chest £7 10s approx.	8	0	0
Automatic repeating fowling piece, 5 shot, 12 bore, full choke.	12	12	0
Double barrel fowling piece, 12 bore, right cylinder, left choke.	15	0	0
Winchester repeating carbine, 12 shot. (40-41)	5	5	0
Colt repeating pistol ·45.	6	6	0
Sundries, and cartridges for testing same.	3	10	0
Two axes.		12	0
Carborundum sharpening stone.		2	0
Camp bed x pattern.	1	15	0
Pillow for same.		5	0
Camp table and chair x pattern.	1	10	0
Rubber bath.	1	15	0
Oilskin coat and sou'wester.	1	15	0
Palm and needles for leather work.		5	0
Field note books, stationery etc.	1	10	0
Sheath knives.		7	6
Leather cases for mule travel. approx.	6	0	0
Boots, special clothing etc.	25	0	0
A sufficient supply of stout linen-lined envelopes for forwarding seeds, address (to be given later) printed, also a number of smaller stout paper envelopes for the seeds themselves, price indefinite?	?	?	?
Also 3-5,000 labels plus price of envelopes.			
	£141	9	6

	£	s	d
Ruby Reflex camera for hand work, also wide angle lens.	15	15	0
Plates.	3	0	0
Cans for same, approx.		1	0
P.O.P [?]	1	10	0
Chemicals etc., approx.		2	0
Seed envelopes, printing.	1	15	0
	£166	9	6

Articles best bought in Rangoon

	£	s	d
Two Willesden canvas tents @ Rps 400.	20	0	0
Ammunition.	10	0	0
Mosquito curtain for camp bed.	1	0	0
Water Bottle.		10	0
Spare drugs, lancets, etc., approx.	3	0	0
Hotel expenses in Rangoon for 7 days.	7	0	0
Fare to Bhamo, cooly and cart hire & extras.	10	0	0
Stores to be bought at Bhamo and Rangoon.	80	0	0
	£131	10	0
Saddle and bridle.	3	10	0
	135	0	0
Additional £6 14s for [?]	6	14	0
Saddle and bridle.		10	0
	£142	4	0

	£	s	d
Stores Rangoon.	131	10	0
England.	141	9	6
Salary, allowance, etc.	2,750	0	0
	£3,022	19	6

Publications by George Forrest

★Each of these items largely comprises notes of GF and one of his full-page illustrations. The material is credited to him in the text, but his name does not appear at the foot of the note.

G.C. = *The Gardeners' Chronicle*

1905	6 Nov. Lama disturbances in North-west Yunnan: Destruction of a French Mission. A Scotsman's personal narrative, *The Scotsman*.
1907	Gentianaceae from eastern Tibet and south-west China, *Notes R.B.G. Edinburgh* **4**: 69-81.
1908	Primulaceae from western Yunnan and eastern Tibet, *Notes R.B.G. Edinburgh* **4**: 213-239.
1908	Journey on the Upper Salwin, October-December 1905, *The Geographical J.* **32**: 239-266.
★1909	20 Nov. Chinese primulas [*Primula listera, Primula vincaeflora* and *Primula poissonii*], *G.C.* **46**: 344-345.
1909	18 Dec. *Cypripedium tibeticum* and *C. margaritaceum*, *G.C.* **46**: 419.
1910	The land of the crossbow, *National Geographic Magazine*, **21**: 132-156.
1910	1 Jan. *Lycoris aurea, G.C.* **47**:12.
1910	8 Jan. *Androsace spinulifera, G.C.* **47**: 27.
1910	15 Jan. *Crawfurdia Trailliana, G.C.* **47**: 44.
1910	22 Jan. *Primula sonchifolia, G.C.* **47**: 58.
★1910	5 Mar. Our supplementary illustration [*Primula denticulata*], *G.C.* **47**:152.
1910	26 Mar. Our supplementary illustration, Scenes in Tibet and China, *G.C.* **47**: 202.
1910	21 May. The perils of plant-collecting, *G.C.* **47**: 325-326.
	28 May. The perils of plant-collecting (cont.), *G.C.* **47**:344.
1910	28 May. *Rhododendron racemosum, G.C.* **47**: 343.
1910	Gentianaceae novae Orienti-Tibeticae atque Austro-Occidentali-Chinenses, *Repert. Sp. Nor. Fedde* **8**: 152-157. (A republication of the descriptions of 10 species, originally published in Forrest, G., 1907.)
★1911	22 July. *Meconopsis delavayi G.C.* **50**: 51-52.
★1911	19 Aug. Our supplementary illustration [*Incarvillea lutea*], *G.C.* **50**:130.
1911	16 Sept. Chinese primulas, *Primula membranifolia* and *P. dryadifolia, G.C.* **50**: 207-209.
1911	30 Sept. *Primula Beesiana*, Forrest, *G.C.* **50**: 242-243.
★1911	11 Nov. Our supplementary illustration [*Meconopsis integrifolia*], *G.C.* **50**: 339.
1911	2 Dec. *Isopyrum grandiflorum, G.C.* **50**: 391.
★1911	30 Dec. Our supplementary illustration [*Primula lichiangensis*], *G.C.* **50**: 473.
1912	11 Jan. Plant collecting in Western China, *J. Horticulture and Home Farmer*, **64**: 34-36.
1912	10 Feb. *Saussurea gossypiphora* and *S. leucoma, G.C.* **51**:85.
1912	13 April. Our supplementary illustration [*Primula forrestii*], *G.C.* **51**: 240.
1912	4 May. Rhododendrons in China, *G.C.* **51**: 291-292.
1912	11 May. *Primula vincaeflora* and *P. pinnatifida, G.C.* **51**: 320.
1915	The flora of north-western Yunnan, *J. Royal Horticultural Soc., London* **41**: 200-208.
1916	13 May. *Primula blattariformis, G.C.* **59**: 254.
1916	27 May. *Meliosma cuneifolia*, Fr., *G.C.* **59**: 279-280.
1916	2 Sept. New Chinese plants [*Aster staticefolius*], *G.C.* **60**: 116.
1916	9 Sept. New Chinese plants [*Delphinium likiangense*], *G.C.* **60**: 129.
1916	28 Oct. *Didissandra lanuginosa*, Clarke, *G.C.* **60**: 205-206.
1916	Notes on the flora of north-western Yunnan, *J. Royal Horticultural Soc., London* **42**: 39-46.
1917	Contribution to Millais, J.G., *Rhododendrons and the various hybrids*, Longman, pp.18-25.
1917	15 Sept. Flora of the Chinese-Tibet borderland, *G.C.* **62**: 105.
1917	27 Oct. Plant collecting in China, *G.C.* **62**: 165-166.
1917	Plant hunting in Upper Burmah. The flora of Yunnan and Upper Burmah, *Garden* **81**: 346-347.
1918	26 Jan. Plant collecting in China, *G.C.* **63**: 31-33.
1920	A lecture by Mr. George Forrest on recent discoveries of rhododendrons in China, *Rhod. Soc. Notes* **2**: 3-23.
1923	Some Meconopsis of Yunnan, (I), *Country Life* **54**: 614-615. (II), *Country Life* **54**: 652-653.
1923	Rhododendrons of 1921 and 1922 and some trees and shrubs of Yunnan, *Rhod. Soc. Notes* **2**:147-158.
1924	Exploration of N.W. Yunnan and S.E. Tibet, 1921-1922, *J. Royal Horticultural Soc., London* **49**: 25-36.
1924	The explorations and work of George Forrest (pp.16-19) and Exploration for Rhododendron, 1917-22 (pp.19-26) in Millais, J.G., *Rhododendrons and the various hybrids*, Longman, 2nd edition.
1927	Magnolias of Yunnan. In Millais, J.C., *Magnolias*, Longman, pp.31-40.
1932	*Primula klaveriana, New Flora & Silva* **5**: 51-52.

Joint publications by W.W. Smith and G. Forrest

1916	New garden Dracocephalums from China, *Trans. Bot. Soc., Edinburgh* **27**: 89-93.
1923	New Primulaceae, *Notes R.B.G. Edinburgh* **14**: 31-56.
1927	Some new Asiatic Primulaceae, *Notes R.B.G. Edinburgh* **15**: 247-258.
1928	The sections of the genus Primula, *Notes R.B.G. Edinburgh* **16**: 1-50. (Reprinted with alterations in *J. Royal Horticultural Soc., London* **54**: 4-50 (1929))

Joint publication by H.F. Tagg and G. Forrest

1927	New species and varieties of Asiatic rhododendrons, *Notes R.B.G. Edinburgh* **15**: 305-320.

Publications by others in which Forrest's help is acknowledged

Stevenson, J.B. (Edit.), *The species of Rhododendron*, The Rhododendron Society, 1930.

Taylor, George, *An account of the genus Meconopsis*, New Flora and Sylva Ltd., London, 1934.

Plants introduced to Britain by Forrest and available today

This is not a comprehensive list, but the following are all available in commerce in the UK and most of the plants have many suppliers, according to the *RHS Plant Finder*, a Plant Directory compiled by The Royal Horticultural Society. Forrest may not have been the first person to introduce them to cultivation, nor does it follow that stocks available today are derived from his introductions, but at some stage he did introduce all of them. Plants with awards (particularly the AGM) and with names related to Forrest have been given priority.

Non Rhododendrons

Abies forrestii (syn. A. delavayi)
Acer davidii (particularly 'George Forrest' AGM)
★*Adenophora bulleyana*
★*Allium beesianum* AGM
★*Allium forrestii*
Anemone rupicola
★*Arisaema candidissimum*
Arisaema consanguineum
★*Berberis jamesiana*
Buddleja fallowiana (var. *alba* has AGM)
★*Buddleja forrestii*
Camellia saluenensis
Cardiocrinum giganteum var. *yunnanense*
Clematis armandii
Clematis chrysocoma
★*Codonopsis bulleyana*
Cynoglossum amabile AGM
Daphne odora
Daphne tangutica Retusa group (syn. *D. retusa*) AGM
Gentiana oreodoxa
★*Gentiana sino-ornata* AGM
★*Hypericum forrestii* (syn. *H. patulum* var. *forrestii*) AGM
Incarvillea delavayi
★*Incarvillea delavayi* 'Bees' Pink'
Incarvillea mairei var. *grandiflora*
★*Iris bulleyana*
Iris chrysographes AM AGM
Iris delavayi AGM
★*Iris forrestii* AM AGM
★*Jasminum beesianum*
Jasminum polyanthum
Lilium davidii AGM
Lilium lankongense
★*Magnolia campbellii* subsp. *mollicomata* (syn. *M. mollicomata*)
Meconopsis integrifolia
Nomocharis aperta (syn. *N. forrestii*)
Nomocharis pardanthina (syn. *N. mairei*)
Nomocharis saluenensis
Osmanthus delavayi (syn. *Siphonosmanthus delavayi*) AGM
Osmanthus yunnanensis (syn. *O. forrestii*)

Paeonia delavayi AGM
Paeonia delavayi var. *lutea*
Paraquilegia anemonoides
Picea likiangensis
★*Pieris formosa* var. *forrestii* (some forms AM FCC AGM)
Pinus armandii
★*Primula aurantiaca*
★*Primula bulleyana* ssp. *beesiana*
★*Primula bulleyana* AGM
Primula burmanica
Primula cernua AM
Primula chionantha subsp. *sinopurpurea*
Primula chionantha subsp. *chionantha* AM AGM
Primula chungensis AGM
Primula deflexa
Primula flaccida (syn. *P. nutans*) AGM
★*Primula forrestii*
Primula malacoides
Primula muscarioides
Primula obconica
Primula poissonii
Primula polyneura
★*Primula prolifera* (syn. *P. helodoxa*) AGM FCC
Primula secundiflora
Primula sikkimensis
Primula sonchifolia
Primula vialii (syn. *P. littoniana*) AGM
★*Primula wilsonii* var. *anisodora* (syn. *P. anisodora*)
Rheum alexandrae
Rhododendron – see separate list
Roscoea cautleyoides AGM
★*Roscoea humeana* AGM
★*Salvia bulleyana*
★*Sorbus forrestii*
Trollius chinensis
Trollius pumilus
Trollius yunnanensis

Through specialist societies and certain individuals it is possible to obtain hardy Chinese plant material (plants or seeds) by exchange or as a gift. For example, the following plants, that were introduced by Forrest, are not now generally commercially available, but may be obtained.

★*Androsace bulleyana*
Androsace spinulifera
★*Camellia forrestii*
Camellia reticulata
★*Codonopsis forrestii*
★*Cotoneaster forrestii*
Daphne aurantiaca
Daphne calcicola
★*Dracocephalum forrestii*
★*Gentiana georgei*
★*Incarvillea forrestii*
★*Hemerocallis forrestii*
★*Magnolia nitida*
★*Magnolia rostrata*
Meconopsis delavayi
Meconopsis pseudointegrifolia
Pleione albiflora
★*Pleione* x *confusa*
Pleione grandiflora
★*Podocarpus forrestii*
★*Rheum forrestii*

Rhododendrons

This list has a bias towards plants that have received awards (AGM, AM or FCC), those with particular connection to Forrest, perhaps by the name, those with very distinctive character, and those that are commonly available.

★*adenogynum*
★*arizelum* (*rex* ssp. *arizelum*)
★*balfourianum*
bureavii AM
calostrotum ssp. *keleticum* (syn. *radicans*)
campylogynum AGM
★*clementinae*
★*cuneatum*
cyanocarpum AM
decorum AGM
★*dichroanthum* AM
★*forrestii* var. *repens* FCC
★*fulvum* AM AGM
★*glischrum*

★*griersonianum* FCC
haematodes FCC
heliolepis
hippophaeoides AM
★*impeditum* AM
irroratum
lacteum FCC
lepidostylum
maddenii ssp. *crassum* (syn. *crassum*)
megeratum
★*oreotrephes*
★*orthocladum*
phaeochrysum
★*pronum*
proteoides
★*protistum*
pubescens
★*rex* ssp. *fictolacteum*
★*roxieanum* var. *oreonastes* AGM
rubiginosum
★*rupicola*
★*russatum* FCC AGM
saluenense AM
★*saluenense* ssp. *chamaeunum*
scabrifolium
selense
★*sinogrande* FCC AGM
★*sperabile*
★*taggianum*
★*telmateium*
tephropeplum AM
★*traillianum*
trichocladum
trichostomum
★*valentinianum* AM
wardii AM
yunnanense

AGM	Award of Garden Merit
AM	Award of Merit
FCC	First Class Certificate
★	New species

With thanks to David Rankin and Peter Cunnington for Non Rhododendron lists.
With thanks to David Rankin and Ken Hulme for Rhododendron list.

The most important cultivars raised directly from Forrest's Rhododendron species

(a) *Rhododendron griersonianum* has been the direct parent of 159 garden hybrids. Introduced in 1917, it is sensitive to low temperatures. Hybridising with hardier species has combined its qualities of colour and floriferousness with an ability to grow in a wide range of conditions. As it flowers later than most species, its hybrids also extend the season of garden display. Thirty-four of the 159 hybrids with *R. griersonianum* as a direct parent have been given horticultural awards by the RHS:

'Aladdin'	AM	'Guielt'	AM	'Romany Chal'	AM, FCC
'Arthur Osborn'	AM	'Ivanhoe'	AM	'Romarez'	AM
'Dorinthia'	FCC	'Jeritsa'	AM	'Rosabel'	AM
'Elizabeth'	AM, FCC	'Jibuti'	AM	'Saltwood'	AM
'F.C.Puddle'	AM	'Karkov'	AM	'Sarita Loder'	AM
'Fabia'	AM	'Laura Aberconway'	AM	'Tally Ho'	FCC
'Fire Flame'	AM	'Master Dick'	AM	'Tensing'	AM
'Fusilier'	AM, FCC	'Matador'	AM, FCC	'Tortoiseshell Wonder'	AM
'Glamour'	AM	'May Day'	AM	'Vanessa'	FCC
'Goblin'	AM	'Mrs Leopold de Rothschild'	AM	'Vulcan'	AM
'Grenadine'	AM, FCC	'Ouida'	AM	'Winsome'	AM
'Gretia'	AM	'Romany Chai'	AM		

(b) *Rhododendron forrestii* has been the direct parent of thirty-eight hybrids, of which eight have been acclaimed by horticultural awards by the RHS:

'Badeilsen'	AM	'Little Ben'	FCC	'Red Lacquer'	AM
'Ethel'	FCC	'Little Bert'	FCC	'Spring magic'	AM
'Fascinator'	AM	'Red Carpet'	AM		

(c) Four well-known hybrids with *Rhododendron impeditum* as a direct parent:

'Blue Star'		'Little Imp'	
'Blue Tit'		'St Tudy	AM

(d) *Rhododendron russatum* is a direct parent of 'Bue Chip'

(e) *Rhododendron roxieanum* is a direct parent of 'Blewbury'

(f) *Rhododendron sinogrande* is a direct parent of 'Fortune'

Source: H.E. Salley & H.E. Greer, *Rhododendron Hybrids*, 1992, Batsford.

With thanks to Ken Hulme

People honoured in the names of Forrest's plants

Forrest's newly discovered plants had to be named. He had a large network of friends and relatives to whom he felt indebted for their assistance and support. Naming plants after them was a plant collector's way of saying 'thank you'. The list gives examples, and includes some named after Bulley or Bees for commercial purposes. Most, but not all of the names are still used today.

Forrest's Family
Wife:
Chirita trailliana
Gentiana trailliana
Rhododendron clementinae
Trailliaedoxa

Brother and sisters:
Androsace graceae
Berberis jamesiana
Dracocephalum isabellae

Father-in-law:
Rhododendron traillianum

Missionaries
Primula dubernardiana
Rhododendron genestierianum
Rhododendron roxieanum
Rhododendron valentinianum

Others in the Far East
Primula littoniana   (British Consul, Tengyueh)
Rhododendron albertsenianum
                            (Customs officer, Tengyueh)
Rhododendron griersonianum
                            (Customs officer, Tengyueh)
Rhododendron mackenzianum   (Friend, Rangoon)
Rhododendron meddianum
        (Agent of the Irrawaddy Flotilla Co., Bhamo)

RBGE gardeners killed in WWI
Buddleja fallowiana
Roscoea humeana

Sponsors
Bulleyia yunnanensis
Androsace bulleyana
Diapensia bulleyana
Iris bulleyana
Primula bulleyana
Beesia calthaefolia
Allium beesianum
Jasminum beesianum
Primula bulleyana spp. *beesiana*
Rhododendron beesianum
Salvia bulleyana and others

Primula coryana
Ligustrum coryanum
Rhododendron coryanum

(J.C. Williams put an embargo on any of Forrest's plants being named after him.)

Sponsor's gardener
Rhododendron martinianum
                (J.C. Williams' gardener at Caerhays)

Plants and animals named after George Forrest

An impressive tally of plant species is named *forrestii* after George Forrest, with variations of *forrestiana* and *georgei*. On the basis of *Index Kewensis*, more than one hundred genera have species named after George Forrest. The following list gives a guide, although the exact number is not given, as through time some species have been put into a different genus, and are mentioned twice. There are many subspecies and varieties named after him, but only a few famous ones in cultivation are given.

Some animals were named after him as *forresti*. As in the plants, many of the names have been changed more recently, or the species reduced to subspecies. Examples of mammals named *forresti* in the Natural History Museum, London, are listed in Appendix 10. Birds and a dragonfly named after him are given below.

PLANTS
Genera with a *forrestii* species named after George Forrest:

Abies	*Caragana*	*Duhaldea*	*Isodon*	*Onosma*	*Polygonum*	*Serratula*
Abutilon	*Carex*	*Dumasia*	*Itea*	*Orchis*	*Potentilla*	*Sinarundinaria*
Acer	*Carum*	*Epilobium*	*Jurinea*	*Oreocharis*	*Primula*	*Sloanea*
Aconitum	*Caryopteris*	*Euonymus*	*Lactuca*	*Ornithoboea*	*Pseudotsuga*	*Smilacina*
Acronema	*Cheiranthus*	*Euphrasia*	*Laportea*	*Osmanthus*	*Pteracanthus*	*Sorbus*
Actinodaphne	*Chelonopsis*	*Festuca*	*Leptodermis*	*Otochilus*	*Pterocarya*	*Staphylea*
Adenophora	*Chirita*	*Galium*	*Lespedeza*	*Parasenecio*	*Pueraria*	*Strobilanthes*
Agapetes	*Chrysosplenium*	*Garuga*	*Lilium*	*Paris*	*Pyrorchis*	*Swertia*
Ajuga	*Cirsium*	*Gentiana*	*Linnaea*	*Parrya*	*Rabdosia*	*Symplocos*
Allantodia	*Clematis*	*Geranium*	*Liparis*	*Pentapanax*	*Randia*	*Syzygium*
Allium	*Cnicus*	*Gueldenstaedtia*	*Litsea*	*Perantha*	*Rhamnella*	*Taraxacum*
Amitostigma	*Corallodiscus*	*Gutzlaffia*	*Lloydia*	*Peristylus*	*Rheum*	*Thea*
Angelica	*Cotoneaster*	*Habenaria*	*Lomatogonium*	*Petrocosmea*	*Rhodiola*	*Theopsis*
Arenaria	*Craibiodendron*	*Hedychium*	*Loxostigma*	*Phlomis*	*Rhododendron*	*Tibetia*
Artemisia	*Cremanthodium*	*Hemerocallis*	*Lysionotus*	*Phlomoides*	*Rhodoleia*	*Tovaria*
Arundinaria	*Cymbidium*	*Hemipilia*	*Maianthemum*	*Phoebe*	*Roettlera*	*Trachydium*
Aster	*Cynanchum*	*Heracleum*	*Manglietia*	*Phyllanthus*	*Rosa*	*Tremacron*
Astragalus	*Cypripedium*	*Herminium*	*Margbensonia*	*Physospermopsis*	*Roscoea*	*Tripterygium*
Begonia	*Daiswa*	*Hibiscus*	*Meconopsis*	*Pieris*	*Salix*	*Tsuga*
Berberis	*Delphinium*	*Hirculus*	*Meliosma*	*Pimpinella*	*Salvia*	*Utricularia*
Betula	*Didymocarpus*	*Hydrocotyle*	*Microula*	*Piptanthus*	*Saxifraga*	*Vaccinium*
Braya	*Diospyros*	*Impatiens*	*Monorchis*	*Plectranthus*	*Schima*	*Vernonia*
Buddleja	*Distephanus*	*Incarvillea*	*Nomocharis*	*Pleione*	*Scrophularia*	*Veronica*
Cacalia	*Dolomiaea*	*Indigofera*	*Omphalodes*	*Pleurogyne*	*Scutellaria*	*Vincetoxicum*
Camellia	*Dracocephalum*	*Inula*	*Omphalogramma*	*Podocarpus*	*Sedum*	*Vladimiria*

Popular plants in cultivation named *forrestii* after George Forrest

Acer pectinatum subsp. *forrestii*
Pieris formosa var. *forrestii*

Genera with a *forrestiana* species named after George Forrest

Androsace
Aristolochia
Jasminum
Leontopodium
Pedicularis
Pyrola
Rosa
Rubus
Viola
Vittara

Genera with a *georgii* or *georgei* species named after George Forrest

Dolomiaea
Gentiana
Jurinea
Saxifraga
Vladimiria

The author is grateful to the Trustees of the RBG Kew for use of the *Index Kewensis* on CD-ROM and *Index Filicales*, with thanks to John Edmondson, Rosemary Davies and Peter Edwards.

DRAGONFLY named after George Forrest

Temnogomphus forresti

BIRDS named after George Forrest

Dryocopus forresti
Fulvetta chrysotis forresti
Ianthocincla forresti
Phylloscopus proregulus forresti
Streptopelia chinensis forresti
Xiphirhynchus superciliaris forresti

With thanks to Edward Dickinson and Mary LeCroy.
Source: M. LeCroy & E. C. Dickinson, 'Systematic notes on Asian birds. 17. Types of birds collected in Yunnan by George Forrest and described by Walter Rothschild.' *Zool. Verh. Leiden* 335, 2001, 183-198.

Forrest's mammal collection
at the Natural History Museum, London

20 Taxa described as new:

Original names	Current names	English names
Apodemus ilex Thomas	*Apodemus sylvaticus ilex*	wood mouse
Crocidura praedax Thomas	*Crocidura fuliginosa*	shrew
Dremomys pernyi Iichiensis Thomas	*Dremomys pernyi pernyi*	Perney's long- nosed squirrel
Eothenomys fidelis Hinton	*Eothenomys melanogaster miletus*	vole
Eothenomys melanogaster confinii Hinton	*Eothenomys melanogaster sleusis*	vole
Eothenomys proditor Hinton		vole
Microtus clarkei Hinton★★		field vole
Nasillus investigator Thomas	*Uropsilus soricipes investigator*	Chinese shrew-mole
Neodon forresti Hinton★	*Pitymys Irene forresti*	vole
Nyctereutes procyonoides orestes Thomas		raccoon dog
Ochotona forresti Thomas★	*Ochotona (?) pusilla forresti*	pika
Ochotona thibetana sacraria Thomas	*Ochotona thibetana thibetana*	pika
Pteromys alborufus ochraspis Thomas	*Petaurista alborufus alborufus*	giant flying squirrel
Petaurista clarkei Thomas★★	*Petaurista elegans clarkei*	giant flying squirrel
Rattus eha ninus Thomas	*Niniventer eha*	rat
Rupestes forresti Thomas★	*Sciurotamias forresti*	Forrest's rock squirrel
Tadarida teniotis caecata Thomas		free-tailed bat
Tamiops clarkei Thomas★★	*Tamiops swinhoei clarkei*	Swinhoe's striped squirrel
Tamiops maritimus forresti Thomas★		
Trogopterus edithae Thomas	*Trogopterus xanthipes edithae*	flying squirrel

★named in honour of George Forrest
★★named in honour of his patron Col. Stephenson R.Clarke

All these animals were collected by George Forrest, in Yunnan, S.W. China, 1918–22.
Original names from the Mammal Section Register, Natural History Museum, London.

Select Bibliography

Books

Bishop, George, *Travels in imperial China: The exploration and discoveries of Père David,* Cassell, 1990

Briggs, Roy W., *'Chinese' Wilson: A life of Ernest H. Wilson,* HMSO, 1993

Coats, Alice, *The plant hunters,* McGraw-Hill, 1969

Cowan, J. Macqueen, *The journeys and plant introductions of George Forrest, VMH,* Oxford University Press for the RHS, 1952

Cox, E.H.M., *Plant-hunting in China,* Oxford University Press, 1945

Cox, Kenneth (Edit.), *Frank Kingdon Ward's Riddle of the Tsangpo Gorges,* Antique Collectors' Club, 2001

Elwes, H.J., *Memoirs of travel, sport and natural history,* Ernest Benn, London, 1930

Fletcher, H.R., *The story of the Royal Horticultural Society, 1804-968,* Oxford University Press for the RHS, 1969

Fletcher, Harold R. and Brown, William H., *The Royal Botanic Garden Edinburgh, 1670-1970,* HMSO, 1970

Handel-Mazzetti, Heinrich, *A botanical pioneer in South West China,* David Winstanley, 1996

Illingworth, John and Routh, Jane (Edits.), *Reginald Farrer, Dalesman, planthunter, gardener,* Centre for North-West Regional Studies, University of Lancaster, 1991

Lancaster, Roy, *Travels in China: A plantsman's paradise,* Antique Collectors' Club, 1989

Lyte, C., *Frank Kingdon-Ward: The last of the great planthunters,* John Murray, 1989

McLean, Brenda, *A Pioneering Plantsman: A.K. Bulley and the Great Plant Hunters,* HMSO, 1997

Mearns, Barbara and Richard, *The bird collectors,* Academic Press, 1998

Pim, Sheila, *The wood and the trees: A biography of Augustine Henry,* Boethius Press, Kilkenny, Ireland, 1984

Postan, Cynthia (Edit.), *The Rhododendron story,* RHS, 1996

Robertson, Forbes W. and McKelvie, Alistair, *Scottish rock gardening in the 20th Century,* Scottish Rock Garden Club, 2000

Rothschild, Miriam, *Dear Lord Rothschild,* ISI Press, Philadelphia, 1983

Scottish Rock Garden Club, *George Forrest, VMH, 1873-1932,* Scottish Rock Garden Club, 1935

Ward, F. Kingdon, *The land of the blue poppy,* Cambridge University Press, 1913 (also Cadogan Books Ltd., 1986)

Wilson, E.H., *A naturalist in Western China,* Methuen, London, 1913. (also Cadogan Books Ltd., 1986)

Articles

A special George Forrest centenary issue of *J. Scottish Rock Garden Club,* Vol.13, Part 3, No.52, 1973 was devoted entirely to Forrest. See especially the articles by Aitken, James T., Forrest, George (jnr), Hulme, J.K. and Keenan, J.

Aitken, James T., 'George Forrest in perspective' (The Clark Memorial Lecture given at West Kilbride on 14 October 1973), *J. Scottish Rock Garden Club,* 14, 1974-75, 33-43

Fraser, Alison, 'George Forrest – my great-uncle', *Royal Caledonian Horticultural Soc. J.,* 1994, 7-11

Keenan, J., 'George Forrest, 1873-1932', *J. Royal Horticultural Soc.,* 98, 1973, 112-117

Papers on the exploration of China, *Proc. Linnean Soc.,* London, 156, 1943-44, 3-44. See especially the articles by Li, H-L., Smith, M.A. and Stern, F.C.

Obituaries

Anon., 'Mr. George Forrest', *Nature,* Vol.129, No.3251, 1932, 270

Anon., 'George Forrest, VMH', *Gardeners' Chronicle,* 23 January 1932, 53-54.

Anon., 'George Forrest', *Kew Bulletin,* 1932, 106-107.

Anon., 'George Forrest', *Ibis,* Vol.2 (13th Ser.), 1932, 354-355

E.H.M. Cox, 'George Forrest', *New Flora & Silva* 4, 1931-32, 180-186.

Smith, W. Wright, 'George Forrest', 1873-1932, *Rhododendron Soc. Notes,* Vol.3, No.5, 1929-1931, 271-275 (reprinted in *J. Horticultural Soc.,* 57 (2), 1932, 356-360 and in *Trans. Bot. Soc. Edinburgh,* 31, 1932, 239-243)

Taylor, G, 'George Forrest (1873-1932)', *J. Botany,* 70, 1932, 79-81.

Papers on the identification of Forrest's plants

These are by various authors (including Forrest himself) and appeared from 1907 to 1934 in *Notes, RBG Edinburgh* Vols. 4, 5 and 7-18

Papers on the identification of Forrest's birds

LeCroy, Mary and Dickinson, Edward C., 'Systematic notes on Asian birds, 17: Types of birds collected in Yunnan by George Forrest and described by Walter Rothschild', *Zoologische Verhandelingen (Leiden),* 335, 2001, 183-198

Rothschild, Lord, 'On a collection of birds from West-Central and North-Western Yunnan', *Novitates Zoologicae,* 28, 1921, 14-67

Rothschild, Lord, 'On a second collection sent by Mr. George Forrest from N.W. Yunnan', *Novitates Zoologicae,* 30, 1923, 33-58

Rothschild, Lord, 'On a third collection of birds made by Mr. George Forrest in North-West Yunnan', *Novitates Zoologicae,* 30, 1923, 247 – 267.

Rothschild, Lord, 'On a fourth collection of birds made by Mr. George Forrest in North-Western Yunnan', *Novitates Zoologicae,* 32, 1925, 292-313.

Rothschild, Lord, 'On the avifauna of Yunnan, with critical notes', *Novitates Zoologicae,* 33, 1926, 189-343.

Papers on the identification of Forrest's mammals

Hinton, M.A.C., 'On the voles collected by Mr. G. Forrest in Yunnan; with remarks upon the genera *Eothenomys* and *Neodon* and upon their allies,' *Ann. Mag. nat. Hist.* 1923, (9) 11, 145-162

Thomas, O., 'Four new squirrels of the genus *Tamiops*', *Ann. Mag. nat. Hist.,* 1920, (9) 5, 304-308

Thomas, O., 'On mammals from the Yunnan Highlands collected by Mr. George Forrest and presented to the British Museum by Col. Stephenson R. Clarke', *Ann. Mag. nat. Hist.* 1922, (9) 10, 391-403

Thomas, O., 'On mammals from the Li-kiang Range, Yunnan, being a further collection obtained by Mr. George Forrest', *Ann. Mag. nat. Hist.* 1923, (9) 11 655-663

Thomas, O., 'Geographical races of *Petaurista alborufus*', *Ann. Mag. nat. Hist.* 1923, (9) 12, 171-172.

Notes

PROLOGUE

1. Hooker, J.D., *Himalayan Journals*, 2 vols., John Murray, 1854
2. Elwes, H.J., *A monograph of the Genus Lilium*, London, 1880

INTRODUCTION

1. Wood, Frances, *No dogs and not many Chinese: Treaty Port life in China 1843-1943*, John Murray, 1998, p.86
2. Cox, E.H.M., *Plant-hunting in China*, OUP, 1986, p.115
3. Le Lievre, A., 'Carl Johann Maximowicz (1827-1891) explorer and plant collector', *New Plantsman*, 1997, vol.4, 3, pp.131-143
4. Franchet, A., 'Notice sur les travaux du R.P. Delavay', *Bulletin du Muséum d'Histoire Naturelle,* no.1, 1896, pp.148-151
5. Rix, M., *The Art of Botanical Illustration*, Bracken Books, 1989, p.199
6. Curtis's *Botanical Magazine,* vol. 124, t.7621, 1898
7. 'Upper Burma during 1886', *Scottish Geographical Magazine*, vol.3, 1887, p.412
8. Kipling, R., 'Mandalay' in *Rudyard Kipling's Verse*, inclusive edn., 1885-1918, Hodder & Stoughton Ltd, pp.476-478
9. Hosie, A., *Three Years in Western China*, London, George Philip & Son, 1890, p.135

CHAPTER ONE

1. Eliot, T.S., from 'Burnt Norton' in *Four Quartets*, Faber paper covered edn. 1959, p.13
2. G. Forrest to J.C. Williams, 11 Aug. 1914, Archives of RBGE
3. Watters, B., *Where Iron Runs Like Water!*, John Donald Publishers Ltd, Edin., 1998, p.190
4. PRO: ADM 33/3350, with grateful thanks to Pat Collis who researched the *Duncan* connection
5. Lyons, D., *The Sailing Navy List*, Conway Maritime, London, 1993
6. *Falkirk Herald,* 23 Mar. 1876
7. Devine, T.M., *The Scottish Nation, 1700-2000*, Allen Lane The Penguin Press, 1999, pp.370-378
8. Ibid. p.402
9. Boyd, Wm., *Education in Ayrshire through seven centuries*, Univ. of London Press Ltd, 1961, p.186
10. The Revd D. Landsborough, at the Annual Meeting of the Kilmarnock Philosophical Institution, reported in a newspaper cutting found in a Minute Book, in the Dick Institute, Kilmarnock
11. Information provided by Neil Dixon, teacher at Kilmarnock Academy
12. Ibid.
13. McNaughton, Wm.D. (Revd Dr), *The Scottish Congregationalist Ministry 1794-1993*, Glasgow, 1993, p.47
14. Ibid.
15. George Forrest, VMH, 1873-1932, *The Scottish Rock Garden Club*, 1935, re-issued 1973, p.10
16. *Kilmarnock Glenfield Ramblers' Society, Annals No. 11,* Jubilee Number 1884-1934
17. Woodward, C., *The Grand Old Man of Kilmarnock*, Dick Institute, p.3

18. William Landsborough (1825-1886) led one of the expeditions in search of the missing explorers, R.O. Burke and W.J. Wills, and was fêted as the first explorer to cross Australia from north to south. He was given a gold watch by the Royal Geographical Society in London
19. Local Magnates No.3, *Auld Killie*, 1 Dec. 1893, p.9
20. D. Landsborough to J.H. Balfour, 3 Aug. 1880, Archives of RBGE
21. Aitken, James, 'George Forrest – The Man and his Work,' *J. Scottish Rock Garden Club*, XIII, no.52, 1973, pp.185-196
22. George Forrest, VMH, 1873-1932, *The Scottish Rock Garden Club*, 1935, re-issued 1973, p.10
23. Information supplied by the Museum of the Royal Pharmaceutical Society of Great Britain
24. Research carried out by Alys Forrest
25. George Forrest, VMH, 1873-1932, *The Scottish Rock Garden Club*, 1935, re-issued 1973, p.11
26. G. Taylor's obituary of G. Forrest in *J. Botany* 70 (1932), pp.79-81
27. 1901 census
28. Valuation Roll for the County of Mid-Lothian, 1902-3, in the Parish of Lasswade, p.349
29. G. Forrest to 'Dear Mother and all of you', 4 Jul. 1905, Patrick papers
30. Correspondence with George Campbell, resident of Loanhead
31. Thanks to Marjorie Robertson, expert on the Abercromby archive, Univ. of Edin.
32. Abercromby, The Hon. John, 'Excavation of Three Long Cists at Gladhouse Reservoir, Midlothian,' *Procs. of the Soc. of Antiquaries of Scotland*, vol. 38, 14 Dec. 1903, pp.96-98
33. Thanks to Gordon Barclay, archaeologist
34. Hon. John Abercromby to I.B. Balfour, 21 Jun. 1903, Archives of RBGE
35. N.H. Hooker to I.B. Balfour, 10 Jan. 1890, Archives of RBGE
36. I.B. Balfour to G. Forrest, 1 Sept. 1903, Archives of RBGE

CHAPTER TWO

1. Obit. Dr William Traill of Woodwick, *Nature*, v. 35, 1887, p.419
2. Obit. William Traill, *Trans. Bot. Soc.*, XVII, 1886-89, p.17
3. Archives Executive Office, Standard Life House, Edin.
4. Traill, G.W., 'Supplementary Notes on the Marine Algae of the Orkney Islands,' *Trans. Bot. Soc. Edin*. XX, 1895, pp.341-345
5. Balfour, I.B., *J.Bot.* XXXV, 1897, p.440
6. Named by Batters, E.A., 1896
7. Traill, G.W., 23 letters 1889-1896, to I.B. Balfour, Archives of RBGE
8. Traill, G.W., *A Monograph of the Algae of the Firth of Forth, illustrated with herbarium specimens of some of the rarer species*, Edin. Co-op. Printing Co. Ltd, 1885
9. Matthews, J.R., George W. Traill's 'Algae Boreali-Americanae', *Trans. Bot. Soc. Edin.* 39 (1960-64), pp.396-398

10. Obituary notice of Balfour, I.B., 1853-1922, *Proc. Roy. Soc.*, XCVI 1924, pp.xii-xvii
11. Forbes, F.B. and Hemsley, W.B., 'Enumeration of all the plants known from China proper, Formosa, Hainan, The Corea, The Luchu archipelago and the island of Hongkong', *J. Linn. Soc.,* vol. XXVI (1889), pp.36-43
12. McLean, B., *A Pioneering Plantsman, AK Bulley and the Great Plant Hunters,* The Stationery Office, 1997
13. Bulley family scrapbook, in the Special Collections of the Archives, Univ. of Liverpool
14. Nelson, E. Charles, 'Augustine Henry and the exploration of the Chinese flora', in *Arnoldia*, 43, 1983, pp.21-38
15. Henry, A., 'Botanical Exploration in Yunnan', *Kew Bulletin*, 1897, p.99
16. A.K. Bulley to A. Henry, 29 Aug. 1897, Henry mss. Glasnevin, Dublin
17. Pim, S., *The Wood and the Trees* (2nd edn.), Boethius Press, 1984, p.225
18. A.K. Bulley to A. Henry, 29 Aug. 1897, Henry mss. Glasnevin, Dublin
19. Henry, A., in the *Kew Bulletin*, 1899, pp 47-48
20. Fairchild, D., *The World was my Garden*, Charles Scribner's Sons, New York and London, 1943, p.157
21. I.B. Balfour to A.K. Bulley, 28 Apr. 1904, Archives of RBGE
22. I.B. Balfour to A.K. Bulley, 30 Apr. 1904, Archives of RBGE

CHAPTER THREE

1 .G. Forrest to I.B. Balfour, received Jun. 1904, Archives of RBGE
2. Coates, P.D., *The China Consuls 1843-1943*, OUP, 1988, p.314
3. Keay, J., *The Great Arc*, Harper Collins, 2000
4. G. Forrest to I.B. Balfour, 5 Jul. 1904, Archives of RBGE
5. G. Forrest to Mrs G. Forrest and family, 3 Jul. 1904, Patrick papers
6. G. Forrest: Diary from Bhamo to Tengyueh, 13 Jul. to 12 Aug. 1904, Patrick papers, 28pp
7. G. Forrest to Mrs G. Forrest, 11 Aug. 1904, Patrick papers
8. Ibid.
9. Coates, P.D., *The China Consuls 1843-1943,* OUP, 1988, p.318
10. Not to be confused with General Sir Charles James Napier (1782-1853), commemorated by a statue in Trafalgar Square, who announced his conquest of a region of India with the Latin pun, *Peccavi* (I have Sind)
11. This campaign is described in *The Blue Nile* by Alan Moorhead
12. With thanks to the Forrest family for reference to the artefacts of George Forrest
13. With thanks to Helen Wang, Curator of East Asian Money, The British Museum
14. Cribb, J., *A Catalogue of Sycee in the British Museum,* British Museum Press, 1993, p.40
15. Sir Francis Younghusband (1863-1942) led a misguided British invasion of Tibet, 1903-4
16. FO 228/1562. Letter from Sir Ernest Satow from HM Consulate, Tengyueh, 11 Apr. 1904, Archives of PRO, Kew

17. G. Forrest to his brother James, 5 Nov. 1904, Patrick papers
18. FO 228/1562 Report from Litton, 15 Nov. 1904
19. G. Forrest to I.B. Balfour, 8 Nov. 1904, Archives of RBGE
20. Forrest, G., 'Gentianaceae from Eastern Tibet and South-West China', Notes RBGE XVII, Apr. 1907
21. G. Forrest to 'Dear Mother and all of you', 21 Nov. 1904, Patrick papers
22. FO 228/1562. Report from Litton, 15 Nov. 1904
23. Prince Henry of Orleans (1867-1901), French explorer and naturalist, was the great-grandson of the last French king, Louis-Philippe. He made two journeys through western China in the 1890s, collecting plants and animals
24. FO 228/1562. Report from Litton, 15 Nov. 1904, p.31
25. G. Forrest to 'Dear Mother and all of you', 21 Nov. 1904, Patrick papers
26. Le Lievre, A., 'Prince Henri of Orléans explorer and plant-hunter (1867-1901)', The New Plantsman, Vol.1, Dec. 1994, pp.238-247
27. G. Forrest to I.B. Balfour, 8 Nov. 1904, Archives of RBGE
28. G. Forrest to 'Dear Mother and all of you', 21 Nov. 1904, Patrick papers

CHAPTER FOUR

1. G. Forrest to I.B. Balfour, 5 Jan. 1905, Archives of RBGE
2. G. Forrest to I.B. Balfour, 4 Apr. 1905, Archives of RBGE
3. I.B. Balfour to G. Forrest, 9 May 1905, copy in the Patrick papers
4. A.K. Bulley to I.B. Balfour, 25 Jun. 1905, Archives of RBGE
5. I.B. Balfour to A.K. Bulley, 28 Jun. 1905, Archives of RBGE
6. I.B. Balfour to G. Forrest, 13 Feb. 1905, copy in the Patrick papers. This primula was named muscarioides by Hemsley of Kew in 1907, Kew Bull. 8, 319
7. I.B. Balfour to G. Forrest, 9 May 1905, copy in the Patrick papers
8. G. Forrest to I.B. Balfour, 28 Apr. 1905, Archives of RBGE
9. G. Forrest to I.B. Balfour, 27 May 1905, Archives of RBGE
10. G. Forrest to 'Dear Mother and all of you', 21 Nov. 1904, Patrick papers
11. G. Forrest to I.B. Balfour, 27 May 1905, Archives of RBGE
12. G. Forrest to 'Dear Mother and all of you', 4 Jul. 1905, Patrick papers
13. Ibid.
14. G. Forrest to I.B. Balfour, 3 Jul. 1905, Archives of RBGE
15. G. Forrest to 'Dear Mother and all of you', 13 Jul. 1905, Patrick papers
16. G. Forrest to I.B. Balfour, 13 Jul. 1905, Archives of RBGE
17. G. Forrest to 'Dear Mother and all of you', 4 Jul. 1905, Patrick papers
18. F.O. to I.B. Balfour, 17 Aug. 1905, Archives of RBGE
19. I.B. Balfour to A.K. Bulley, 17 Aug. 1905, Archives of RBGE
20. A.K. Bulley to I.B. Balfour, 19 Aug. 1905, Archives of RBGE

21. Sir E. Gorst to I.B. Balfour, 19 Aug. 1905, Archives of RBGE
22. A.K. Bulley to G. Forrest, 21 Aug. 1905, Forrest family papers
23. G. Litton to G. Forrest, 19 Aug. 1905, Forrest family papers
24. G. Litton to I.B. Balfour, 19 Aug. 1905, Archives of RBGE
25. W.J. Embery to I.B. Balfour, 17 Aug. 1905, Archives of RBGE
26. There is more than one version of this story. This account to Clementina does not mention a spike through his foot
27. Cowan, J. Macqueen, Ed., The Journeys and Plant Introductions of George Forrest, OUP, 1952, p.14
28. C.I.M. Directory, 1 Jan. 1904, S.O.A.S. Special Collections. The China Inland Mission was founded by J. Hudson Taylor in 1866 and by 1904 it was the largest missionary society in China. The Tali mission was founded in 1881 and was only one of three CIM stations in the whole of Yunnan
29. Forrest, G., 'Journey on Upper Salwin, Oct.-Dec. 1905', The Geographical Journal, Sept. 1908, pp.239-266
30. Ibid. p.246-7
31. G. Forrest to I.B. Balfour, 30 Dec. 1905, Archives of RBGE. Forrest was using the common terminology of the time when a 'savage' was wild or uncivilised and perceived as existing in the lowest stage of human culture. In that post-Darwinian period, the evolution of man had become a synonym for 'progress', a view modified in our day to being more akin to a copiously branching bush
32. Forrest, G., 'The land of the crossbow', The National Geographic Magazine, 21, 1910, pp.132-156
33. G. Litton to I.B. Balfour, 13 Dec. 1905, Archives of RBGE
34. G. Forrest to J. Forrest, 30 Dec. 1905, Patrick papers
35. I.B. Balfour to G. Litton, 25 Sept. 1905, Archives of RBGE
36. G. Forrest to J. Forrest, 30 Dec. 1905, Patrick papers
37. G. Forrest to J. Forrest, 13 Jan. 1906, Patrick papers
38. Coates, P.D., The China Consuls, 1843-1943, OUP, 1988, p.386
39. G. Forrest to J. Forrest, 27 Jan. 1906, Patrick papers
40. Ibid.
41. G. Forrest to 'Dear Mother and all of you', 7 Feb. 1906, Patrick papers. It is possible that Consul Litton had helped Forrest to write the article in the Scotsman, as he promised in his letter to Forrest on 19 Aug. 1905
42. China's Millions, 1905, S.O.A.S. Special Collections
43. G. Forrest to I.B. Balfour, 8 May 1906, Archives of RBGE
44. G. Forrest to I.B. Balfour, 21 Jun. 1920, Archives of RBGE
45. G. Forrest to Mrs Forrest, 24 Mar. 1905, Archives of RBGE
46. G. Forrest to Mrs Forrest, 28 Mar. 1905, Archives of RBGE
47. G. Forrest to I.B. Balfour, 17 Apr. 1906, Archives of RBGE
48. Forrest, G., 'Primulaceae from Western Yunnan and Eastern Tibet', Notes RBGE No.XIX., Apr. 1908, p.228-229

49. Ibid., p.232
50. Ibid., p.225
51. G. Forrest to I.B. Balfour, 1 Sept. 1906, Archives of RBGE

CHAPTER FIVE

1. Memorandum 6159/06 'Reemployment of George Forrest.' Archives of RBGE
2. I.B. Balfour to A.K. Bulley, 31 May 1907, Archives of RBGE
3. G. Forrest to I.B. Balfour, 2 May 1907, Archives of RBGE
4. A.K. Bulley to I.B. Balfour, 3 Jun. 1907, Archives of RBGE
5. G. Forrest to Miss H.C.M.W. Traill, undated letter (1905), Archives of RBGE
6. With thanks to Mr and Mrs K. Ross; for rent at £30 a year, see valuation roll for the County of Mid-Lothian, 1907-8, in the Parish of Lasswade
7. With thanks to the late George Campbell, resident of Loanhead
8. With thanks to Dr Mary Noble and Miss Purves
9. Forrest, G., 'Primulaceae from Western Yunnan and Eastern Tibet', Notes RBGE No. XIX. 1908, pp.215-239
10. Grace Forrest to I.B. Balfour, 5 Mar. 1908, Archives of RBGE
11. Forrest, G., 'Journey on Upper Salwin, Oct.-Dec. 1905, The Geographical J., 32 (1908) pp.239-266
12. G. Forrest to I.B. Balfour, 12 Aug. 1908, Archives of RBGE
13. I.B. Balfour to G. Forrest, 14 Aug. 1908, Archives of RBGE
14. I.B. Balfour to G. Forrest, 26 Aug. 1908, Archives of RBGE
15. Sutton, S.B., Charles S. Sargent and the Arnold Arboretum, Harvard Univ. Press, 1970
16. I.B. Balfour to G. Forrest, 5 Sept. 1908, Archives of RBGE
17. I.B. Balfour to G. Forrest, 18 Nov. 1908, Archives of RBGE
18. G. Forrest's proposal for a second expedition of three years. Archives of RBGE
19. G. Forrest to I.B. Balfour, 26 Nov. 1908, Archives of RBGE
20. G. Forrest to I.B. Balfour, 26 Feb. 1909, Archives of RBGE
21. G.C. Vol. 44, Dec., 1908, p.396-7, 416
22. G.C. Vol. 45, 1 May 1909, p.274
23. G.C. Vol. 46, 10 Jul. 1909, p. 15
24. G.C. Vol. 46, 27 Nov. 1909, p.353
25. Fairchild, D., The World was my Garden, Charles Scribner's Sons, N.Y. and London, 1943, p.359
26. D. Fairchild to G.H. Grosvenor, 26 Nov., 1909, National Geographic Society (NGS) Archives
27. Statement of Accounts, Archives of RBGE
28. Their wives were both daughters of Alexander Graham Bell, the former president of the NGS
29. G.H. Grosvenor to D. Fairchild, 14 Oct. 1909, NGS Archives
30. G. Forrest to G.H. Grosvenor, 2 Nov. 1909, NGS Archives
31. G.H. Grosvenor to G. Forrest, 4 Jan. 1910, NGS Archives
32. G. Forrest to I.B. Balfour, 13 Oct. 1909, Archives of RBGE
33. G. Forrest to Oldfield Thomas, 22 Dec. 1909, Letters on Mammalia, Archives of the N.H.M.

34. G. Forrest to I.B. Balfour, 4 Jan. 1910, Archives of RBGE

35. G. Forrest to I.B. Balfour, 3 Feb. 1910, Archives of RBGE

36. G. Forrest, 'The Perils of Plant Collecting', *GC,* May 1910, vol. 47, pp.325-326 and 344

37. G. Forrest to I.B. Balfour, 3 Mar. 1910, Archives of RBGE

38. G. Forrest to I.B. Balfour, 25 Mar. 1910, Archives of RBGE

39. G. Forrest to W.W. Smith, 24 Jun. 1913, Archives of RBGE

40. G. Forrest to I.B. Balfour, 23 May 1910, Archives of RBGE

41. G. Forrest to I.B. Balfour, 12 Jul. 1910, Archives of RBGE

42. G. Forrest to I.B. Balfour, 17 Sept. 1910, Archives of RBGE. (This primula is classified under *P. chionantha* Balf.f. & Forrest in John Richard's 1993 edn. of *Primula,* pubd. by B.T. Batsford Ltd.)

43. G. Forrest to I.B. Balfour, 12 Jul. 1910, Archives of RBGE

CHAPTER SIX

1. J.C. Williams to I.B. Balfour, 24 Mar. 1917, Archives of RBGE

2. Accounts in Forrest's hand for expenditure of Bees Ltd on 2nd Expedition, filed in letters between Forrest and Balfour in 1911, Archives of RBGE

3. G. Forrest to I.B. Balfour, 22 Mar. 1911, Archives of RBGE

4. Williams F.J., 'J.C. Williams – an enthusiast', *J. Royal Institution of Cornwall,* 1999, pp.9-32

5. G. Forrest to J.C. Williams, 18 Jul. 1914, Archives of RBGE

6. G. Forrest to J.C. Williams, 23 Oct. 1911, Archives of RBGE

7. G. Forrest to I.B. Balfour, 1 Nov. 1911, Archives of RBGE

8. Tab.2875 *Impatiens arguta,* Hk.f., et Thoms. var. *bulleyana,* Hk.f. in *Icones Plantarum,* Sept. 1908, and letter from I.B. Balfour to G. Forrest, 6 Aug. 1909

9. G. Forrest to J.C. Williams, 27 Nov. 1911, Archives of RBGE

10. Forrest family papers

11. Forrest family papers

12. Forrest family papers

13. G. Forrest to W.W. Smith, 23 Jan. 1912, Archives of RBGE

14. G. Forrest to J.C. Williams, 26 Jan. 1912, Archives of RBGE

15. 'Rhododendrons in China', *G.C.* 51, 4 May 1912, p.291-292

16. G .Forrest to J.C. Williams, 17 Apr. 1912, Archives of RBGE

17. G. Forrest to J.C. Williams, 18 May 1912, Archives of RBGE

18. G. Forrest to J.C. Williams, 29 Jun. 1912, Archives of RBGE

19. G. Forrest to J.C. Williams, 31 May 1912, Archives of RBGE

20. G. Forrest to J.C. Williams, 14 Jun. 1912, Archives of RBGE

21. G. Forrest to I.B. Balfour, 31 Aug. 1912, Archives of RBGE

22. G. Forrest to J.C. Williams, 10 Oct. 1912, Archives of RBGE

23. G. Forrest to J.C. Williams, 25 Oct. 1912, Archives of RBGE

24. G. Forrest to J.C. Williams, 28 Dec. 1912, Archives of RBGE

25. G. Forrest to J.C. Williams, 31 Aug. 1912, Archives of RBGE

26. G. Forrest to J.C. Williams, 17 Feb. 1913, Archives of RBGE

27. G. Forrest to J.C. Williams, 10 Jun. 1913, Archives of RBGE

28. Yung to G. Forrest, Archives of RBGE

29. G. Forrest to J.C. Williams, 26 Jun. 1913, Archives of RBGE

30. A view with which Williams concurred: 'J.C. Williams visited Bulley in 1911 and wrote to Wilson that he was "quite sad to see stuff so knocked about, thousands of things are dead through sheer ignorance of how to handle them."'. Williams, F.J in 'J.C. Williams – an enthusiast', *J. Royal Institution of Cornwall,* 1999, pp. 9-32

31. *J.R.H.S.* 39, 1913-1914,

32. G. Forrest to J.C. Williams, 26 Jun. 1913, Archives of RBGE

33. G. Forrest to J.C. Williams, 9 Nov. 1913, Archives of RBGE

34. G. Forrest to J.C. Williams, 6 Jan. 1914, Archives of RBGE

35. I.B. Balfour to J.C. Williams, 30 May 1914, Archives of RBGE

36. G. Forrest to J.C. Williams, 29 Nov. 1913, Archives of RBGE

37. I.B. Balfour to J.C. Williams, 27 Jul. 1912, Archives of RBGE

38. G. Forrest to J.C. Williams, 24 Jul. 1913, Archives of RBGE

39. I.B. Balfour to R. Farrer, 28 Sept. 1913, Archives of RBGE

40. Camillo Schneider was the General Secretary of the Austro-Hungarian Dendrological Society

41. I.B. Balfour to J.C. Williams, 27 Jul. 1914, Archives of RBGE

42. Extract from the Register of Vital Statistics kept at the Consulate of the Netherlands in Canton in the year 1914. Archives of RBGE

43. C.O. Schneider to J.C. Williams, 24 Jul. 1914, Archives of RBGE

44. Handel-Mazzetti, H., *A Botanical Pioneer in South West China*, translated by D. Winstanley, 1996

45. G. Forrest to J.C. Williams, 18 Jul. 1914, Archives of RBGE

46. G. Forrest to J.C. Williams, 31 Jul. 1914, Archives of RBGE

47. Because it was too difficult for him to leave China, he actually travelled in South-West China until 1919

48. C.O. Schneider to I.B. Balfour, 3 Dec. 1915, Archives of RBGE

CHAPTER SEVEN

1. I.B. Balfour to R. Farrer, 6 Feb. 1915, Archives of RBGE

2. Sir D. Prain to I.B. Balfour, 13 Oct. 1914, Archives of RBGE

3. J.C. Williams to E.A. Bowles, 22 Nov. 1914, Bowles correspondence, Archives of RHS

4. I.B. Balfour to J.C. Williams, 1 Apr. 1915, Archives of RBGE

5. J.C. Williams to I.B. Balfour, 4 Apr. 1915, Archives of RBGE

6. Sir F.W. Moore to J.C. Williams, 6 Apr. 1915, Forrest family papers

7 I.B. Balfour to Sir D. Prain, 7 Apr. 1915, Archives of RBGE

8. I.B. Balfour to J.C. Williams, 19 Apr. 1915, Archives of RBGE

9. I.B. Balfour to Sir D. Prain, 25 Apr. 1915, Archives of RBGE

10. Fletcher, H.R. & Brown, W.H., *The Royal Botanic Garden Edinburgh 1670-1970*, HMSO, 1970, p.228

11. H.J. Elwes to I.B. Balfour, 3 Jun. 1915, Archives of RBGE

12. I.B. Balfour to H.J. Elwes, 5 Jun. 1915, Archives of RBGE

13. H.J. Elwes to I.B. Balfour, Wednesday (presumably 9 Jun. 1915), Archives of RBGE

14. G. Forrest to I.B. Balfour, 2 Jun. 1915, Archives of RBGE

15. G. Forrest to J.C. Williams, 6 Jan. 1914, Archives of RBGE

16. J.C. Williams' offer to Balfour is dated 9 Jun. 1915. Balfour replied the next day. Both letters are in Archives of RBGE

17. I.B. Balfour to H.J. Elwes, 21 Jun. 1915, Archives of RBGE

18. Jarvis, S.D. & D.B., The cross of sacrifice series, Vol.1, *Officers who died in the service of British, Indian and East African Regiments and Corps 1914-19*, 1993

19. I.B. Balfour to H.J. Elwes, 15 Jul. 1915, Archives of RBGE. Balfour's comment about work refers to the Latin motto, *Labor omnia vincit*

20. The plant is now named *Primula chionantha* subsp. *sinopurpurea.* The comment is from I.B. Balfour to D. Prain, 28 Apr. 1916, Archives of RBGE

21. G. Forrest to F.J. Chittenden, 20 Jun. 1918, Archives of RBGE

22. G. Forrest to E.H. Wilson, 14 Jun. 1915, Archives of the Arnold Arboretum, Boston, USA

23. *J. Roy. Hort. Soc.* XLI (1915) 200-208

24. J.C. Williams to H.J. Elwes, 26 Jun. 1916, in Balfour – Elwes correspondence, Archives of RBGE

25. H.J. Elwes to I.B. Balfour, 30 Jun. 1916, Archives of RBGE

26. H.J. Elwes to I.B. Balfour, 26 Jun. 1916, Archives of RBGE

27. I.B. Balfour to H.J. Elwes, 27 Jun. 1916, Archives of RBGE

28. RHS Minutes of Council, Vol.27, p.279, 1 Aug. 1916

29. H.J. Elwes to I.B. Balfour, 3 Sept. 1916, Archives of RBGE

30. I.B. Balfour to H.J. Elwes, 4 Sept. 1916, Archives of RBGE

31. I.B. Balfour to J.C. Williams, 22 Sept. 1916, Archives of RBGE. Williams replied on 25 Sept.

32. I.B. Balfour to H.J. Elwes, 11 Sept. 1916, Archives of RBGE

33. Sir H.J. Veitch to Rev. W. Wilks, 11 Oct. 1916, in Forrest correspondence, Archives of RBGE

34. G. Forrest to I.B. Balfour, 19 Nov. 1916, Archives of RBGE

CHAPTER EIGHT

1. *Rhododendron Soc. Notes,* Vol.3 No.1, 1925, p.15

2. Forrest, G., 'Rhododendrons in China', *Gardeners' Chronicle*, 4 May 1912, p.291

3. *Rhododendron Soc. Notes*, Vol.1 No.3, 1917, pp.145-149
4. I.B. Balfour to G. Forrest, 22 Apr. 1917, Archives of RBGE
5. Forrest, G., 'Plant collecting in China', *Gardeners' Chronicle*, 27 Oct. 1917, pp.165-166
6. I.B. Balfour to G. Forrest, 1 Oct. 1917, Archives of RBGE
7. Forrest, G., 'Plant collecting in China', *Gardeners' Chronicle*, 27 Oct. 1917, pp.165-166
8. Forrest, G., 'Plant collecting in China', *Gardeners' Chronicle*, 26 Jan. 1918, pp.31-33
9. J.C. Williams to I.B. Balfour, 12 Jan. 1919, Archives of RBGE
10. J.G. Millais, *Rhododendrons*, Longman, Green & Co., London, 1917
11. Père Valentin to G. Forrest, 20 May 1919, Archives of RBGE
12. W.W. Smith to G.Forrest, 21 Oct. 1919, Archives of RBGE
13. I.B. Balfour to G. Forrest, 4 Jan. 1919, Archives of RBGE
14. I.B. Balfour to G. Forrest, 15 Oct. 1919, Archives of RBGE
15. *Ibid*
16. Downie, D.G., 'Chinese species of *Tsuga*', *Notes RBGE* Vol.XIV, 1923-24, pp 13-19
17. G. Forrest to F.J. Chittenden, 12 Jan. 1919, Wisley Archives of RHS, and G. Forrest to W.W. Smith, 12 Jul. 1919, Archives of RBGE
18. G. Forrest to F.J. Chittenden, 16 and 23 Aug. 1919 and 28 Oct. 1919, all in Archives of RBGE
19. G. Forrest to I.B. Balfour, 27 Sept. 1919, Archives of RBGE
20. G. Forrest to F.J. Chittenden, 7, 15 and 30 Jan. 1920, all in Archives of RBGE
21. Balfour, I.B., 'New species of Rhododendron', *Notes RBGE* Vol.XI, Jan. 1919, and I.B. Balfour to G. Forrest, 28 Sept. 1918, Archives of RBGE
22. J.C. Williams to I.B. Balfour, 13 Feb. 1920, Archives of RBGE
23 G. Forrest to W.W. Smith, 12 Jul. 1919, Archives of RBGE
24. Edmonds, Frances, *Another bloody tour: England in the West Indies 1986*, Fontana
25. I.B. Balfour to the Headmaster of George Watson's College, 25 Aug. 1919, Archives of RBGE
26. W.W. Smith to Mrs Forrest, 10 Mar. 1921, Archives of RBGE
27. Forrest ,G., 'Rhododendrons of 1921 and 1922 and some trees and shrubs of Yunnan', *Rhododendron Soc. Notes*, Vol.2, No.4, 1923, 147-158

CHAPTER NINE

1. The Family papers of John and Joan Farrer, The Farrer archive
2. I.B. Balfour to R. Farrer, 15 Aug. 1917, Archives of RBGE
3. R. Farrer to his mother, 17 Apr. 1919, The Farrer archive
4. G. Forrest to I.B. Balfour, 16 Apr. 1919, Archives of RBGE
5. I.B. Balfour to R. Farrer, 15 Aug. 1917, Archives of RBGE
6. J.C. Williams to I.B. Balfour, 3 Jun. 1919, Archives of RBGE
7. R. Farrer to his mother, 29 May 1919, The Farrer archive

8. R. Farrer to his mother, 1 Oct. 1919, The Farrer archive
9. I.B. Balfour to R. Farrer, 2 Jan. 1920, The Farrer archive
10. R. Farrer to W.W. Smith, 11 Apr. 1920, Archives of RBGE
11. Forrest, G., 'Rhododendrons discovered recently in China', *Rhododendron Soc. Notes*, II, No.I. 1920, pp.3-23
12. Forrest family papers
13. G. Forrest to R. Cory, 7 Dec. 1920, Archives of RBGE
14. G. Forrest to R. Cory, 23 Aug. 1920, Archives of RBGE
15. G. Forrest to R. Cory, 19 Aug. 1920, Archives of RBGE
16. G. Forrest to W.W.Smith, 17 Mar. 1921, Archives of RBGE
17. I.B. Balfour to Mrs Forrest, 27 May 1921, Archives of RBGE
18. G. Forrest to R. Cory, 7 Sept. 1921, Archives of RBGE

CHAPTER TEN

1. Forrest family papers
2. Stephenson Clarke to W.W. Smith, 26 Jun. 1924, *Archives of RBGE*
3. Stephenson Clarke to W.W. Smith, 15 Jul. 1930, *Archives of RBGE*
4. Obituary of Col. Stephenson R. Clarke, *Ibis* 91, 1949, pp.353-355
5. Rothschild, Lord, 'On a collection of birds from west-central and north-western Yunnan', *Novitates Zoologicae* 28, 1921, pp.14-67
6. Information kindly provided by E.C. Dickinson
7. Mearns, Barbara and Richard, *The Bird Collectors*, Academic Press, 1998, p.197
8. George Rippon (1861-1927) Obituary, *Ibis*, 1927, pp.527-8
9. G. Forrest to Stephenson Clarke, 7 Jul. 1918, Box 38, Tring Museum Corresp. Archives of Natural History Museum (NHM), London
10. G. Forrest to Stephenson Clarke, 12 Sept. 1919, Box 38, Tring Museum Corresp. Archives of NHM, London
11. G. Forrest to Stephenson Clarke, 30 Jan. 1920, Box 39, Tring Museum Corresp. Archives of NHM, London
12. Rothschild, Miriam, *Dear Lord Rothschild*, 1983, *ISI Press*, p.122
13. LeCroy, M. & Dickinson, E.C., 'Systematic notes on Asian birds. 17. Types of birds collected in Yunnan by George Forrest and described by Walter Rothschild,' *Zool. Verh. Leiden* 335, 2001, pp.183-198
14. The Ornithology Department of the NHM is now at Tring
15. R. Cory to G. Forrest, 17 Jan. 1921, Archives of RBGE
16. G. Forrest to R. Cory, 19 Jan. 1921, Archives of RBGE
17. R. Cory to G. Forrest, 22 Jan. 1921, Archives of RBGE
18. C.W. Beebe, *A Monograph of the Pheasants*, Vol. I, 1918, Witherby & Co., p.156
19. Rothschild, Lord, 'On the Avifauna of Yunnan, with critical notes', *Novitates Zoologicae*, XXXIII, Dec. 1926, p.211
20. G. Forrest to Stephenson Clarke, 14 Nov. 1921, Box 43, Tring Museum Corresp. Archives of NHM, London
21. *Bull. Ornithologists' Club*, 43, 1922-1923

22. Forrest family papers
23. LeCroy, M. & Dickinson, E.C., 'Systematic notes on Asian birds. 17. Types of birds collected in Yunnan by George Forrest and described by Walter Rothschild,' *Zool. Verh. Leiden*, 335, 2001, pp.183-198
24. See *Novitates Zoologicae*, Vols. 28, 30, 32 and 33 (1921-1926)
25. Ward, F. Kingdon, *The Land of the Blue Poppy*, CUP, 1913
26. Hinton, M.A.C., 'On the Voles collected by Mr G. Forrest in Yunnan; with Remarks upon the Genera *Eothenomys* and *Neodon* and upon their Allies', *Ann. & Mag. N. Hist.*, 11, 1923, pp.45-162
27. Thomas, O., 'Four new squirrels of the Genus *Tamiops*', *Ann. & Mag. N. Hist.*, 5, 1920, pp.304-308
28. G. Forrest to Stephenson Clarke, 14 Nov. 1921, Box 43, Tring Museum Corresp. Archives of NHM, London
29. Information kindly supplied by Andrew Whittington.
30. Riley, N.D., 'A new species of *Armandia* (Lep. *Papilionidae*)', *The Entomologist*, vol. LXXII, 1939, pp.207-208
31. Keenan, J., JARS vol.98, 1973, p.116
32. Morton K.J., 'Notes on the *Odonata* of Yunnan, with descriptions of new species', *Trans. Ent. Soc. London*, 1928, pp.109-118
33. G. Forrest to R. Cory, 23 Aug. 1920, Archives of RBGE
34. G. Forrest to Messrs Janson & Son, 17 Dec. 1923, Box 19, Janson Family mss. Corresp., Entomological library, NHM
35. *Janson Letter Book* 1923-24, Index pp.224,237, Entomological Library, NHM

CHAPTER ELEVEN

1. G. Forrest to H.J. Elwes, 3 Jul. 1916, Forrest family papers
2. G. Forrest to I.B. Balfour, 13 Sept. 1920, Archives of RBGE
3. I.B. Balfour to H.J. Elwes, 10 Nov. 1920, Archives of RBGE and 'A lecture by Mr. George Forrest on recent discoveries of rhododendrons in China', *Rhododendron Soc. Notes*, Vol.2 No.1 (1920) pp.3-23
4. G. Forrest to W.W. Smith, 18 Sept. 1927, Archives of RBGE
5. G. Forrest to W.W. Smith, 26 Sept. 1927, Archives of RBGE
6. W.W. Smith to Lord Headfort, 23 Apr. 1928, Headfort boxfile 3, Glasnevin archives
7. Smith, W.W. & Forrest, G., 'The Sections of the Genus Primula, *Notes RBGE*, Vol. XVI, No.lxxvl, Mar. 1928, pp.1-50
8. Stephenson Clarke to W.W. Smith, 29 May 1928, Archives of RBGE
9. Based at Glenveg, Tweedsmuir, Peeblesshire
10. At 14 Drumshough Gardens
11. McLaren, H.D., 'Asiatic Primulas for the Garden', The Fourth Primula Conference 1928, *JRHS*, vol.LIV, pt.I 1929, pp.63-68
12. Handel-Mazzetti, H., 'The Natural Habitats of Chinese Primulas, The Fourth Primula Conference 1928, *JRHS*, vol. LIV, pt.I, 1929, pp.51-62
13. Forrest, G., 'Rhododendrons of 1921 and 1922 and some trees and shrubs of Yunnan', *Rhododendron Soc. Notes* Vol.2 No.4 (1923) pp.147-158

14. H.D. McLaren to L.de Rothschild, 8 Jun. 1928, 'Digby file, section Y-Z, 1928 Forrest corresp. of the Hon. H.D. McLaren, in Lord Aberconway's archive, Bodnant. The letters are from now on referred to as the McLaren papers
15. G. Forrest to H.D. McLaren, 1 Apr. 1929, McLaren papers
16. G. Forrest to W.W. Smith, 8 Sept. 1929, Archives of RBGE
17. G. Forrest to W.W. Smith, 8 Aug. 1929, Archives of RBGE
18. G. Forrest to H.D. McLaren, 31 Aug. 1929, McLaren papers
19. G. Forrest to McLaren, 5 Oct. 1929, McLaren papers
20. 'Headfort' to H.D. McLaren, 5 Jan. 1930, McLaren papers
21. H.D. McLaren to W.W. Smith, 24 Feb. 1930, McLaren papers
22. G. Forrest to H.D. McLaren, 13 Apr. 1930, McLaren papers
23. F. Stern to H.D. McLaren, 20 Apr. 1930, McLaren papers
24. G. Forrest to H.D. McLaren, 20 Apr. 1930, McLaren papers
25. G. Forrest to H.D. McLaren, 1 May 1930, McLaren papers
26. W.W. Smith to Mr Holms, 13 Dec. 1929, Archives of RBGE
27. W.W. Smith to Mrs Berry, 27 Aug. 1930, Archives of RBGE
28. J.C. Williams to I.B. Balfour, 28 Nov. 1918, Archives of RBGE
29. Vol. 1927-1935, Archives of Lady Londonderry, National Trust
30. G. Forrest to G. Taylor, 4 Oct. 1930, Accession No.9533, Box 1, File 1, General Correspondence, National Library of Scotland

CHAPTER TWELVE
1. Tennyson, Alfred Lord (1809-1892), Ulysses in *Poems of Alfred Lord Tennyson, 1830-1870,* OUP 1950, p.182
2. Clarke, E., *Hidcote – the making of a garden,* Michael Joseph, 1989, p.81
3. L. Johnston to H.D. McLaren, 21 Oct. (1929?) Bodnant archives
4. L. Johnston to H.D. McLaren, 14 Oct. (1929?) Bodnant archives
5. Interview with Sir George Taylor
6. Ibid.
7. Pavord, A., *Hidcote Manor Garden,* The National Trust, 1993, p.14
8. Brown, J., *Eminent Gardeners,* Viking, 1990, p.2
9. G. Forrest to W.W. Smith, 26 Feb. 1931, Archives of RBGE
10. Ibid. p.6
11. W.W. Smith to G. Forrest, 11 Mar. 1931, Archives of RBGE
12. Probably this was *Camellia saluensis,* which Forrest introduced. (Cowan, J.M., *George Forrest: Journeys and Plant Introductions,* OUP 1952, p.119)
13. Curtis's *Botanical Magazine* t 9590, v.162, 1939-40
14. Pavord, A., *Hidcote Manor Garden,* The National Trust,1993, p.11
15. G. Forrest to W.W. Smith, 26 Feb. 1931, Archives of RBGE
16. G. Forrest to W.W. Smith, 26 Feb. 1931, Archives of RBGE

17. Forrest thought *Paeonia trollioides* and *Paeonia potanini* were probably distinct species, but the first of these is now considered just a highly desirable form of the other. (Fearnley-Whittingstall, J., *Peonies The Imperial Flower,* Seven Dials, Cassell & Co., 2000, p.20)
18. W.W. Smith to H.C.M.W. Forrest, 23 Mar. 1931, Archives of RBGE
19. W.W. Smith to G. Forrest, 6 Apr. 1931, Archives of RBGE
20. In the hands of the National Trust for Scotland
21. Roosevelt, T. and Roosevelt, K., *Trailing the Giant Panda,* Scribners, New York, 1929, pp.225-226
22. G. Forrest to H.D. McLaren, 14 Apr. 1931, Bodnant archives
23. G. Forrest to W.W. Smith, 26 Feb. 1931, Archives of RBGE
24. H.C.M.W. Forrest to W.W. Smith, 18 Mar. 1931, Archives of RBGE
25. G. Forrest to W.W. Smith, 31 Mar. 1931, Archives of RBGE
26. G. Forrest to H.D. McLaren, 14 Apr. 1931, Bodnant archives
27. G. Forrest to Lord Headfort, 16 Apr. 1931, Archives of RBGE
28. Stevenson, J.B., *The Species of Rhododendron,* The Rhododendron Society, 1930, p.309
29. G. Forrest to W.W. Smith, 31 Mar. 1931, Archives of RBGE
30. Chamberlain, D.F., 'Revision of Rhododendron: subgenus Hymenanthes', *Notes* RBGE 39(2), p.250
31. Sutton, S.B., *In China's Border Provinces, The Turbulent Career of Joseph Rock, Botanist-Explorer,* 1974, p.52
32. Cox, E.H.M., *Plant Hunting in China,* O.U.P., 1986, p.196
33. G. Forrest to I.B. Balfour, 25 Sept. 1922, Archives of RBGE
34. J. Rock's diary, Archives of RBGE
35. Sutton, S.B, *In China's Border Provinces,* New York: Hastings House, 1974, p.214
36. W.W. Smith to G. Forrest, 28 Oct. 1931, Archives of RBGE
37. W.W. Smith to G. Forrest, 3 Jul. 1931, Archives of RBGE
38. W.W. Smith to G. Forrest , 16 Jun. 1931, Archives of RBGE
39. W.W. Smith to G. Forrest, 18 Nov. 1931, Archives of RBGE
40. Stephenson Clarke to W.W. Smith 18 Dec. 1931, Archives of RBGE
41. G. Forrest to W.W. Smith, 31 Mar. 1931, Archives of RBGE
42. G. Forrest to the British Legation, Peking, 16 Oct. 1931, Archives of the NHM, London, Folder DF1004 /CP422, Forrest, George, 1932-1933
43. Extract from letter from Mr Forrest, 26 Dec. 1931, Forrest family papers
44. Cowan, J.M., *The Journeys and Plant Introductions of George Forrest VMH,* OUP. 1952, p.35
45. W.W. Smith to G. Forrest, 4 Jan. 1932, Archives of RBGE

CHAPTER THIRTEEN
1. Archives of RBGE
2. H. Prideaux Brune (H.M. Consul) to Mrs Forrest, 8 Jan. 1932, Forrest Family Archive

3. Forrest, G. jnr., 'George Forrest. "The Man"', *J. Scottish Rock Garden Club,* vol. 13, No.52., 1973, pp.169-175
4. A. Grove to Mrs Forrest, 13 Feb. 1932, Forrest family papers
5. Interview with William MacKenzie
6. Interview with Helen Miller (née Maxwell)
7. *Nature,* vol.129 (no.3251) 1932, p.270
8. British Consul, Tengyueh to Foreign Office London, 13 Jan. 1932, Folder DF1004/CP422, Forrest, George, 1932-1933, Archives of the NHM
9. Folder DF1004/CP719 (Tring), Archives of the NHM
10. Memorandum stamped 1632, dated 22 March 1932, in above folder of the NHM
11. Mearns, B. and R., *The Bird Collectors,* Academic Press, 1998, p.300. Rothschild, Miriam, *Dear Lord Rothschild: Birds,Butterflies and History,* 1983, ISI Press, Philadelphia
12. Barbara Blood (who helped divide the seeds for shareholders): script of talk given to Botanic Section, Natural History Society, Northampton, 15 Dec. 1977

CHAPTER FOURTEEN
1. I.B. Balfour to A.K. Bulley, 15 Apr. 1912, Archives of the RBGE
2. I.B. Balfour to J.C. Williams, 30 May 1914, Archives of the RBGE
3. Cox, E.H.M., *New Flora and Silva,* vol. 4, 1931- 32, pp.180-186
4. J.C. Williams to I.B. Balfour, 12 Jan. 1919, Archives of the RBGE
5. I.B. Balfour to J.C. Williams, 22 Jan. 1919, Archives of the RBGE
6. J.C. Williams to I.B. Balfour, 29 Aug. 1919, Archives of the RBGE
7. Curtis's *Botanical Magazine,* Vol. 148, 1922
8. I.B. Balfour to J.C. Williams, 21 Dec. 1918, Archives of the RBGE
9 I.B. Balfour to J.C. Williams, 6 Dec. 1919, Archives of the RBGE
10. *The land of the blue poppy,* 1913
11. I.B. Balfour to J.C. Williams, 1 Jan. 1915, Archives of the RBGE
12. G. Forrest to W.W. Smith, 1 Feb. 1918, Archives of the RBGE
13. De Zhu, Li and Paterson, David, 'Rhododendron conservation in China' in Argent, George and McFarlane, Marjory, *Rhododendrons in horticulture and science,* Royal Botanic Garden Edinburgh, 2003

APPENDIX 3
1. Forrest family papers and, for the fourth expedition, archives of RBGE
2. Accounts in Forrest's hand in archives of RBGE
3. Archives of RBGE
4. *Field Notes of trees, shrubs and plants – other than Rhododendrons – collected in Western China by Mr. George Forrest 1917-19,* pubd. by RHS, 1929
5. The only information on M. Yorke that I have found is that he was an Original Member of The Garden Society
6. Forrest family papers
7. G. Forrest to Stephenson Clarke, 14 Nov. 1921, Box 43, Tring Museum Corresp., Archives of Natural History Museum, London
8. Both are in Forrest family papers
9. McLaren papers

Acknowledgements

As in the work of George Forrest, the research and production of this book has been a team effort. It is a pleasure to thank everyone, named and unnamed, who has helped in any way. Learning from them has made the project a stimulating and enjoyable adventure.

The wealth of new information in the book would not have been brought to light without a generous grant from the Trustees of the Stanley Smith (UK) Horticultural Trust towards the expenses of my research. I also thank the Friends of the RBGE for kindly contributing towards my travel costs and the Friends of Ness Gardens for funding additional photography. Further illustrations were made possible by a grant from the Robert Turner Memorial Trust, whilst a grant from the Trustees of the Orcome Trust assisted the production of the book. I am also grateful to Diana Steel of Antique Collectors' Club for publishing it.

The Royal Botanic Garden Edinburgh has been the headquarters of my research, and I am grateful to successive Regius Keepers, Professor David Ingram and Professor Stephen Blackmore, for their support. It has been a privilege and delight to work in the library and I thank successive Heads of Library, Colin Will and Jane Hutcheon for their guidance and expertise, together with Graham Hardy, Leonie Paterson and all the library staff for their patience in answering many questions. Sid Clarke and Debbie White expertly reproduced Forrest's photographs, and took ones of their own for the book; Norma Gregory and Ida Maspero helped administratively. Alan Bennell, David Chamberlain, James Cullen and Henry Noltie have greatly sustained me by their long-term encouragement, help and advice. David Knott, Mark Watson and many other staff willingly gave assistance. Former staff and students of the RBGE provided memories and stories of George Forrest: Barbara Blood, H.H. Davidian, Edward Kemp, William Mackenzie, Helen Miller, Mary Noble and Jennifer Woods. Volunteers gave extra help, especially Margaret Elliott, Sally Heron and Eileen and Bill Marshall.

I am indebted to the University of Liverpool for the privileges of a Fellow of the University in the Department of Geography. Sandra Mather skilfully drew all the maps and diagrams, Ian Qualtrough and Suzanne Yee helped with scanning and photography. I have received ready assistance from former and present staff of Ness Botanic Gardens, especially Peter Cunnington, Ken Hulme and Hugh McAllister.

Expert help came from the staff of the following institutions: American Museum of Natural History (Mary LeCroy), Arnold Arboretum (Carol David), British Museum (Joe Cribb and Helen Wang), Dick Institute, Kilmarnock (Jason Sutcliffe), Falkirk Museum Services (Carol Sneddon), Hunt Institute for Botanical Documentation, Pittsburgh (Angela Todd), Kilmarnock Academy (Neil Dickson), Linnean Society (Gina Douglas), Liverpool Museum (Simon Bean, John Edmondson, Clem Fisher and Leander Wolstenholme), Massachusetts Horticultural Society (Eric Frazier), Museum of the Royal Pharmaceutical Society (Lorraine Jones), National Botanic Gardens, Glasnevin, Dublin (Sarah Ball), National Geographic Society (Renee Braden), National Museums of Scotland (Helen Nicoll, Geoffrey Swinney, Andrew Whittington, Jane Wilkinson), National Trust (Anne Casement), Natural History Museum (Phillip Ackery, Mark Adams, David Carter, Richard Harbord, Julie Harvey, Daphne Hills, Paula Lucas, Robert Prys-Jones, Susan Snell, John Thackray, Michael Walters, Effie Warr), Public Record Offices of Kew and Belfast, Royal Botanic Garden Kew (Marilyn Ward), Royal Geographical Society, Royal Horticultural Society (Brent Elliott and the picture librarians), and the School of Oriental and African Studies. I also thank Edward Dickinson for his advice and expertise on Forrest's birds.

Members of the Forrest family have kindly encouraged and helped by leading me to new material and allowing me to use it. Gillie and Hugh Cameron and Alison Fraser gave hospitality and shared Forrest letters, photographs, documents and artefacts. I also thank Alys Forrest for the stimulus of her research as she delved into the family history, on which she is now the expert. Elspeth Dutch, George and Eric Forrest, Ian and Richard Forrest, Marion Leadbetter, Beth Patrick and Celia Smith all made contributions. The relatives of others in the Forrest story kindly provided hospitality and access to their family archives: Rupert Eley, John and Joan Farrer and Lord and Lady Aberconway (Charles M. McLaren).

Help has also been given by Ted Brabin, Darren Crook, Yan Dong, Mary Forrest, Pat Hollis, Andrew Hill, Peter Hutchison, Richard Kirkby, Charles Nelson, Cynthia Postan, Charles and Martin Puddle, Mike Snowden, George Taylor, Julian Williams. In the search for Forrest's former houses, George Campbell, Faith Pullin, Mary Purves, Marion Richardson, Mr and Mrs K. Ross, Mr and Mrs J. Smith all assisted.

I thank friends and relatives whose understanding, support and encouragement have been hugely appreciated over many years. Sue Manley and Mrs Yoh have given practical help. Others have given advice, hospitality, helped with research or read and improved numerous draft texts: Eve Bennett, Anne Dennier, John Dickenson, Alys Forrest, Richard McLean, David Rankin, Dick and Winifred Sillitto and Ben Wilson. Others again, from their experience of life, have offered wisdom and friendship of an unseen and invaluable kind.

From the beginning, I have had the backing of my mother, who at ninety-four still retains her sense of fun in endeavour. The eager and generous spirit of my twin brother Robert has always been behind me. The love and loyalty of my husband Robin has seen the book to completion: he became co-researcher, organiser and co-author, writing Chapters Seven and Eight and contributing to others. When, like a yacht, the project was becalmed or nearly hit the rocks, our sons, Andrew and Richard, willed us on and gave helpful advice. When extra crew were needed, they, and Geraldine, joined in, while Robin kindly shared the tiller, put up the spinnaker, and guided the ship to the finishing post. We have enjoyed the challenge and hope that readers, too, take pleasure in stepping back in time and sharing in the life of a remarkable plant collector of another era.

Picture Credits

The author is grateful to the following people and institutions for permission to reproduce illustrations. Copyright resides with them:

Royal Botanic Garden Edinburgh (RBGE), George Forrest photographic archive:
  Frontispiece and Plates 18, 20, 21, 22, 26, 31, 33, 34, 38, 43, 45, 47, 48, 49, 51, 52, 56, 57, 60, 65, 66, 68, 71, 74, 76, 78, 80, 84, 85, 87, 92, 99, 102, 104, 106, 110, 116, 118, 119, 129, 136, 139, 140, 141, 143, 144, 145, 147, 149, 151, 152.
RBGE: Plates 11, 12, 13, 17, 54, 100, 158.
Sid Clarke, RBGE: Plate 10 (Loaningdale, Peebles).
David Knott, RBGE: Plates 28, 70, 109.
Leonie Paterson, RBGE: Plate 155.
Mark Watson, RBGE: Plates 35, 42, 67, 108.
Debbie White, RBGE: Colour photographs in Plate 10 (except Loaningdale, Peebles and 17, Inverleith Place, Edinburgh) and Plates 14, 111.

Lady Aberconway: Plate 134.
Eve Reid Bennett: Plate 58.
Bodnant Garden & Jarrold Publishing: Plate 133.
Peter Cunnington: Plates 30, 32, 37, 82, 83, 130.
Anne Dennier: Plate 10 (17, Inverleith Place, Edinburgh).
East Ayrshire Council (Museums, Arts & Theatre section): Plates 7, 8.
H.W.G.Elwes: Plate 94.
David Farnes: Plates 53, 89, 101.
Eileen Farnes: Plate 142.
Forrest family: Plates 23, 24, 25, 46, 75, 117, 127, 131, 132, 137, 156.
Derek Harris Associates Ltd.: Plates 73, 150.
Ken Hulme: Plates 77, 91, 98.
John Hutchinson: Plates 36, 81.
David Leadbetter: Plate 55.

Gill Lewis: Plates 16, 107.
Liverpool Record Office, Liverpool Libraries & Information Services: Plate 15.
Brenda McLean: Plates 113, 115.
Geraldine McLean: Plate 62.
National Museums of Scotland: Plates 50, 72, 126.
Natural History Museum: Plates 2, 112, 114, 120, 121, 122, 123, 124, 125.
Beth Patrick: Plate 23.
David Rankin: Plates 29, 69, 79, 88, 93, 148, 154.
Rosslyn Chapel Trust: Plate 59 (photograph by Antonia Reeve).
Royal Botanic Gardens, Kew, the Board of Trustees: Plates 41, 62, 63, 97, 128.
Also (from *Curtis's Botanical Magazine*): Plates 1, 39, 40, 138, 153, 160.
Royal Horticultural Society, the Lindley Library: Plates 64, 90, 96, 157.
Celia L.Smith: Plate 6.
Jennifer Trehane: Plates 146, 161.
Joan Wilkinson: Plate 103.

Copyright of maps and diagrams
Alys Forrest: Plate 5.
Brenda McLean: Plates 4, 10, 19, 95, 105.

Other sources
Atlas of false-colour satellite photographs of the land surface of China, 3 vols., Beijing: Kexue Chubanshe, 1983, 2, pp.141-2: Plate 3.
Davies, H.R., *Yun-nan, the link between India and the Yangtze*, Cambridge University Press, 1909: Plate 27.

Index

Page numbers in **bold** refer to illustrations